MAGNIFYING
GOD in CHRIST

MASON Wheely
    Suicide

MAGNIFYING GOD IN CHRIST

A Summary of New Testament Theology

Thomas R. Schreiner

Baker Academic

a division of Baker Publishing Group
Grand Rapids, Michigan

Published by Baker Academic
a division of Baker Publishing Group
P.O. Box 6287, Grand Rapids, MI 49516-6287
www.bakeracademic.com

Printed in the United States of America

Library of Congress Cataloging-in-Publication Data
Schreiner, Thomas R.
    Magnifying God in Christ: a summary of New Testament theology / Thomas R. Schreiner.
        p.   cm.
    Includes bibliographical references (p.   ) and indexes.
    ISBN 978-0-8010-3826-6 (pbk.)
    1. Bible. N.T.—Theology. I. Title.
BS2397.S468 2010
225′.61—dc22   2009029866

10   11   12   13   14   15   16   7   6   5   4   3   2   1

To Daniel and Ashley,
and to
Patrick and Hannah,
with love

Contents

Preface

I am grateful to Jim Kinney from Baker Academic, who invited me to write an abbreviated version of my *New Testament Theology: Magnifying God in Christ*. Naturally, this more compact version cannot examine the issues of the larger volume in the same depth, for the former book was intended for seminarians and pastors who desired a detailed study of NT theology. I hope that this slimmer edition will make the main argument of the book available to laypeople, students, and pastors who are also interested in the message of the NT. The fundamental argument of my larger book is summarized here in shorter scope. I have eliminated virtually all footnotes and invite readers to consult my larger work for more in-depth discussion, but the present work contains a digest of what is found in the larger work. Finally, I would like to dedicate this book to two of my sons, Daniel and Patrick, and to their respective wives, Ashley and Hannah. Both Daniel and Patrick have been married in the last year, and Diane and I have been filled with joy in seeing the pure devotion to Christ in the lives of Ashley and Hannah.

Abbreviations

Bibliographic and General

AD	anno Domini, in the year of the Lord
AT	author's translation
BC	before Christ
ca.	circa, approximately
e.g.	exempli gratia, for example
esp.	especially
ESV	English Standard Version
HCSB	Holman Christian Standard Bible
LXX	Septuagint
m.	Mishnah
NRSV	New Revised Standard Version
NT	New Testament
OT	Old Testament
par./pars.	parallel(s) included
RSV	Revised Standard Version

Old Testament

Gen.	Genesis
Exod.	Exodus
Lev.	Leviticus
Num.	Numbers
Deut.	Deuteronomy
Josh.	Joshua
Judg.	Judges
Ruth	Ruth
1–2 Sam.	1–2 Samuel
1–2 Kings	1–2 Kings
1–2 Chron.	1–2 Chronicles
Ezra	Ezra
Neh.	Nehemiah
Esth.	Esther
Job	Job
Ps.	Psalms
Prov.	Proverbs
Eccles.	Ecclesiastes
Song	Song of Songs
Isa.	Isaiah

Jer.	Jeremiah	1–2 Tim.	1–2 Timothy
Lam.	Lamentations	Titus	Titus
Ezek.	Ezekiel	Philem.	Philemon
Dan.	Daniel	Heb.	Hebrews
Hos.	Hosea	James	James
Joel	Joel	1–2 Pet.	1–2 Peter
Amos	Amos	1–3 John	1–3 John
Obad.	Obadiah	Jude	Jude
Jon.	Jonah	Rev.	Revelation
Mic.	Micah		
Nah.	Nahum		
Hab.	Habakkuk		
Zeph.	Zephaniah		
Hag.	Haggai		
Zech.	Zechariah		
Mal.	Malachi		

Old Testament Apocrypha and Pseudepigrapha

2 Bar.	2 Baruch (Syriac Apocalypse)
1 En.	1 Enoch
1–4 Esd.	1–4 Esdras
2–3 Macc.	2–3 Maccabees
Pss. Sol.	Psalms of Solomon
Sir.	Sirach
T. Mos.	Testament of Moses
Wis.	Wisdom of Solomon

New Testament

Matt.	Matthew
Mark	Mark
Luke	Luke
John	John
Acts	Acts
Rom.	Romans
1–2 Cor.	1–2 Corinthians
Gal.	Galatians
Eph.	Ephesians
Phil.	Philippians
Col.	Colossians
1–2 Thess.	1–2 Thessalonians

Qumran / Dead Sea Scrolls

1QS	1QRule of the Community
3Q15	3QCopper Scroll
4QFlor	4QFlorilegium
4QMMT	4QHalakhic Letter

Introduction

Why Study New Testament Theology?

Studying NT theology is valuable because NT students are inclined to see the parts and neglect the whole. We may spend considerable time interpreting individual texts or books of the NT without reflecting on larger themes, so that we fail to step back and survey the landscape as a whole. Naturally our vision of the whole will be distorted if we do not attend diligently to the parts. In-depth exegesis must function as the foundation of the larger picture. At the same time, if we fail to look at the NT through a wider lens and view it only through the narrow lens of intensive exegesis, we may end up making mistakes in our exegesis as well. For looking at the whole assists us in understanding the parts.

Thus NT theology surveys the landscape. What is the NT all about? What are the major themes? How do they fit together? Not all scholars think that the NT has a coherent message. I would argue that there is a beauty and coherence in what is now called the NT canon. When we survey the landscape, we see the same central themes in the various writers, even though they addressed different situations and communities. So NT theology helps us understand the message of the entirety of the NT, and surely it is the desire to understand the message of the NT that motivates us to invest time in studying it.

How Should We Study New Testament Theology?

How should a NT theology be written? For readers who are interested in a more in-depth discussion of this matter historically and in terms of method, I recommend the appendix from the larger volume (see Schreiner 2008: 867–88).

I have chosen a thematic approach in this work because a thematic structure has some advantages. The coherence and the unity of NT theology are explained more clearly if a NT theology is presented thematically. Is a study of each individual writer truly a NT theology, or is it a theology of Matthew, Mark, Luke, Paul, and so forth? I am not saying, however, that a study of each book separately is illegitimate. Such an approach opens vistas onto the text that are obscured, at least in part, by a thematic approach. I reject the claim that there is one correct way to write a NT theology. The subject matter of NT theology is too vast and comprehensive to be exhausted by any single approach. Barr (1999: 61) rightly says that "there can be no such thing as the one appropriate method for biblical theology" (see also his remarks at 1999: 342). No NT theology will ever do justice to the complexity and beauty of the NT. Each of the various approaches and perspectives casts a different light upon the NT, and in that sense having a number of different approaches is helpful. Fruitful NT theologies could be written from the standpoint of eschatology, the people of God, Christology, ethics, and so on.

In Defense of a Thematic Approach

I believe, however, that a thematic approach is particularly needed today, with the proviso that it is truly rooted in biblical theology. Many NT scholars shy away from such an approach today, fearing that it too closely resembles systematic theology. They worry about domesticating the text by our own categories. A thematic approach runs the danger of domesticating the text and squeezing out the diversity of the NT. Still, it is a risk worth taking. Our Western world is worried about metanarratives, and hence much of the work in NT studies examines a small part of the NT, or even a single verse in the NT. It is safer to present one's conclusions on a single verse than it is to say what the entire NT is about. Perhaps it is saner as well! And no NT theology is helpful if the writer has not "gotten dirty" by studying the text inductively, piece by piece.

  And yet there is another side to the story. We understand each of the pieces in the NT by our understanding of the whole, by our worldview, by our own metanarrative. We can fall into the illusion that if we study a part, then we are dealing with just the "evidence," "the hard phenomena" of the text. But our understanding of any piece of evidence is also affected by our standpoint, our worldview. We do not assess any piece of evidence from a neutral and objective standpoint. Hence, there is a dialogue between the inductive and deductive that constantly occurs. If we do not venture to consider NT theology as a whole, we are in danger of skewing the particular piece of evidence that we study. Examining the NT thematically, then, may assist us in understanding the pieces that make up the NT.

I have already noted the benefit of considering each writer individually. But there is another liability in studying each writer individually. We need to recall that none of the NT documents claims to be the "theology" of the writer in question. This is particularly obvious in the case of the Epistles. The Epistles are occasional writings directed to specific situations and circumstances in the lives of churches. It is somewhat distorting, then, to write a theology of, say, Jude or James. We can hardly claim that they have packaged the whole of their theology into such short letters. Yet Paul is different in that he wrote thirteen Letters, and so we have a larger corpus from which to construct his thought.[1] But even in Paul's case we do not have a complete map of his convictions. Some holes still exist.

In the same way, more can be said about Matthew and Mark, Luke-Acts, and the Johannine writings than can be said about Jude. Useful studies of the particular emphases of these writings have been produced. We need to remember, however, the constraints under which the Gospel writers composed their works. At this juncture, I am assuming that they were historians *and* theologians. They were not free, in other words, to construct a theology sundered from the actual words and works of Jesus. When we compare John with the Synoptic Gospels, it is obvious that the different perspectives add tremendous richness to our understanding of Jesus Christ. The diversity of perspectives indicates neither a lack of interest in history nor the presence of a freeness to compose in accord with one's desires. We have four Gospels because the depth and breadth of Jesus Christ could not be captured by a single writer.

The Gospels, then, are theological history, containing an interpretation of the works and words of Jesus of Nazareth. Nevertheless, they are *Gospels*, which bear witness to Jesus Christ and his historical work. They are located at a certain juncture in the history of salvation. When considering the theology of the Gospels, we must attend to the location of the writer on the redemptive-historical timeline. Some matters in the Gospels remain undeveloped because God's promises are not realized until the death and resurrection of Christ. Hence, the Gospels conclude with the expectation and promise that the Spirit will be poured out on God's people. This blessing of the Spirit is not given, however, in the Gospels themselves. In this sense, the rest of the NT should be located in a different place in salvation history than the Gospels.

In summary, none of the NT writings contains the whole of what is taught in the NT. They are accurate but partial and fragmentary witnesses. They witness truly but not exhaustively to the gospel of Jesus Christ. Hence, a the-

---

1. In my judgment, all the letters attributed to Paul are authentic. The Pastoral Epistles are the first to be contested, but solid reasons exist to support authenticity. See Mounce 2000: lxvi–cxxix; Knight 1992: 21–52; Ellis 1992.

matic approach to NT theology is invaluable because it attempts to capture the whole of what is taught by considering all twenty-seven books.

The Question of a Center

Is there a single center for NT theology? The question of a center has long been debated, and many different centers have been proposed. I think it is safe to say that no alleged center will ever become the consensus. In one sense, having several different centers is useful, since NT theology can be studied helpfully from a number of different perspectives. Since the various perspectives are interlocking and not mutually exclusive, there is a diversity of ways by which the NT can be explored. Furthermore, examining the NT from different angles allows new light to be shed upon the text. Since the subject matter of NT theology is God himself, we are not surprised to learn that none of our scholarly endeavors ever exhausts the subject matter.

It is illuminating to consider NT theology from a twofold perspective. First, God's purpose in all that he does is to bring honor to himself and to Jesus Christ. The NT is radically God-centered. We could say that the NT is about God magnifying himself in Christ through the Spirit. We could easily fail to see the supremacy of God and the centrality of Christ in the NT precisely because these themes are part of the warp and woof of the NT. Sometimes we fail to see what is most obvious, what is right before our eyes. Any NT theology that does not focus on what God has done in Christ, however, fails to see what is fundamental to and pervasive in the text of Scripture.

Second, the centrality of God in Christ leads to abstraction if it is not closely related to the history of salvation, to the fulfillment of God's promises. In the Scriptures, we have the story of God's saving plan (which includes judgment). The NT unfolds the fulfillment of the promises made in the OT. One of the striking themes in the NT is that of the "already–not yet." God has inaugurated his kingdom, but he has not consummated it. He has begun to fulfill his saving promises, but he has not yet completed all that he has started. No one can grasp the message of the NT if redemptive history is slighted. Redemptive history is fundamental to grasping the message of the NT. God's ultimate purpose is reflected in the fulfillment of his plan. He must have a purpose, an aim, a goal in such a plan. Here the purpose of all of salvation history emerges. God works out his saving plan so that he would be magnified in Christ, so that his name would be honored.[2] Hence, contrary to what some have said, God's glory and humans' salvation are not in conflict. Rather, God is glorified in the salvation of his people.

2. In most instances when citing a text from the Synoptic Gospels for which there are parallels, I cite only Matthew. No significance should be ascribed to my citation of Matthew.

A Short Tour of the Book

Every NT theology has its own distinctive slant. My goal in this book is not to argue a novel thesis but to attempt to discover inductively what was most important to NT writers. The book begins in chapter 1 with the already–not yet theme in the NT. The OT closes with unfinished business. The Lord made promises that were not yet fulfilled for his people and for the world. When we read the NT, we find that God's saving promises are fulfilled, and yet these promises are realized in a surprising fashion. There is an already-but-not-yet character to the fulfillment. Hence, the kingdom is inaugurated but not consummated. Believers enjoy eternal life now, and yet they will enjoy the fullness of such life only on the day of resurrection. Understanding the tension between the inauguration and consummation of God's promises is indispensable for grasping the message of the NT.

Chapters 2 through 8, which represent the heart of the book, focus on the Father (chap. 2), Jesus Christ (chaps. 3–7), and the Holy Spirit (chap. 8). Again, we are asking the question: what is the NT fundamentally about? The promises of God come to fruition through the Father, the Son, and the Holy Spirit. They are the main actors in the drama, and hence praise goes to them for their saving work.

We shall see in chapter 2 that the Father is the sovereign creator and the merciful Lord. He works out both his saving and judging purposes in history. Chapters 3 through 7 examine the Christology of the NT. The subject is vast, for surely Jesus Christ is the central character of the NT witness. God's saving promises become a reality through him. Virtually the whole NT answers the question: who is Jesus Christ, and what has he accomplished? We shall see that the identity of Jesus Christ cannot be captured merely by his titles, and yet the titles given to him are of great significance. He is the Messiah, the Son of Man, the Son of God, the Lord, and the Logos. The Gospels all culminate with the story of the cross and resurrection, indicating that God's salvation is secured through Jesus' death and resurrection. The Epistles and Revelation continue to focus on the identity of Jesus Christ. We see Paul's high Christology in Phil. 2:5–11 and Col. 1:15–20. The high Christology of Hebrews is apparent in Heb. 1:1–14. And Jesus as the Lamb of God is regularly accorded the same status as God in Revelation. The significance of the cross is featured throughout the NT. In the Synoptics, Jesus explains his death at his last Passover meal with his disciples, and Paul practically bursts at the seams in using a variety of terms to describe what God has accomplished in Christ: justification, sanctification, propitiation, redemption, reconciliation, and so on. The centrality of the cross is also featured in 1 John, 1 Peter, Hebrews, and Revelation. There is little doubt that we have a found a main artery in NT teaching.

The work of the Holy Spirit is explored in chapter 8. The Gospels emphasize that Jesus is anointed by the Spirit, and Luke in Acts teaches that this same

Jesus who was filled with the Spirit also pours out his Spirit on his disciples, so that they are empowered to bring the good news of Jesus to the ends of the earth. A consistent theme throughout the NT is that the Spirit has come to honor Jesus Christ, that he is the Spirit of Jesus Christ. Hence, the Spirit's ministry is not an independent one. He empowers and sanctifies God's people so that Jesus Christ will be praised.

Chapter 9 steps back and asks why the great saving work of the Father, Son, and Spirit is needed. The NT answer is that human beings are in desperate straits. Human beings have failed to honor God as they should. The Synoptics emphasize that we are rotten trees. Paul teaches that we have not praised and thanked God as we should, and John teaches that sin is lawless rebellion (1 John 3:4). The salvation accomplished is astonishingly great, for it overcomes human rebellion.

How should human beings respond to what God has accomplished in Christ through the Spirit? The NT proclaims that we must believe and obey. In chapter 10, I argue that both of these themes are pervasive in the NT. Faith and obedience may be distinguished, but they are inseparable. No one will enjoy final salvation without believing and obeying. A careful examination of the NT reveals that all obedience flows from faith, and that there is no salvation apart from a changed life.

The already–not yet theme and the call for obedience raise the question of the place of the OT law in the life of believers. Now that Jesus Christ has come, what is the relationship between the covenants? How do believers in Jesus Christ relate to the laws of the Sinai covenant? In chapter 11, I defend the notion that there is both discontinuity and continuity with the OT law. Believers are no longer under the Mosaic covenant, but they now observe the law of love, which is the law of Christ.

The call to faith and obedience should not be understood individualistically. God always intended to bless the whole world (Gen. 12:3), to form a new community for his own glory and praise. So in chapter 12, I explore what the NT says about the church of Jesus Christ. Finally, God will consummate his purposes. The not-yet will not last forever. Jesus will return and reward those who obey him and punish those who resist him. A day of resurrection is coming. The new exodus, the new creation, and the new covenant will be fulfilled. And believers will praise and honor God forever.

1

The Fulfillment of God's Saving Promises

The Already–Not Yet

———◈———

The thesis advanced in this book is that NT theology is God-focused, Christ-centered, and Spirit-saturated, but the work of the Father, Son, and Spirit must be understood along a salvation-historical timeline; that is, God's promises are already fulfilled but not yet consummated in Christ Jesus. We will see that the ministry of Jesus Christ and the work of the Spirit are fundamental for the fulfilling of God's promises. The coming of Jesus Christ and the gift of the Spirit are the prime indications that God is beginning to fulfill the saving promises made to Abraham.

I will argue for the centrality of God in Christ in the concrete and specific witness of the NT as it unfolds God's saving work in history. Another way to put this is that God will receive all the glory for his work in Christ by the Spirit as he works out his purpose in redemptive history. Furthermore, redemptive history is characterized by inaugurated but not consummated eschatology; thus the glory that belongs to God has not yet reached its zenith, but it will.

In this chapter, the already-but-not-yet theme in the NT will be explored. What is quite remarkable is that inaugurated (but not yet consummated) eschatology pervades the NT. We shall see in this chapter that in the Synoptic Gospels the kingdom of God comes to the forefront: the kingdom is present in Jesus' ministry, and yet at the same time there is a future fulfillment. The Johannine writings emphasize that believers now enjoy eternal life, but the physical resurrection still awaits believers. Similarly, the already–not yet theme pervades the Pauline writings. Believers are saved now, and yet salvation will be fully realized in the future. Believers are now redeemed but await the resurrection of their bodies on the last day, and so forth. In the same way, the other writings in the NT maintain the tension between the present fulfillment of God's promises and the future realization of those promises. For instance, the author of Hebrews proclaims that atonement has been secured through the death of Christ, but his severe warnings to believers demonstrate that the promises are not yet fully realized. The signature of the arrival of the age to come is the gift of the Holy Spirit. On the other hand, believers await the final resurrection, indicating that the Spirit is a foretaste of greater things to come. Before examining the theme of the already–but not yet in the NT, we must consider briefly the OT background.

The Old Testament Backdrop

Before surveying the NT witness, we need to take a cursory look at the OT. We could summarize the OT under the rubrics of creation, fall, and redemption. The centrality of God is featured in the fact that he is the creator of all. God's sovereign creation of the universe is a pervasive theme in the OT, indicating that he is Lord of the cosmos and the central actor of the OT story. He made human beings in his image so that they would display his glory, reflect his character, and rule the world for God (Gen. 1:26–27; 2:15–17). Adam and Eve rejected God's lordship and struck out on their own. God's judgment of Adam and Eve also communicates his lordship and is a preview to the pervasive theme of judgment in the OT. Every act of God's judgment demonstrates that he is sovereign and Lord. Still, the story line of the OT concludes not with judgment but with the promise of redemption.

The OT is animated with an eschatological hope. Thus Gen. 3:15 forecasts a day when the seed of the woman will triumph over the seed of the serpent. Subsequent history appeared to mock the promise, for the seed of the serpent ruled over human beings during the days of Noah so that evil reigned over the world. God revealed his lordship over history by destroying those who rebelled against him with a flood, but the tower of Babel illustrated that human beings had not fundamentally changed. God's promise of blessing for the whole world focused thereafter upon one man, Abraham. The Lord promised Abraham and his descendants land, seed, and a blessing that would encompass the entire world (e.g., 12:1–3; 18:18; 22:17–18; 26:3–4; 28:14–15; 35:12–13). The promise began to be fulfilled in the days of the patriarchs and Moses, for the people of Israel multiplied in accord with God's promise. Then the promise of the land of Canaan became theirs during the days of Joshua. It seemed that the nation was poised to become the vehicle for worldwide blessing, but a cycle of sin and judgment ensued in the days of the judges. David's accession as king and the everlasting covenant made with him (2 Sam. 7) demonstrated that universal blessing would become a reality through a Davidic descendant. But the story of the kings of Judah, not to mention the kings of Israel, sadly disappointed. The nation spiraled downward until it was carried into exile by Babylon in 586 BC. Yahweh promised through the prophets, however, the dawning of a new covenant (Jer. 31:31–34), a coming kingdom (Obad. 21), a rebuilding of David's fallen booth (Amos 9:11–15), a new day for Jerusalem and Zion (Joel 3:15–21; Zeph. 3:15–20), a pouring out of God's Spirit (Joel 2:28), a day when the Lord would give his people a new heart and Spirit so that they would obey him (Ezek. 36:26–27), a new exodus when God would liberate his people once again (e.g., Isa. 43:5–9), and a new creation (Isa. 65:17–25; 66:22). None of these promises were fulfilled during the OT era, and so this brings us to the NT witness.

Kingdom of God

In considering the already-but-not-yet theme, we begin with the kingdom of God, which certainly is of prime importance in NT theology. Goldsworthy (2000: 618) remarks, "The idea of the rule of God over creation, over all creatures, over the kingdoms of the world, and in a unique and special way, over his chosen and redeemed people, is the very heart of the message of the Hebrew scriptures."

The Synoptic Gospels make it apparent that the kingdom of God is central to Jesus' teaching. The importance of the kingdom of God in Jesus' teaching is also apparent by the location of the sayings about the kingdom. Both Matthew and Mark introduce Jesus' teaching ministry with pregnant sayings about the kingdom of God (Matt. 4:17; Mark 1:14–15). Jesus proclaimed the imminence of the kingdom, the fulfillment of the good news that God would redeem his people. This promise of good news (*euangelion*) reaches back to Isaiah, where the good news is the new exodus from Babylon, the return from exile (Isa. 40:9; 52:7). The importance of the kingdom is also attested by the summary statements that epitomize Jesus' ministry and prominently feature the kingdom (Matt. 4:23; 9:35; 24:14; Luke 4:43–44; 8:1; 9:11). Jesus' ministry in Galilee consisted of teaching, healing, and proclaiming the good news of the kingdom. The healing of every disease signifies that the old order is passing away and a new era has arrived.

How should we understand what Jesus meant by the "kingdom of God"? The expectation of a future rule of God in which he fulfills his promises to Israel and subjugates his enemies is found in both the OT (Isa. 24:23; Dan.

2:44; 7:14, 18, 23, 27; Amos 9:11–15; Obad. 21; Zeph. 3:15; Zech. 14:9) and
in Second Temple literature (T. Mos. 10.1; 2 Bar. 73.1–7; Pss. Sol. 17–18).
Interestingly, the desire for Israel to triumph and to see surrounding nations
defeated is expressed in a thoroughly Jewish way in Luke 1–2, indicating
Luke's faithful rendering of early Jewish piety before the coming of the Messiah (Luke 1:52–55, 68–75).

When we turn to the teaching of Jesus, we see that he too expected a future
kingdom, an end-time kingdom where God would fulfill his saving promises.
This is evident from the Lord's Prayer, in which believers are to pray, "Your
kingdom come" (Matt. 6:10). Jesus also speaks to the disciples of the day when
he will come "in his kingdom" (16:28; cf. Luke 23:51), which clearly refers
to the future fulfillment of the kingdom promise. When the kingdom comes,
the judgment will commence, and all will be appraised for the way they have
lived (Matt. 25:31–46). The coming kingdom can be described as a great end-
time feast in which the righteous will rejoice but others will be cast out into
the darkness (8:11–12; 26:29; Mark 14:25; Luke 14:15; 22:16, 18, 29–30; cf.
Isa. 25:6–8). The futurity of the kingdom is evident in the call to "inherit the
kingdom" that has been prepared by God from the beginning (Matt. 25:34).
Jesus did not believe that the kingdom had come in its fullness in his day; he
envisioned a future day when he would enjoy the messianic banquet in God's
kingdom (Mark 14:25; Luke 22:18). Clearly, Jesus anticipated a period of time
in which believers awaited the fulfillment of God's saving promises and the
unleashing of his terrible judgments.

The kingdom of God cannot be restricted to the future in the ministry and
teaching of Jesus. It is also a present reality. Yet there is a sense in which God
always and invariably rules as king over all. This is illustrated by Ps. 103:19:
"The LORD has established his throne in the heavens, and his kingdom rules
over all." God reigns at all times and in all places over all that occurs in history
(cf. Pss. 47:8; 93:1; 97:1; 99:1). Nevertheless, the unique element in Jesus' teaching about God's kingdom is its presence in Jesus' ministry. In other words, the
OT promises of a new covenant and a new creation and a new exodus were
beginning to be fulfilled in the ministry of Jesus. How does the presence of
the kingdom in Jesus' ministry fit together with the prayer for the kingdom
to come? Why pray for the kingdom to come if it has already arrived in the
person of Jesus? Many scholars now agree that the kingdom of God in Jesus'
teaching is both present and future. In other words, the kingdom is already
inaugurated but not yet consummated.

One of the most remarkable statements in the Gospels is found in Matt.
12:28, where Jesus says, "But if it is by the Spirit of God that I cast out demons,
then the kingdom of God has come upon you." What is remarkable is that
Jesus saw in his exorcisms a sign that the kingdom of God had broken into
history. Matthew indicates that the eschatological Spirit promised in the OT
was active in Jesus' ministry. Here we have evidence for the already–not yet

tension that informs the NT. The kingdom had already arrived in the person and ministry of Jesus, but God's enemies had not yet been entirely removed, and the people of God did not yet possess all the blessings pledged to them in the OT.

The kingdom of God was present also in Jesus' miraculous signs and preaching. A programmatic text is Luke 4:16–30, for here Luke portrays the inauguration of Jesus' public ministry and almost certainly relates Jesus' customary message. Jesus began by citing the OT Scriptures and claiming that they reach fulfillment in his person and ministry (cf. Isa. 61:1–2; 58:6; 29:18). The good news of release from exile had now been realized through him. The year of the Lord's favor and the liberty of God's people had arrived. It does not appear here that Jesus merely states that these promises will be fulfilled at the consummation of all things. Even now, through his healing ministry, the blind were receiving sight. The gospel that he proclaimed means that the poor were hearing the glad tidings in the present. Indeed, Jesus skipped over the line in Isa. 61 that speaks of the Lord's vengeance and referred only to the time of his favor. This suggests that the era of Jesus' ministry was not a time of vengeance but the day of salvation.

A text that points in the same direction is Matt. 11:2–6. John the Baptist voiced doubts about Jesus, presumably because he languished in prison, and his expectations regarding the kingdom were not being realized. John perceived that the political impact of Jesus' ministry was relatively inconsequential and so began to question whether he was truly "the coming one." Jesus did not reply to John's messengers directly but pointed them to what was being accomplished in his ministry: the blind seeing, the lame walking, lepers cleansed, the deaf hearing, and the dead raised. Indeed, the good news was being preached to the poor. Once again Jesus cited texts in Isaiah that related what the Lord would do when he freed his people from exile (35:1–10; cf. 40:9; 42:6–7; 52:7). What stands out is that many of the prophecies found in Isaiah remained unfulfilled in Jesus' ministry. Israel did not reside in Jerusalem with everlasting joy, nor were they free from their enemies. The Romans were still menacingly present in Jesus' day. No vengeance was meted out to Israel's enemies. The world was not transformed into a new creation. All of these facts must have contributed to John's doubts about whether Jesus was truly the coming one.

Jesus responds by instructing John about the nature of his ministry. His work among the blind, the lame, the deaf, and the poor reveal that God is fulfilling his promises in Jesus. The new exodus and return from exile promised by Isaiah are a reality for those who respond to Jesus' message—the good news of the gospel is being proclaimed. And yet Jesus himself recognizes that the fulfillment astonishes. He says, "Blessed is the one who is not offended by me" (Matt. 11:6). The prophecies of Isaiah are beginning to be fulfilled, but they are not yet fulfilled in their totality. The kingdom really is present in Jesus' ministry, and yet all that God has promised to do has not become a reality. If John had eyes to see, he would perceive the eschatological tension. Something unexpected has arisen. The promises were not coming to pass in the way John or anyone else expected. God was working remarkably in Jesus' ministry, and yet only some of what was predicted had been realized. The kingdom had arrived, and yet Israel must await the day of vengeance and the completion of all that God promised (cf. also Luke 17:20–21).

In Matt. 13:11 Jesus says that the parables reveal the "secrets" or "mysteries" of the kingdom. The parable of the four soils (13:1–9, 18–23) teaches a number of different truths. What we are seeking here is what it teaches about the kingdom of God. A striking feature of the parable is that when the kingdom is proclaimed, not all accept its message. There are four different kinds of soil, and only the last bears genuine fruit. All the other soils do not continue to bear fruit, and they represent people who are unsaved on the day of judgment. One of the mysteries of the kingdom communicated here is that the word of the kingdom will not immediately have overwhelming success in this world. Many will reject the good news about the kingdom, but they will not be judged instantly. The Jews expected the kingdom to arrive in apocalyptic power, sweeping away all opponents. But this parable reveals that the message of the kingdom does not operate initially in this manner. In and through the preaching of Jesus, the kingdom is successful only in some hearts. The whole world is not changed dramatically, and yet the kingdom is at work; it is operating in the world, transforming hearts through Jesus' message (cf. Mark 4:26–29; Matt. 13:24–30, 36–43).

The nature of the kingdom is captured well by the parables of the mustard seed and the leaven (Matt. 13:31–33). These parables likewise present the mystery of the kingdom. Again we must remind ourselves that the Jews thought that the kingdom would demolish their enemies, arrive with overwhelming force, and be evident to all. Jesus, however, taught that the kingdom does not arrive as a massive tree that holds sway over the earth, like the kingdom of Nebuchadnezzar (Dan. 4). The kingdom's coming is as inconspicuous and small as a mustard seed—the smallest known seed of Jesus' day. The parable of the leaven should be interpreted like the parable of the mustard seed, and its placement immediately after the latter suggests that the two make basically the same point. The kingdom does not arrive manifestly and clearly but rather is nearly invisible, like leaven in flour. In other words, the watching world does not perceive the presence of the kingdom. Still, Jesus maintained that the kingdom had arrived in his ministry even though it was hidden and obscured. Jesus contrasted what the kingdom is like in this present age with its consummation in the age to come. Only at the end will the kingdom rule over all, and then it will be as comprehensive and complete as leaven permeating dough.

Even though the kingdom is nearly invisible, it is incomparably precious. The value of the kingdom is communicated in the parable of the hidden treasure (Matt. 13:44). Jesus concluded the parables in Matt. 13 by comparing the kingdom of heaven to a scribe "who brings out of his treasure what is new and what is old" (13:52). Here Jesus considered the OT, the many prophecies about the kingdom of God. The disciple of Jesus, however, must interpret the prophecies in light of what is new, the dawning of the kingdom of God in the ministry of Jesus. The wise disciple, then, both grasps the meaning of the OT prophecy and discerns its fulfillment in Jesus. The new and the old are rightly related and correlated to one another. The new is not imposed upon the old, nor does the old squelch the new. Both the new and the old have their proper place, but the old, ultimately and finally, can be grasped only by those who understand the newness present in Jesus.

The inauguration of the kingdom is manifested by signs, wonders, and healings. Jesus' miracles are not just the promise of the kingdom; they are themselves the actualization, at least in part, of the kingdom. In many texts in the Synoptic Gospels, the proclamation of the gospel is accompanied by physical healing and the exorcism of demons (e.g., Matt. 4:23; 9:35; 10:7–8; Luke 9:11; 10:9, 17; 11:20). Jesus' exorcisms instantiate his victory over Satan and demons, indicating that the kingdom is now present and that Jesus has triumphed over the reign of evil. Indeed, we see from Isa. 35 that such healings are indications of the presence of the kingdom—of the kingdom already exerting its power in this present evil age.

Adherents of rationalistic liberalism denied the reality of the miraculous because of their Enlightenment worldview, which denied the intervention of God in the cosmos. Their problem with miracles arose from their philosophical standpoint and cannot be derived from a study of the text. It is clear that the Gospel writers believed that the miracles truly occurred. The miracles are not merely spiritual realities that can be reduced to spiritual lessons or moral truths. Indeed, there are sound reasons for believing that the miracles actually occurred in Jesus' ministry, that the stories go back to the historical Jesus.

Meier (1994: 630) says about the miracles "that total fabrication by the early church is, practically speaking, impossible"; and, "the tradition of Jesus' miracles is more firmly supported by the criteria of historicity than are a number of other well-known and often readily accepted traditions about his life and ministry. . . . Put dramatically but with not too much exaggeration: if the miracle tradition from Jesus' public ministry were rejected *in toto* as unhistorical, so should every other Gospel tradition about him." Indeed, Meier (1994: 773–873) does not shrink back from saying that, as far as one can determine matters historically, there are solid grounds for believing that Jesus raised people from the dead.[1] The miracles, then, testify to the already–not yet character of the kingdom. They demonstrate that the kingdom has

1. Meier (1994: 968) is not claiming that these accounts are actually miracles but only that what occurred was thought to be miraculous by some of Jesus' contemporaries. It is not my purpose here to examine Meier's philosophical approach, which is, I think, too limiting. My point is simply that even within the bounds of his criteria, solid reasons exist to believe that

entered into this world, and yet not everyone is healed, which shows that the kingdom is not yet consummated. Death and evil still cast their long shadow over the world.

The kingdom of God is a central theme in Jesus' ministry, and the meaning of the concept must be discerned from the OT because Jesus nowhere defines it. When Jesus referred to God's kingdom, he had in mind God's saving power, the fulfillment of his saving promises. When God's saving promises become a reality, then those who are God's enemies will be judged. Still, Jesus called attention to God's saving work on behalf of his people. The surprising element in Jesus' teaching on the kingdom is its ambiguous character. The kingdom can be explained in terms of the already–not yet. The kingdom was inaugurated in Jesus' ministry but not yet consummated. It had arrived, but the full salvation and judgment promised had not yet come to pass.

Eternal Life and Eschatology

One of the primary themes in John's Gospel is life. Life in John is not an abstract entity but is rooted in John's Jewish worldview. Life belongs to the age to come, which is inaugurated by the resurrection. What is remarkable in reading John is his emphasis on the gift of life now. He does not focus on the future age, when the resurrection will occur. He fixes his gaze on what believers in Christ possess even now through faith in Jesus as the Christ. The gift of life in the present age is available only because Jesus is the resurrection and the life (11:25). The life of the age to come has dawned because Jesus of Nazareth has risen from the dead (John 20). In the resurrection of Jesus, the coming age has invaded the present age. Life has penetrated where only death reigned. Light has dawned where darkness shrouded all. Truth has arrived to conquer falsehood.

The triumph over death is achieved in Jesus' resurrection, and in John the resurrection of Jesus is rooted in history. John does not hang his teaching about life upon a gnostic hope of life in some ethereal sphere. He does not conceive of life as spiritual over against the material. Life is inaugurated in the space-time sphere by the physical resurrection of Jesus from the dead.

The emphasis on the present fulfillment of God's promises in John is rooted in the cross and resurrection of Jesus Christ. Hence, those who enjoy eternal life now eat Jesus' flesh and drink his blood (6:53–54). Life in the age to come is available only through Jesus, who possesses life in himself (5:26) and is the way, the truth, and the life (14:6). Participation in life does not stem from abstract faith in God but rather comes by a faith that eats Jesus' flesh and drinks his blood. In other words, the life of the age to come becomes a reality as one trusts in the work of Jesus as the crucified and risen Lord.

Jesus performed many miracles. Incidentally, Meier (1994: 874–1038) is more skeptical about the historical reliability of the nature miracles, except for the miraculous feedings.

In Jesus, life has been introduced into the world, and that life shines in the darkness (1:4–5). He is the light of life (8:12) and came so that people could have life (10:10). The life of the age to come is, therefore, radically Christ-centered. Eternal life comes by knowing Jesus Christ and by knowing the one true God (17:3). Human beings must come to Jesus in order to enjoy life (5:40). Indeed, the purpose of this Gospel is enunciated in the claim that one must believe in Jesus in order to obtain eternal life (20:30–31). We are not surprised to learn that John frequently emphasizes that those who believe enjoy life eternal (3:15–16, 36; 5:24; 6:47). The teaching of 1 John is similar.[2] Jesus is the life, and the life was manifested in history through the incarnation (1 John 1:1–2). The promise of eternal life is realized in him (2:25), and such life is secured by his death (3:16), in which he yielded up his life for others. Hence, all those who believe in the Son enjoy eternal life now because such life is bound up with Jesus and his self-revelation (5:11–13). As the epistle says in closing, Jesus himself "is the true God and eternal life" (5:20).

First John 2:8 demonstrates that the new age has arrived, for "the darkness is passing away and the true light is already shining." The overlap between the present and future age is evident in this verse, for the darkness and light exist concurrently. The age to come has arrived by virtue of the death and resurrection of Christ, but its arrival does not spell the immediate removal of evil and darkness. The Jews expected that when the coming age dawned, the evil age would be set aside immediately. The fulfillment of the OT promises is realized, however, in a surprising way. The light shines without instantaneously quenching the darkness. We would be mistaken, though, to conclude that light and darkness are now equivalent, as if the two balance each other with equal force. John emphasizes the defeat of evil (it is passing away) and the triumph of the light (it is shining). Ultimately the light that has dawned in Christ will shine triumphantly over all.

A similar theme is communicated powerfully in John 5:24–25. The final judgment is reserved for the future, and yet those who believe in the Son will never face such a judgment, for they have already entered into life. They face the day of reckoning with confidence because of their trust in the Son. Interestingly, 1 John 3:14 communicates the same truth: "We know that we have passed out of death into life, because we love the brothers. Whoever does not love abides in death." The same verb (*metabainō*) is used in John 5:24, again conveying the truth that believers currently possess life. The great transaction has occurred so that the reign of death has ended, even though believers still await physical death. Nevertheless, they have now passed into life and abide in life, and hence the age to come is now a reality. As Jesus declares in 10:28,

---

2. With most scholars, I maintain that the author of the Gospel of John and 1–3 John is the same person.

"I give them eternal life." Such life is not reserved for a future time but is the present gift of the Son of God to his sheep.

The age to come has arrived since believers are forgiven of their sins and know God (1 John 2:12–14), and therefore they are assured that they are his children (3:1–3). The world still exists and continues to allure believers. And yet believers now enjoy victory over the world by faith (5:4–5). The Synoptic Gospels emphasize the fulfillment of God's promises by speaking of the kingdom of God, but in John the focus is not on God's kingdom but on eternal life. Still, the two notions are remarkably similar. As Köstenberger (2004: 123) says, "That the expressions 'kingdom of God' and 'eternal life' are essentially equivalent is suggested by their parallel use in Matthew 19:16, 24 pars." John particularly emphasizes that this life is available now for those who believe in Jesus; conversely, those who do not put their trust in Jesus stand under God's judgment even now.

Inaugurated Eschatology in Paul

The tension between inaugurated and consummated eschatology identified in the Synoptic Gospels and in the Johannine literature also informs the remainder of the NT. Indeed, the prominence of the already–not yet in Paul confirms that eschatological tension was a characteristic feature of NT theology.

Jewish thought distinguished between this age and the age to come. This age is marred by sin, disease, and death, whereas the age to come brings life, abundance, and joy (2 Esd. 2:36, 39; 4:27; 7:113; 9:18–19). The distinction between the two ages, as we have already observed, is found in the Gospels. Matthew contrasts "this age" with "the age to come" (12:32). Mark and Luke place eternal life in the age to come (Mark 10:30; Luke 18:30). Jesus contrasts the "sons of this age" who marry with those who "attain" the coming age, where marriage is no longer practiced (Luke 20:34–35). Those who belong to "this age" are consumed with wealth (Luke 16:8 NRSV), and hence Jesus speaks of the worries and concerns that animate people during this age (Matt. 13:22; Mark 4:19). Since there is an age to come, the present age is temporary and will come to an end (Matt. 13:39–40, 49; 24:3; 28:20).

The term "kingdom" and the phrase "kingdom of God" are not common in Paul, and yet the instances where they do occur indicate that the already–not yet theme, so characteristic of the teaching of Jesus, is present in these Pauline texts as well (Rom. 14:17; 1 Cor. 4:20; 6:9–10; 15:24, 50; Gal. 5:21; Eph. 5:5; Col. 1:13; 4:11; 1 Thess. 2:12; 2 Thess. 1:5; 2 Tim. 4:1, 18). In most instances the "kingdom of God" refers to the future kingdom that awaits believers (see esp. 1 Cor. 6:9–10; 15:24; Eph. 5:5), but in Col. 1:13 believers are now transferred to God's kingdom, and Rom. 14:17 suggests that the power of the kingdom is now at work because believers enjoy the gift of the Spirit, and hence righteousness, joy, and peace are theirs.

Paul also believed in two ages: this present evil age and the coming age of righteousness. The clearest example is found in Eph. 1:21, where he specifically differentiates between "this age" and "the one to come," claiming that Jesus rules over all during the present age and will continue his reign in the coming era.

Paul often contrasts the values and behavior of those living in this age with those of the coming one. Satan is described as the god of this age (2 Cor. 4:4), indicating that those under the dominion of the devil engage in false worship. Since Satan rules as the god of this age, it follows that unbelievers live in accord with the standards of this world (Eph. 2:2). The impact of the old world order displays itself in the domain of scholarship and the intellect. The rhetoricians and debaters of this age are celebrated (1 Cor. 1:20). Those endowed with rhetorical ability are deemed wise (1:20; 3:18–19). But Paul was unimpressed with the dazzling skills of orators because the rulers of this age, with all their so-called wisdom, crucified the glorious Lord (2:6, 8), demonstrating their failure to grasp true wisdom.

Paul taught that Christians live in between the times inasmuch as the present evil age lingers, even as the new age has invaded history. "The ends of the ages have come" (1 Cor. 10:11 NRSV), signifying the fulfillment, at least in part, of God's saving promises. The cross and resurrection of Christ are the turning point in history. Believers have been set "free from the present evil age" by virtue of the death of Christ (Gal. 1:4 NRSV). The form of this present world is passing away (1 Cor. 7:29–31), so that the activities of everyday life are relativized in light of the coming eschaton. Joy and sorrow, buying and selling, marriage and education—all must be viewed in light of the shortness of the time, the temporary character of human history (see Schreiner 2008: 755–801). Therefore, Paul did not criticize riches per se, but he did warn the rich in the present era not to pin their hopes on that which is fleeting (1 Tim. 6:17).

Christians live in, so to speak, the twilight zone, for they have experienced the saving power of the age to come, and yet they still reside in the present evil age. Even now Jesus reigns, but the consummation of his rule and the destruction of every enemy have not yet occurred (Eph. 1:21; 1 Cor. 15:26–28). Because of the cross of Christ, believers are a new creation (Gal. 1:4; 6:14–15; 2 Cor. 5:17), and yet the redemption that they enjoy (Rom. 3:24) is not yet completed, for they endure the anguish of death and await the redemption of the body (8:23; cf. Eph. 1:14). In the meantime, as believers inhabit the interval between inauguration and consummation, they must resist the blandishments of this world (Rom. 12:2). The world allures and captivates even those who have the firstfruits of the Spirit, but those in whom the Spirit dwells must surmount fleshly desires and live in the realm of the Spirit (8:13).

The Spirit constitutes the "firstfruits" of God's work (Rom. 8:23). Just as Christ is the firstfruits of the resurrection (1 Cor. 15:20, 23), guaranteeing the physical resurrection of believers, so the gift of the Spirit ensures that God will fulfill the remainder of his saving promises. The Spirit constitutes a pledge (*arrabōn*) that God will redeem the bodies of believers by raising them from the dead on the last day (Eph. 1:14; cf. Rom. 8:23; 2 Cor. 1:22). All of this fits with the main point being argued here: the presence of the Spirit indicates that the new age has dawned, but believers have not yet obtained all that God has promised.

The inauguration of the new creation in the present age (2 Cor. 5:17; Gal. 6:15) points forward to the future, for Christians anticipate with confidence and joy the life of the age to come, when they will enjoy eternal life (e.g., Rom. 2:7; 5:21; 6:23; Gal. 6:8; Titus 1:2). As the messianic and Davidic king (Ps. 110:1), Jesus now rules over every enemy (Eph. 1:19–23; 1 Cor. 15:26–28). But the fullness of his power will be evident on the final day of judgment and salvation. Then believers will celebrate and commemorate forever the grace bestowed on them in Christ Jesus (Eph. 2:7).

The Gift of the Spirit in Acts

The gift of the Spirit signals the arrival of the eschaton. According to the prophet Joel, God pledged to pour out his Spirit (Joel 2:28). Joel anticipated the day of the Lord, when Yahweh would reverse the fortunes of Israel by vindicating his people and punishing the nations that opposed Israel (Joel 3). Those who curse Israel would be cursed, and those who bless Israel would be blessed, in accordance with God's promise to Abraham (Gen. 12:3). Joel prophesied about the day when Jerusalem would become holy, and the land would burst with fruitfulness as wine and milk flow in abundance and a fountain springs up from the Lord's house (Joel 3:17–18).

The signature of such promises is the dispensing of the Spirit; according to Acts, Peter proclaimed that the day of fulfillment had come (Acts 2:16–21). The Spirit was poured out by Jesus, the crucified and risen Lord (2:33), for at his exaltation he was crowned as Lord and Christ (2:36), and he granted the Spirit to his people. The enthronement of Jesus of Nazareth as Lord and Christ fulfilled the Davidic covenant, indicating that he reigns as the Davidic king (cf. 2 Sam. 7; 1 Chron. 17; Pss. 89; 132). As the messianic king, he confers the Spirit on his people, and the gift of the Spirit indicates that God's promises are now being fulfilled. Luke, however, did not envisage the coming of the Spirit as the completion of all of God's promises. History will reach its culmination and climax at the coming of Jesus Christ, when God will fulfill everything promised in the prophetic writings (Acts 3:20–21). Jesus now reigns, and the Spirit now indwells the hearts of believers, but in the interim before Jesus comes again, he rules from heaven. The apostles' question to Jesus about when the kingdom would be restored to Israel (1:6) should not be dismissed as a mistaken departure into nationalistic ideology. Jesus' promise of the Spirit naturally precipitated the question, since in the OT the restoration of Israel was indissolubly joined with the promise that God would pour out his Spirit (cf. Isa. 32; 44:1–5; Ezek. 36–37). The disciples did not yet comprehend the already–not yet tension that informed Jesus' earthly ministry. Jesus answered the question by implying that the restoration of Israel and the fulfillment of all of God's promises are not coterminous with the granting of the Spirit (Acts 1:7–8). An interval exists between the gift of the Spirit and the consummation.

Hebrews

At first glance, it seems that Hebrews does not share the same eschatological viewpoint evident in the rest of the NT. The linear eschatology found elsewhere in the NT appears to be replaced by a vertical contrast between what is below and what is above. Indeed, Hebrews could be interpreted along Platonic lines, with the earthly representing the heavenly, so that the latter is the archetype of the former. The true tent was not the tabernacle erected by Moses (8:2), for the earthly tent points to and represents the very presence of God in heaven (9:24). The holy place and the inner sanctum of the temple (the holy of holies) are merely copies and anticipations of God's dwelling. The author of Hebrews drew upon Exod. 25:40, where Moses was instructed to make the tabernacle in accord with the pattern revealed to him on Mount Sinai. The earthly articles of the tabernacle (Heb. 9:1–5), it seems, mirror heavenly reality. Similarly, the sacrifices and gifts offered, along with the various regulations relating to foods and drinks and washings, relate only to the physical and symbolic sphere (9:8–10). They point to something greater and higher, for they cannot effect forgiveness of sins. The earthly sacrifices purify the copies of the heavenly things, but they fail to secure forgiveness in God's very presence (9:23–24). Only the sacrifice of Christ truly and definitively achieves full atonement for sin. Just as the tabernacle and the articles in it point to a vertical reality, so also the earthly priests from the tribe of Levi anticipate a superior priesthood, a Melchizedekian one. The priests "serve a copy and shadow of the heavenly things" (8:5; cf. 10:1). Hence, the ritual duties of the priests symbolize access into God's presence (9:6–8). The holy of holies may be entered only once a year by priests, signifying the unavailability of regular and unhindered admission to God.

Even though Hebrews has superficial affinities with Platonic thought, the "vertical" language of the letter should be plotted into its eschatological world-view. The already–not yet tension found elsewhere in the NT permeates Hebrews as well. The focus on eschatology surfaces in the opening verses of the letter, where "these last days" have arrived with the coming of God's Son (1:2) and the fulfillment of OT prophecy (1:5–14). Final and definitive forgiveness of sins has been accomplished by the work of Christ (1:3; 10:12); the power of the coming age has invaded this present era (6:5). Forgiveness of sins must be understood eschatologically, along the lines of promise and fulfillment. The author of Hebrews argues that forgiveness signals the fulfillment of the new covenant (8:6–13; 10:16–18; cf. Jer. 31:31–34). Inevitably, therefore, the old covenant has become obsolete and is no longer in force for Christians. The contrast between the old and new covenants certifies that the timeline of redemptive history is crucial for the author.

The eschatological cast of the author's mind is apparent in Heb. 9:26 as well. Christ "appeared once for all at the end of the ages to put away sin by the sacrifice of himself." The "end of the ages" is another way of speaking of "these last days" (1:2). The forgiveness of sins "at the end of the ages" confirms the fulfillment of the new-covenant promises found in Jeremiah. The end of redemptive history has dawned by virtue of the work of Christ. The author fixes our attention on the work of Christ that is featured at the beginning of the letter, where after accomplishing cleansing for sins, Christ sat down at God's right hand (1:3). The author's thought cannot be restricted to vertical categories; it also operates horizontally, on a redemptive-historical timeline. Hebrews does not dismiss OT revelation as a mistake or substandard but conceives of history in terms of promise and fulfillment. The OT sacrifices point toward and anticipate the sacrifice of Christ. God ordained the Aaronic priesthood but never intended it to last forever. The Aaronic priesthood functions as a type of the Melchizedekian priesthood, which is superior because it is based on God's oath (7:11–28). The old covenant prepares the way for and even prophesies the coming of the new.

We might conclude that Hebrews swallows up the not yet into the already because it emphasizes Jesus' reign and final forgiveness of sins. Hebrews, however, maintains the same eschatological tension as is found in the rest of the NT witness. Jesus now reigns, but enemies still remain and have not yet been subjected under his feet (1:13; 10:12–13; cf. Ps. 110:1). Christ has dealt with sin definitively once for all, and yet the day of judgment has not yet commenced; believers await Jesus' return, when he will complete the salvation already accomplished (Heb. 9:26–28). Psalm 8 reflects upon humanity's role in the universe—the high honor of ruling the entire world for God. Hebrews 2 engages in a commentary on the psalm, acknowledging that the world is not ruled by human beings the way it should be (2:8). We know that the world has gone awry because of death (2:14–15), and death can be traced to the wickedness of human beings. Jesus, however, succeeded where Adam and the rest of humanity failed. As the sinless one, he lived as the perfect "Adam" (4:15; 7:26). Moreover, because of his suffering and death, he is exalted and now "crowned with glory and honor" (2:9). The already–not yet tension infuses Heb. 2. Jesus reigns as the second Adam, but the work of his reign is incomplete. He has defeated death for believers, and yet believers are not exempted from physical death (2:14–15).

The believing recipients of Hebrews have been forgiven; they have been sanctified once and for all by the sacrifice of Christ (10:14), and yet the whole of Hebrews indicates an eschatological reserve. The readers are urgently warned not to forsake the salvation that they have embraced. They must not drift away from "such a great salvation" (2:1–4; 3:12–4:13; 5:11–6:12; 10:19–12:3; 12:25–29). Homiletical warnings permeate the letter, demonstrating that believers inhabit the period between the already and the not yet. Salvation is eschatological, and believers await its consummation, and hence they are called to believe, obey, and endure in the interval. The heavenly city and country have not yet arrived (11:10, 13–16). Believers in Christ do not find a lasting city on this earth (13:14). The tension between what has already been received and the final reception of salvation is reflected well in the teaching on entering God's rest. Hebrews 4:3 claims that those who believe in Christ have already entered God's rest. Furthermore, the use of the word "today" (4:7) emphasizes the present realization, at least in part, of the promise. And yet 3:12–4:11 emphasizes repeatedly that the promised rest still remains for God's people (4:1, 6). The rest is fundamentally eschatological since those who rest cease from their works as God ceased from his (4:10). When believers enter the heavenly city, they cease activity because the day of striving has come to an end.

Soundings from the Rest of the New Testament

The already–not yet theme is not as pervasive in the rest of the NT (James, 1–2 Peter, Jude, and Revelation). The purpose and occasional nature of the documents furnish an adequate explanation. The book of Revelation, being a prophetic-apocalyptic work, naturally focuses on the day of future judgment and salvation when God vindicates his people and condemns the wicked. During the present age the church suffers and dies for its witness to Jesus, and the beast and Babylon oppress the people of God. Still, believers should shun fear and embrace hope because the beast's hour of triumph will not endure. Satan's opportunity to persecute Christians is limited to three and one-half years (12:14)—that is, forty-two months (11:2; 13:5) or one thousand two hundred and sixty days (11:3; 12:6). Scholars dispute whether the interval of time should be construed literally or whether the number is symbolic. The latter seems more likely because the number "seven" symbolizes perfection and completeness, as in 1:4, where the seven spirits stand for the Holy Spirit. One-half of seven denotes a time in which evil dominates and rules over the world, the time when Satan has been cast from heaven to earth after the victory accomplished by Christ at the cross (12:7–12). He persecutes the people of God during this interval (12:14); it thus seems that the evil period designated by half of seven years refers to the entire era between the cross of Christ and his return.

Since believers suffer in the interval between the cross and resurrection, Revelation looks forward to the consummation of God's purposes, to the day when Satan, the beast, and the false prophet are consigned to the lake of fire (19:20; 20:10), when Babylon will be overthrown (17:1–19:5), when the blood of the saints will be avenged (6:9–11)—the day when the kingdoms of the world become the kingdom of our Lord and his Christ (11:15–19). At the consummation God will introduce a new heaven and earth, and he will fulfill his covenant and dwell personally with his people (21:1–22:5).

The book of Revelation fixes our attention on the completion of God's covenantal promises, but the "already" theme is not entirely absent. Christ has delivered believers "from our sins by his blood and made us a kingdom, priests to his God and Father" (1:5–6). The decisive battle for believers has been won. They conquer "by the blood of the Lamb" (12:11). Their robes are glistening white by virtue of Jesus' blood as God's Lamb (7:14). Jesus has expelled Satan from heaven (12:9) and has been exalted to the right hand of God and his throne (12:5) by virtue of his work on the cross. As God's slain Lamb, he has opened the scroll with seven seals (5:1–14), so that the definitive and irrevocable work in salvation history has been done. In the interim period in which Satan attacks believers, they must endure suffering (3:10; 13:10; 14:12) and "conquer" (2:7, 11, 17, 26; 3:5, 12, 21; 15:2; 21:7) to obtain the final reward. The already–not yet schema is present in Revelation. The cross of Christ is the fulcrum of history; he has redeemed believers from sin. Still, they must suffer and endure until Jesus returns and recompenses their enemies.

The letters of James and 1 Peter are addressed to believers undergoing trials and/or persecution. Again, we must recall the occasional and circumstantial character of both letters, since neither constitutes a treatise on Christian theology. Both authors intend to strengthen believers facing difficulties that could quench their faith. James regularly considers the day of judgment as the time when believers will be exalted and unbelievers will face judgment. The "poor" (AT), a term used virtually synonymously with "believer," will be exalted at the judgment, whereas the "rich" will perish (James 1:9–11). The one who shows mercy to others and desists from partiality, particularly to the economically well-off, will obtain mercy on the last day (2:12–13). The wealthy who oppress their workers and deny them their wages in order to live sumptuously are storing up judgment against themselves on the day of reckoning (5:1–6). The righteous should exercise patience because the Lord will come soon, even if his delay seems inordinately long (5:7–8). Since ethical exhortation dominates the letter, the lack of emphasis on realized eschatology is unremarkable.

Still, two texts seem to point toward a realized eschatology. First, there is 1:18: "Of his own will he brought us forth by the word of truth, that we should be a kind of firstfruits of his creatures." Despite some good arguments supporting a reference to physical creation, it is probable that James speaks of the spiritual birth of his readers—their new life in Christ. Even though believers await the judgment of the final day, they are the firstfruits of God's promised work in all his creation. Ultimately, he promises new heavens and a new earth (Isa. 65:17; 66:22), and the new life of believers testifies that they are the first installment of the blessing intended for all of creation. The second indication of realized eschatology is in James 2:5: even now God has chosen that the poor would be "rich in faith and heirs of the kingdom." In this present era they are God's people and trust in him, and yet they await the eschatological gift of the kingdom.

In his First Letter, Peter addressed suffering believers, encouraging them to persevere in their troubles because of the promise of end-time salvation. Sufferings cause grief and represent God's purifying judgment of his flock, but their sorrows are short-lived compared with the final inheritance that believers will receive when Jesus returns (1:4–7; 4:17; 5:10). Peter emphasized the future character of salvation in describing it as an inheritance that believers will receive in the future (1:4). Both husbands and wives share the same destiny as "co-heirs of the grace of life" (3:7 AT). Presently God fortifies believers so that they will obtain a salvation that will be revealed only when Jesus comes again (1:5, 7). In one sense, salvation is incomplete, for believers await "the outcome of" their "faith," which is "the salvation of" their "souls" (1:9), and elders shepherding the flock anticipate receiving a glorious and permanent reward when Jesus appears (5:4). In speaking of loving life and seeing good days (3:10), Peter likely referred to life in the eschaton—the future reward awaiting the righteous. Supporting this interpretation is the judgment awaiting the wicked according to 3:12, for the Lord's face will turn against them forever on the last day.

Peter did not confine himself to future eschatology, for God has caused believers to be born again by means of the word of the gospel (1 Pet. 1:3, 23). Their eschatological hope is grounded in the new life that they have already received (1:3). God has ransomed believers from their vain and futile life by means of Christ's blood (1:18–19). The decisive and fundamental change has already occurred in their lives, so that the redemption that they possess anchors their future hope. The remarkable text about the OT prophets in 1:10–12 verifies that believers live on the fulfillment side of the promise. The prophets searched diligently, wondering when the prophecies about the Messiah would be fulfilled. They discovered that their ministry was not intended for their own times; they prophesied for the sake of the believers of Peter's day. Clearly, the readers should appreciate that they live during the age of fulfillment, in the era when God's promises are coming to pass. The last times have arrived, and their commencement is attested by the coming of Jesus the Christ (1:20).

The letters of 2 Peter and Jude respond to licentious false teachers in the churches. Both of them, therefore, emphasize the eschatological judgment of such opponents. The adversaries in 2 Peter may have collapsed the not yet entirely into the already, so that they deny the second coming of Christ (3:1–13). The transfiguration (1:16–18) functions as a proleptic anticipation of Christ's return, and his coming will commence the day of judgment, when scoffers will be destroyed. Neither Peter nor Jude said much about the already, doubtless because of the circumstances encountered in their churches in responding to teachers who deny a future judgment. Still, Jude reminds believers that they are beloved by God and kept by Jesus Christ (1). Peter taught that believers even now share in the divine nature and have escaped the world's corruption (2 Pet. 1:3–4; 2:20). Both authors proclaim that God keeps those who are his, and that he will guard them from the onslaughts of the false teachers until the last day (2 Pet. 2:9; Jude 24–25).

Conclusion

The tension between the already and the not yet permeates the NT. The authors address the theme in a variety of ways, and hence there is not a set terminology. In some instances we have a contrast between this age and the coming one. Other texts speak of a new creation, of the coming of the kingdom, or of eternal life. The word "salvation" is used to denote both the present fulfillment of God's promises and the final fulfillment. Some pieces of literature (e.g., Revelation) focus on final fulfillment, whereas others (e.g., Ephesians and Colossians) put the emphasis on realized eschatology. The variation is likely accounted for by the purpose of the author and the situation of the readers. Still, in every case we find that God has begun to fulfill his saving promises in Jesus Christ, and yet believers still await the completion of what God has promised. The promises made to Abraham have been fulfilled in a decisive way through the ministry, death, and resurrection of Jesus Christ, but the end of history has not arrived. To use an illustration from the theater, the opening curtain has risen on the play announced so long ago by the OT, but the final curtain has yet to come down on the last act.

Pastoral Reflection

Does the already–not yet emphasis of the NT make any difference in Christian life and ministry? First, we must beware of political utopian schemes. Marxism is a Christian heresy that promises heaven on earth by guaranteeing that the not yet will become a reality now. We must never become satisfied with this world, and yet we must not think that we can ever make it like heaven either. Second, believers *say* that churches are imperfect, but they often live as if they expect them to be perfect, and hence in the Western world they often migrate from church to church, looking for the perfect fit instead of learning to love the brothers and sisters and pastors God has given them. Third, many marriages fall apart because we expect our marriages to satisfy all our needs. Practically, we forget about the not yet, and we expect more of our marriages than they can deliver. Too often the perfect becomes the enemy of the good. Fourth, we can fall into a fundamentalism as Christians where we demand perfection from our children, while forgetting about the log in our own eyes. I have seen too many children rebel against the Christian faith because their parents placed unrealistic demands upon them. Fifth, an overemphasis on the already can lead to perfectionism in our view of the Christian life, and hence we can become overly discouraged about how far we fall short.

Finally, each of the examples above can be reversed. We can so overemphasize the not-yet that we compromise with this sinful world. Or we become comfortable in our churches and lose a passion to see Christ glorified in them. So too, we may become too lax with our children and fail to discipline them wisely. In the same way, we may rationalize sin in our lives. Clearly, the already-but-not-yet theme has many practical ramifications.

2

The Centrality of God
in New Testament Theology

⟡

We tend to look past what constantly stands in front of us. If we see
them every day, we often take for granted verdant trees, stunning
sunsets, and powerful waves thundering on the beach. Similarly, in
reading the NT, we are prone to screen out what the NT says about God himself. God is, so to speak, shoved to the side, and we investigate other themes,
such as justification, reconciliation, redemptive history, and new creation. I
suggest that the centrality of God in Christ is the foundational theme for the
narrative unfolded in the NT. Yet we must beware of abstracting God himself
from the story communicated in the NT. Focusing on God does not mean
that we engage in systematic theology. Biblical theology does not pursue the
philosophical implications of the doctrine of God, for such an enterprise is
distinctive of systematic theology. We may think that nothing further needs
to be said about "God" in a theology of the NT because it is obvious and assumed that our theology is about God. But if we ignore what is obvious and
assumed, we may overlook one of the most important themes in NT theology.
We may gaze past what looms massively in front of us simply because we are
accustomed to the scenery.

It should also be said at the outset that the grounding theme of NT theology
is magnifying God in Christ. Separating the revelation of God in the NT from

Christology, as if God is central and Christ is secondary, is impossible. God is magnified and praised in revealing himself through Christ as God fulfills his saving promises. The coming of Christ does not diminish the centrality of God but rather enhances it.

It might be objected that to speak of the Father, Son, and Spirit is to fall prey to systematic theology and to later trinitarian theology. However, the argument made here is that an inductive study of the NT itself demonstrates that the Father, Son, and Spirit are foundational and central to NT theology. Moreover, our study of the Father, Son, and Spirit must be integrated with the fulfillment of God's saving promises—the already–not yet theme in the NT. The Father fulfills his saving promises in history by sending his Son, and the Son's work is vindicated through the sending of the Spirit. In the work of the Father, Son, and Spirit our focus is directed to the God of the promise and to God's saving work in fulfilling the promises.

In the current chapter we will briefly explore what the NT writers tell us about God. What stands out is that God is the sovereign creator of all, who rules over all of creation. God the creator is also the Father of believers and the Lord Jesus Christ. In his mercy and grace he saves human beings. Those who refuse to obey the Lord will face judgment on the last day. All glory and praise and honor belong to him as the Lord and Redeemer.

The Synoptic Gospels

One of the pervasive themes in the OT, from the very first verse, is that God is the creator of all that exists. Indeed, God's role as creator is woven into the fabric of nearly every piece of literature. Since God is the creator of all, he is the sovereign Lord, who demands to be worshiped above anything or anyone in the universe (Exod. 20:3), for he is the one true and living God. Creatures, by definition, should give primacy to their creator. Deuteronomy 6:4–5 was fundamental to Jewish thought, and the Shema (6:4) was said daily by Israelites. They were reminded by these words that there is only one God, and that their supreme loyalty should be given to him alone. God is not an impersonal creator, and he has shown his mercy and love to his people by redeeming them from slavery in Egypt. Thompson (2001: 54) summarizes well the OT portrayal of God: "God is identified, first, as the Maker and Creator of all that is. God is the life-giving God. Because God is the creator of all, God is also supreme over all other beings, whether heavenly or human. Epithets such as 'Almighty' and 'Most High' indicate God's supremacy over all other figures and underscore the extent of God's sovereignty. As Creator and Sovereign, God therefore merits worship and honor."

Isaiah also repeatedly emphasized that Yahweh is the one and only God, and that idols stem from the futile imagination of human beings (e.g., Isa.

45:20–21). Yahweh is the true and living God, the first and the last, and the ruler of the kingdoms of the world. Similarly, in the book of Daniel the sovereignty and rule of God over all nations is expressed in a number of texts (Dan. 4:34–35). When NT writers speak of God, they refer to the true and living God revealed in the OT, the God who reigns over the nations. God's rule over all things is grounded in the fact that he is the creator of all things, the maker of heaven and earth.

As we consider what the Synoptic Gospels say about God, it is necessary to be selective. What the Synoptics teach about God can be embraced under three major themes: (1) God's sovereignty, (2) God's mercy, and (3) God's glory. The term "heaven" emphasizes God's sovereignty and majesty. He is the one exalted far above human beings. Both "kingdom of heaven" and "kingdom of God" refer to the kingdom that belongs to God. Here there is no need to rehearse how pervasive this theme is in the Synoptics. Yet we stress the fact that the kingdom is *God's*. He is the sovereign one who rules over all.

The kingdom of God suggests God's rule and reign over all, but we have also seen that the kingdom of God in the Synoptics refers to the fulfillment of God's saving promises. The coming of the kingdom in Jesus Christ testifies that God is a promise-keeping God, and hence the coming of the kingdom spells the fulfillment of his promise to bless his people. Matthew's opening genealogy conveys that God is a promise keeper, for Jesus is traced back to David and Abraham (Matt. 1:1–17). He fulfills the covenant made with Abraham to bless the whole world (Gen. 12:3) and the covenant of an eternal dynasty pledged to David (2 Sam. 7; 1 Chron. 17). In the same way, the infancy narratives in Luke 1–2 emphasize that God is fulfilling his covenantal promises relating to his kingdom.

God's kingdom calls attention to both his sovereignty and his mercy, yet it also communicates the goal for human existence. Human beings are to live for the sake of God's kingdom, and nothing should take precedence over the kingdom (e.g., Matt. 6:33). But this means that human beings are to give the whole of their lives over to God. He is the great treasure that is received when the kingdom is found (see 13:44–46). To live for the sake of the kingdom is simply another way of saying that human beings live for God's sake—for his glory.

God's Sovereignty

The word "sovereignty" designates God's rule and control over the world that he has made. He bestows beauty on the lilies and clothes the grass of the field (Matt. 6:28–30). He is the living God (26:63); nothing is outside the realm of possibility for him, so that he can grant conception to a virgin (Luke 1:37) and give eternal life to human beings (Matt. 19:26). Human beings limit God because they do not know his power to raise people from the dead (22:29). If he wills, he can turn stones into the children of Abraham (3:9), and he could, if he so desired, deliver Jesus from death even when he was upon the cross (27:43).

God declares his will authoritatively through his word (e.g., Matt. 4:4; 15:6; Luke 3:2; 5:1; 8:11, 21; 11:28). His authority manifests itself in his control over the course of history. He raised up David and installed him as king over Israel (Luke 1:32). Angels are commissioned by God to carry out his will and purposes (e.g., Matt. 1:20, 24; 2:13, 19; 4:11; Luke 1:19, 26; 2:9–14). Not even a sparrow falls apart from his will, and hence believers can be assured that he watches over and cares for them (Matt. 10:29–31). The infancy narratives also relate God's sovereignty: despite Herod's machinations, Jesus escapes from his clutches (Matt. 2). The story echoes the preservation of Moses and Israel during the time of the Pharaohs, impressing upon the reader God's sovereignty in working out his saving plan. God knows the hearts of all people infallibly (Luke 16:15). He hides the revelation of himself from those who are wise and proud but discloses himself to those who are humble (Matt. 11:25–26).

God's Mercy

The Father rules over all things, but his reign over all reflects his love and mercy. The birds find their daily sustenance from his hand (Matt. 6:26), and he adorns flowers with their spectacular and quiet beauty (6:28–29). God's love cannot be limited to the people of God; he demonstrates his love to unbelievers in sending sunlight and rain to all (5:45). He knows what people need even before they voice their requests in prayer, and hence frantic and superstitious repetitions should be avoided (6:7–8; Luke 12:30). From these texts we see that God's sovereignty expresses his love. God's sovereignty does not signify the harsh rule of a tyrannical and mean-spirited despot. He gives good things to those who make requests of him (Matt. 7:11), or as Luke says, he grants the Holy Spirit to those who entreat him (11:13). God should not be compared to a malicious father who smuggles a serpent that looks like a fish into his child's lunch (Luke 11:11). When asked for an egg, he does not substitute a scorpion that is rolled up so that it appears to be an egg (11:12). His heart is generous and giving, and he is not a crabbed and penurious father. He is good (Mark 10:18), forgiving the sins of those who come to him in repentance (2:7). God's beneficence is captured well in Luke 12:32: "Fear not, little flock, for it is your Father's good pleasure to give you the kingdom." The Father's tender care for his weak and needy people is represented by his giving them the kingdom. He does not give the kingdom reluctantly or grudgingly but joyfully bestows it on his people.

The love of God is remarkably displayed in the parables of Luke 15. The lost sheep, the lost coin, and the lost sons all represent God's overflowing joy when sinners repent and turn to him. In the face of grumbling by Pharisees and scribes, Jesus intended all three parables to defend his table fellowship with social outcasts and sinners (15:1–2). The unforgettable story of the two lost sons communicates this truth powerfully. The father in the parable does not bear a grudge against his returning younger son by recalling how he wasted his inheritance. In Palestinian culture running was considered undignified, but the father does not care about decorum. Filled with compassion, he runs to greet his son and embraces him with kisses. And the father does not allow the son to finish his confession of sin and failure (cf. 15:18–19 with 15:21). He celebrates his son's return by outfitting him with the best robe and with shoes and a ring, and by preparing a fattened calf for a celebratory feast. The younger son represents tax collectors and sinners who have wasted their lives by abandoning the ways of God (15:1–2). The older son, who supposedly was compliant and obedient ("I never disobeyed your command"; 15:29), represents the Pharisees and scribes. He returns from a hard day's work and is scandalized to discover that a party is being thrown to celebrate the return of his brother, who is a scoundrel. The father, however, is unrelenting in his love. He pleads with the older brother to join the festivities. Jesus here communicates God's love for Pharisees, and the parable ends with this question reverberating in the ears of the readers: Will the Pharisees come to the party? Indeed, will the reader?

The love of God cannot be understood apart from the holiness and the judgment of God. Those who refuse to submit to his lordship will face judgment on the last day (Matt. 7:1–2; 10:15; 11:20–24; Luke 10:13–15). Trees that fail to bear good fruit will be cut down and cast into the fire (Matt. 7:19; cf. Luke 3:9). Those who do not have faith will be cast out into the darkness, where there is weeping and gnashing of teeth (Matt. 8:12; cf. Luke 13:25–30). Weeping and gnashing of teeth will also be the lot of those without a wedding garment, those who are not dressed to enter the Messianic banquet (Matt. 22:11–14). Human beings should fear God, who is able to cast them into hell (10:28). If people do not repent, they will perish (Luke 13:1–9). The failure to conquer sin will result in unquenchable fire on the last day (Mark 9:42–48), and those who refuse to forgive others will not receive forgiveness from God (Matt. 6:14–15; 18:21–35). God will punish the tenants in the vineyard who do not bear fruit (21:40–41). The rich who fail to care for the poor and do not repent will suffer forever (Luke 16:19–31). God's mercy, then, can be understood only against the background of his righteous anger against sin and the judgment to come. The day of mercy has arrived in the preaching of the kingdom, and a hand beckoning sinners to repent is extended. In the gospel of Jesus Christ and the preaching of God's kingdom, the "tender mercy" of God has dawned (1:78–79).

God's Glory

Since God is the creator and the sovereign of all, he demands primacy in the lives of all people. In speaking of God's glory, the intention is not to restrict

the theme to the places where the word "glory" appears. The word "glory" is
used broadly to capture the supremacy of God in everything. In other words,
human beings exist to obey, believe in, and praise God. For instance, Jesus did
not fall prey to sentimentality with respect to his family; he maintained that
those who do God's will constitute his family (Matt. 12:50). God exercises
an absolute claim upon the lives of all. Thus the most important thing in life
is that God's name be honored and hallowed (6:9). In the Matthean version
of the Lord's Prayer, hallowing God's name is carried out when his kingdom
comes and when his will is done (6:10). Jesus rejected Satan's invitation to leap
from the pinnacle of the temple because such an act would constitute a testing
of God (4:7; cf. Deut. 6:16). Jesus drew upon Deut. 6 again when Satan tried
to entice Jesus to worship him, replying that he must worship and serve God
alone (Matt. 4:8–10; cf. Deut. 6:13). It seems clear that sin is heinous because
it constitutes a dishonoring of God and a refusal to trust in him.

God's primacy over everything animates Jesus' teaching. Money lurks as a
great danger because it easily becomes one's god. Those entranced with treasures on earth lose out on the treasures in heaven (Matt. 6:19–21). The parable
of the rich fool illustrates the danger of earthly riches (Luke 12:16–21). The
rich man is not faulted for the capital investment of building bigger barns,
as if planning how to increase the profitability of one's business were blame-
worthy. Rather, Jesus identifies the rich man's fundamental sin as his failure
to be "rich toward God" (12:21). The rich man neglected to think about God
at all: he conceived of his life as a perpetual vacation, where he could relax
and enjoy his wealth. Jesus taught that God allows no competitors. Human
beings cannot serve two masters (Matt. 6:24), and so the kingdom of God
must have first claim upon their lives (6:33). The final reward that human beings will receive cannot be equated with earthly blessings, as if heaven were
merely a supercharged version of the pleasures of this world. The greatest
joy, reserved for the pure in heart, is seeing God himself (5:8). No joy can be
compared to the vision of God promised to the faithful.

God's absolute priority is expressed by Jesus' reply to the rich young ruler
(Matt. 19:17; Mark 10:18; Luke 18:19). In all three accounts Jesus declared that
only God is good, calling attention to the beauty of God's moral perfection.
Since God is supreme, it follows that loving God with all of one's being and
strength is elevated as the most important command in the Scriptures (Matt.
22:37–40; Mark 12:28–34; cf. Luke 10:25–27). This command finds its roots
in the Shema (Deut. 6:4). The religious tradition practiced by the Pharisees
irritated Jesus because it substituted rituals for heart devotion and elevated
human traditions above God's word (Matt. 15:1–11). Jesus was not satisfied
with lips that mouth the correct words if the hearts of human beings stray far
from God. He demanded authenticity and affection in the worship of God.

The supremacy of God over all things means that nothing is more important
than glorifying God. Good works are commended not merely because they help

others—though that too is important—but also because they bring glory to God (Matt. 5:13–16). When the ten lepers were cleansed, the Samaritan stood out because he praised and thanked God for his healing (Luke 17:11–19). The Samaritan, who stood outside mainstream Judaism, recognized that God deserves praise for his mercy. The nine who did not give thanks stood condemned because they failed to do what is most important in life. When Jesus raised the only son of the widow of Nain from the dead, people were amazed and glorified God (7:16). The woman disfigured by a disablement for eighteen years glorified God when Jesus healed her (13:13). Jesus' healings often and rightly stimulated people to give praise and glory to God (Matt. 15:29–31).

The Gospel of Luke begins and ends with praise of God. Mary and Zechariah magnified and blessed the Lord for fulfilling his covenantal promises (1:46–55, 68–79). The angels praised God and gave him glory at the birth of the Christ (2:13–14). And the shepherds blessed God because the Christ was revealed to them (2:20). Simeon and Anna also responded with praise and thanksgiving (2:28, 38). Luke's Gospel concludes with the disciples in the temple, praising and blessing God (24:53), thereby fulfilling the true purpose for which the temple existed, in contrast to those who had turned the temple into a place of financial advantage (19:45–48).

God acts in history to fulfill his saving promises, and the fulfillment of such promises reveals how glorious and great and beautiful God is. The gift of salvation is not prized over the Giver. The gift reveals the Giver in all his power, love, and goodness. Hence, people responded by praising and honoring God for the salvation that they received. The heart of NT theology is the work of God in Christ in saving his people, and such saving work brings praise, honor, and glory to God.

God as Father

A theme that is remarkably prominent in the Synoptics is the fatherhood of God. Scholars in the past emphasized the distinctiveness of Jesus' calling God "Father." Jeremias (1967: 11–67) in particular called attention to the uniqueness of Jesus' use of the term "Father" in terms of his experience with God. Some references to God as "Father" exist in Jewish literature before the time of Jesus, but the frequency with which Jesus used the term stands out. Jesus distinctively and emphatically addressed God as "Father." Some have concluded that the frequency and intimacy of the term indicates that "Father" is equivalent to "Abba," which is then rendered "Daddy." Surely Jesus' relationship with God was intimate and unique, and his many references to God as "Father" are distinctive. Still, it goes beyond the evidence, as Barr (1988) has demonstrated, to conclude that "Father" should be equated with "Daddy."

Identifying God as the "Father in heaven" also highlights his authority and sovereignty. This is confirmed by the observation elsewhere in Matthew that heaven is God's throne (5:34; 23:22). The Father is also designated as "Lord of heaven and earth" (11:25; Luke 10:21). Heaven represents that which is transcendent and invisible to human beings, and so it is striking when God speaks from heaven (Matt. 3:16–17). The authority and power of the Father are evident, for he sees what people do in secret and will reward them accordingly (6:4, 6, 18). Nothing is hidden from his gaze, and as Father, he knows what his people need before they voice their requests (6:8, 32). Only the Father knows the day on which the Son is returning, and this date is hidden from angels and even from the Son (24:36). Since God is the sovereign Father, human beings are required to do his will and to obey what he says (7:21; 12:50; cf. 10:32–33).

Jesus testifies to the Father's authority, asking him to remove the cup from him, and such a request would be pointless if God could not change the oncoming circumstances (Mark 14:36). Similarly, Jesus remarked that if he were to appeal to the Father, twelve legions of angels would prevent his suffering and death (Matt. 26:53). Hence, when Jesus died, he commended his spirit to his Father (Luke 23:46). The uniqueness of God as Father is such that no human being should be accorded the title "Father" with the same significance that applies to God (Matt. 23:9). The term "Father" is part of the divine name (28:19), and the Son of Man comes with the glory that belongs only to the Father (16:27).

The Gospel of John

John assumes the monotheism established in the OT (1:1; 17:3). No one has ever seen God, since he is invisible and his glory overwhelms human beings (1:18). When John says "God is spirit" (4:24), he means, according to Barrett (1978: 238), that God "is invisible and unknowable," and thus imperceptible to human beings. Despite God being a spirit and invisible, John does not teach that God is unknowable, for the entire thrust of this Gospel is that God has revealed himself in his Son, and that the Father has sent the Son. The God of the Gospel of John is not a silent God. He has spoken to his people through the OT Scriptures (e.g., 5:45–47; cf. 9:29), and finally and supremely in Jesus (1:18; 14:9). God has not only spoken; he has also acted. In particular, God has demonstrated his love for the world in sending his Son for its salvation (3:16; 20:30–31). God sent the Son to save the world, not to condemn it (3:17), and hence the Son is God's supreme gift to the world (4:10).

The God who has revealed himself to human beings is truth, and hence he is trustworthy (3:33). He has manifested his glory to the world in sending his Son to die as the Lamb of God for the sin of the world (1:29, 36; 11:4, 40; 13:31–32; 17:1, 4, 5). Yet God's love and mercy are not all that can be said of

God. John, with his realized eschatology, emphasizes that unbelievers already stand under God's judgment. Those who do not believe are condemned already, and God's wrath remains on them (3:18, 36), but he also teaches that there will be an end-time judgment for those who practice evil (5:29).

John emphasizes that salvation is God's work and cannot be accomplished or effected by human beings. Those who are saved have been born of God (1:13; 3:3, 5, 7). The new life is bestowed supernaturally by God himself. The gift character of salvation is emphasized in John. Those who come to the Son in belief are given by the Father to the Son (6:37). Jesus grants eternal life only to those whom the Father has given to him (17:2) and reveals God's name to those whom God has given him (17:6, 24). Jesus restricted his prayer to those whom the Father has given him (17:9), fulfilling the Father's will in preserving to the end all those given to him by the Father (6:39). He also prayed that the Father would keep and preserve them until the last day (17:11, 15); hence, they will never apostatize and will be raised from the dead on the last day. If people are not drawn by the Father to the Son, they will be unable to come to Jesus for life (6:44). Conversely, those whom the Father has taught will certainly come to Jesus (6:45). They are part of the flock given to Jesus by the Father (10:29), whereas those who failed to believe were not given by the Father to the Son (6:64–65).

Human beings are called upon to give glory to God in all that they do. Hence, the man born blind to whom Jesus restored sight should glorify and praise God for his healing (9:24). Jesus raised Lazarus (11:4, 40), conducted his ministry, and went to his death (13:31–32; 17:1, 4, 5) to bring glory to God, for God is glorified in the work of his Son. The object and the aim of human existence is to bring glory to God, and so we see that the foundational theme of NT theology—the glory of God—is central in John's Gospel as well. Peter's death, though gruesome, will bring glory to God, presumably because he will die for the sake of Jesus Christ (21:19). The Jews who did not believe in Jesus are indicted because rather than prizing God's glory, they lived for the approbation and respect of human beings (5:44; 12:43). They were not animated by love for God (5:42), but rather they lived to please people.

The fatherhood of God, as in the Synoptic Gospels, is central in John's Gospel. Indeed, the fatherhood of God is emphasized even more in John than in the Synoptics. What is particularly striking, however, is that John does not emphasize that God is the Father of believers. Instead, the focus is on God as the Father of Jesus. Jesus' intimate relationship with God is such that he often refers to God as "my Father." Jesus clearly distinguished between his unique relationship with the Father and the relationship that his disciples enjoyed with the Father. Jesus is the exclusive and unique Son of the Father.

Acts

The God of Acts is the sovereign God, who fulfills his plans in the stream of redemptive history. The time of fulfillment is in God's hands, for he has "fixed by his own authority" "times or seasons" (1:7). Stephen proclaimed God's sovereignty in his speech in Acts 7, and in doing so he reflects the worldview of the OT. A persistent theme in Acts is that God has fulfilled prophecy in the ministry, death, and resurrection of Christ (2:17–36; 3:11–26; 4:9–12; 24:14–15; 26:6–7, 22–23; 28:23). In his sermon at Antioch, Paul emphasized that God's promises fulfilled in Jesus are part and parcel of God's covenant made with Israel from the beginning and that the Davidic covenant reaches its fulfillment in Jesus (13:16–41). The saving promises that are being realized in redemptive history are the promises of *God*; he is acting to carry out his will and purposes.

The narrative in Acts features the spread of the gospel to the Gentiles. Again and again Luke explains that the acceptance of the gospel by the Gentiles is due to the sovereignty of God. That God sovereignly works out his plan is clear from all of Acts. The martyrdom of Stephen was a great tragedy, but it led to the scattering of believers and the spreading of the word (8:1–4). The conversion of Paul, related three times in Acts (9:1–19; 22:1–16; 26:1–23), testified to God's sovereign work in both saving Paul and in appointing him as the missionary to bring the gospel to the Gentiles. Luke concludes the first missionary journey of Paul and Barnabas with the explanation that God "had opened a door of faith to the Gentiles" (14:27; cf. 15:4, 12). At the Jerusalem Council, Peter recalled how God determined that the Gentiles (Cornelius and his friends) heard the gospel and believed through his ministry (15:7). The priority of God's grace is quite clear from the response of the Gentiles to Paul's gospel in 13:48: "And as many as were appointed to eternal life believed." Luke highlights God's grace, which secures the response of belief in the hearts of Gentiles. Acts emphasizes that God is working out his saving plan for the world. He is fulfilling his covenantal promises through Jesus Christ and bringing to pass what he pledged.

God's sovereign rule over all things does not mean that everything that occurs is intrinsically good. For instance, in Acts 12 Herod took action against the church and beheaded James the brother of John. Luke records the event abruptly and without detail. The death of James scarcely led to the conclusion that God is not in control, for Peter was released supernaturally, probably because of the church's fervent prayers. Luke is not suggesting that the church failed to pray for James. He offers no explanation for the deliverance of Peter and the execution of James, proposing no neatly packaged answer for why some suffer and others are spared. God's rule over the world does not lend itself to formulas by which evil can be easily explained. Given Luke's worldview, he must have believed that God *could have* delivered James as well, and yet no reason for God's actions are given. The rationale for much of what happens is obscured from human vision. Still, God's control over all is conveyed powerfully by the conclusion of the story. The same Herod who executed James is struck dead by God when he fails to give God glory (12:23).

God's rule over all is featured supremely in the death of Christ. Christ's death, as Acts 2:23 indicates, was due to God's predestined plan and foreknowledge. God's plan from the beginning was that Christ would die for the sins of his people. And yet 2:23 also declares that those who put Christ to death should not have done so and are held responsible for their evil behavior. This same perspective appears in 4:27–28, where Herod, Pilate, the Gentiles, and even Jewish leaders conspired against Jesus in putting him to death. Nevertheless, what happened to Jesus was in accord with God's plan and predestined purpose (4:28).

One of Luke's themes, therefore, is that God's purpose and plan cannot be thwarted. This perspective is summarized well by the Pharisee Gamaliel, who cautioned his contemporaries from waging an all-out campaign of violence against Christians, lest they find themselves fighting a fruitless battle against God himself (Acts 5:34–39). The nature of God's purpose in Luke-Acts is often denoted by the words "it is necessary" (*dei*). The death and resurrection of Jesus are necessarily part of God's plan (Luke 9:22; 13:33; 17:25; 24:7). Indeed, everything that occurs in the ministry, death, and resurrection of Jesus fulfills God's plan found in the Scriptures (22:7; 24:44). God's plan and purpose will be accomplished because he is the true and living God who made the world (Acts 4:24, 28).

The God of Acts is the God of mission. He sovereignly and lovingly acts to fulfill his saving promises to bless all nations through Abraham. God intervenes in history to carry out his purposes, whether that involves initiating the conversion of Paul, or bringing Peter to Cornelius to proclaim the gospel, or frustrating Jewish attempts to bring the ministry of Paul to an end.

The Pauline Literature

The centrality of God pulsates through Paul's theology. Paul stands in line with his Jewish heritage in confessing that God is one (1 Cor. 8:4, 6; Eph. 4:6; 1 Tim. 2:5). This one God is also the Father (Eph. 4:6), from whom every family on earth receives its name (3:14–15). It is clear, therefore, that Paul, despite his high Christology, does not depart from Jewish monotheism.

Paul defines sin as the "degodding" of God, as the failure to thank and glorify God (Rom. 1:21). The root sin consists in worshiping and serving the creature rather than the creator (1:25). Paul indicts his fellow Jews as sinners because their actions have caused unbelievers to revile God's name (2:24). Idolatry, then, must be shunned (1 Cor. 10:14), for God brooks no competitors

(10:21–22) and will not tolerate those who try to serve him and yet compromise by eating in the temples of idols.

Paul states the truth of God's supremacy in a myriad of different ways. Believers exist for God's sake (1 Cor. 8:6), so that the entirety of their lives should reflect his beauty. This explains why Paul can say that believers are to do all things for God's glory, including eating or drinking (10:31). Elsewhere the same thought is expressed when Paul declares that believers ought to give thanks for all things (Eph. 5:20), and this gratefulness manifests itself when believers acknowledge God's lordship over every area of their lives (Rom. 14:7–9). The importance of gratefulness is confirmed by the thanksgiving introductions in almost every Pauline letter (see also 2 Cor. 2:14; 8:16; 1 Thess. 2:13).

The God and Father of the Lord Jesus Christ is not an abstract entity. He has structured all of history so that it finds its apex, summation, and unification in Christ (Eph. 1:9–10). He is "the King of the ages" (1 Tim. 1:17). Lau (1996: 271) says that in the Pastoral Epistles the emphasis is "on the transcendent sovereignty and majesty of the eternal, invisible and incomprehensible God." Even when he hardens someone like Pharaoh, he continues to be just and righteous (Rom. 9:14–18), and he dulls those who reject his gracious offers so that they have no capacity to discern the truth and be saved (2 Thess. 2:11–12). He is the sovereign Lord, who rules and reigns over history, showing severity to some and kindness to others (Rom. 11:22). The election of Israel, their hardening to the gospel, the inclusion of the Gentiles, and the end-time final salvation of Israel—these are all part of God's wise plan (9:1–11:32). God's work in history and the fulfillment of his saving promises cause Paul's heart to well up in praise to God for his inscrutable wisdom and unsurpassed knowledge (11:33–35). He confesses that God deserves all the glory because "from him and through him and to him are all things" (11:36).

God's grace reveals his mercy and love, which are so great that believers will never come to the end of the wonder about what God has done for them in Christ (Eph. 2:7–8). God's wisdom will be on display forever for the work that he has accomplished in the church and in Christ Jesus (3:9–11). God's ultimate purpose in the church is to evoke the recognition of his glory (3:21). We see, then, God's supremacy in all of the Pauline Letters. Paul does not propound an abstract and philosophical doctrine of God separated from everyday life. The God and Father of our Lord Jesus Christ is the Lord of history, the one who fulfills his saving promises, and the one who is to be praised in all things.

Hebrews

God is the sovereign creator of the entire universe (11:3). He rested after completing his creative work (4:4), not because he was weary, but because his work was completed. The majestic opening to the letter reminds readers that the God whom they worship reveals himself authoritatively in human words. He spoke his word through the prophets in the past, but now he has spoken definitively and finally in the Son (1:1–2). The author of Hebrews clearly believes that God has revealed himself and spoken through the OT Scriptures. The author introduces OT citations with a number of expressions that emphasize God's speech (1:5–8, 13; 4:3, 7; 5:5–6; 7:21; 8:8; 10:5). The author of Hebrews clearly views God as a "talking God," one who exists (11:6) and is not silent. The God who has spoken cannot lie (6:18); hence, the readers must pay heed to what has been uttered (2:1; cf. 11:7).

Human beings should hold God in awe and reverence because he "is a consuming fire" (12:29). Falling into the hands of the God who inflicts his vengeance on those who abandon him is terrifying (10:27–31). His word pierces swiftly and penetratingly, and no human being can hide from the creator God. Hence, humans must continue to trust in God if they wish to avoid the sword of judgment (4:12–13).

As the creator of all things (3:4), the living God has subjected the world to Christ (2:8); God possesses the power to raise the dead (11:19), just as he raised Jesus Christ (13:20); and he has promised to establish a heavenly city in the future (11:10, 16; 12:22). He will shake the world in the future so that his kingdom is established and the wicked are removed from the scene (12:26–28). This God of salvation and judgment is the one "for whom and through whom all things exist" (2:10 NRSV). In other words, all human beings are to live to honor him. They are to praise his name and do good because these are the sacrifices that bring him pleasure (13:15–16). Human beings please God by trusting in him and believing in his existence (11:5–6).

James

James says nothing about God that would surprise anyone rooted in OT piety. The oneness of God is assumed (2:19), though James warns his readers that assent to such is scarcely sufficient, since even demons recognize this truth. In a letter that concentrates on the ethical responsibility of believers, we expect the theme of God's judgment. He is the eschatological judge, who will exalt poor believers and humiliate rich unbelievers, for the rich oppress God's people and revile God's name (1:9–11; 2:6–7; 5:1–5). God will show mercy as the end-time judge only to those who show mercy to those in need (2:12–13). Hence, if believers cast their lot with rich unbelievers, they reveal their antagonism to God. If the rich who revile God's name will be judged for their behavior, then it follows that believers are to honor God's name, particularly by their godly lifestyle.

In the midst of sufferings, James calls attention to God's goodness. If people need wisdom, God is the source of all wisdom, and he grants his gifts gener-

ously and gladly, not grudgingly (1:5). Similarly, in the midst of trials, believers
are inclined to think that God is tempting them. James assures them that God
does not lure humans into sin (1:13). God finds evil utterly repulsive, and so
he would never entice humans to sin. "Every good gift and every perfect gift
is from above" (1:17). Believers can cling to God amid life's pressures because
he longs to bless them. His goodness is reflected in both the old creation and
the new creation. He is the "Father of lights" (1:17). James probably alludes
here to the creation of the sun, moon, and stars in Genesis (1:15–16). The
loveliness of the sun, moon, and stars testifies to God's beauty. Finally, James
1:17 emphasizes that God is unalterably good. He is not changeable—one day
generous and the next day stingy. His character remains the same. God does
not vary from season to season or year to year.

The Letter of James highlights God's just judgment and his generous goodness. Both themes are included so that believers will not depart from God but
instead will put their trust in him.

1 Peter

Peter addresses believers suffering for their faith in Christ, encouraging them
to persevere and maintain a witness by their good works in a hostile world.
He often emphasizes that God is sovereign so it follows that the suffering of
those addressed accords with God's will (3:17; 4:19). Dominion and sovereignty
belong to God forever (5:11). He foreknew the time in salvation history when
Jesus Christ would arrive (1:20), and so the entire course of history is under
his supervision and jurisdiction.

Believers are encouraged to place their trust (4:19) and hope (1:13; cf. 1:21)
in God, knowing that he is sovereign over all things. They know that he is a
God who lifts up the humble and debases the proud (5:5), and so they can
give to God all their worries and concerns (5:7) because they are assured that
he will vindicate them on the last day and grant them eschatological salvation (1:3–9; 5:10). Believers live before a sovereign God and Father who will
reward them on the last day (3:10–12) and will judge them impartially (1:17).
God, therefore, is not to be trifled with but must be feared as the holy one
(1:17; 2:17). Believers must live holy lives in accord with the God who called
them to himself (1:15–16; 5:10). They are summoned to live for the will of
God rather than the pleasures of this age (4:2). They should live consciously
in the presence of God in everything they do (cf. 2:19).

Believers have been the recipients of God's saving mercy (1:3–9; 2:10), and
so they know the wonders of his love. They were foreknown for salvation by
God before the world was inaugurated (1:1–2). As God chose Israel of old, so
also he has elected believers to be his children, his elect sojourners in an evil
world (1:1). God has bestowed his grace upon them and called them to salva-

tion (5:10), and his calling has secured a response from his people. Believers have been born again through the word of the gospel (1:3, 23).

Peter communicates in a variety of ways that salvation is of the Lord: believers are God's elect, foreknown, chosen, and born again. The reference to God's "mighty hand" (5:6) alludes to the exodus, where God delivered his people from Egyptian bondage (e.g., Exod. 3:19; Deut. 4:34; 5:15; 6:21). The salvation given in Jesus Christ is the new exodus, to which the Egyptian liberation pointed (cf. 1 Pet. 1:10–12). Believers are guarded by God's power even now so that they will obtain eschatological salvation (1:5). In response, believers should bless and praise God for his extraordinary mercy and grace in their lives (1:3). They should proclaim his excellencies in worship and evangelism (2:9).

2 Peter and Jude

We will examine the letters of 2 Peter and Jude together because both are brief, and the content of Jude overlaps significantly with 2 Pet. 2. Both letters react to the presence of false teachers in the churches. Therefore, one of the major themes in both letters is God's righteous judgment of sinners (Jude 4–16; 2 Pet. 2:3–16; 3:7, 10). God is ever the holy one, and those who live dissolute lives will not stand in his presence on the eschatological day. The judgments on sinning angels, the flood generation, Sodom and Gomorrah, and Israel anticipate the final judgment that will be meted out by God on the false teachers and those who follow in their wake (Jude 5–7; 2 Pet. 2:4–6). Yet the message of God's judgment is not novel; it is rooted in OT revelation, where God judges those who despise him and fail to do his will.

God's final judgment on evil cannot be separated from his sovereignty. If God were not Lord, he would lack the power to enforce his judgment. Peter particularly calls this fact to the readers' attention by reminding them of creation and the flood (2 Pet. 3:5–6). Both creation and the flood signify God's rule over the universe. He brought the world into existence initially by his word and through water. Similarly, water and the word were the means he employed to destroy the world through a cataclysm. The readers can be assured, then, that God is able to intervene in the world. Contrary to the false teachers who deny the future coming of the Lord (3:4), the cosmos will not continue without interruption. The world is not independent of God but rather is subject to his will, even to his catastrophic interventions. Indeed, history will conclude with a fiery consumption of heaven and earth (3:7, 10, 12) because God is the sovereign ruler of history.

Both 2 Peter and Jude feature God's grace as well. The grace of God frames Jude's Letter, for he commences by reminding readers that they are called by God to be his children. God has specially set his love upon them, and they are protected and kept from the designs of the intruders by Jesus Christ himself (1). The letter concludes with a doxology (24–25) that returns to the theme of God's sustaining love. He is able to keep believers from succumbing to apostasy. By this, Jude likely means that God *will* keep the readers from apostasy. The reference to God's love probably alludes to his saving work in calling believers to himself. Indeed, mercy, peace, and love flow into the lives of believers only from God himself (2). One of the main themes of Jude, then, is that God is the one who saves. He sets his love on believers and guards them from apostasy.

The theme of grace also informs 2 Peter. Those who believe do so because God has granted them the saving gift of righteousness that comes from Jesus Christ (1:1). The term "righteousness" here likely has an OT background, referring to God's saving activity (e.g., Pss. 88:12; 98:2–3; Isa. 42:6; 45:8; 46:13; Mic. 6:5; 7:9). Such an understanding fits with 2 Pet. 1:3–4, where everything that believers need for a godly life has been granted to them. One of Peter's favorite words is "knowledge" (*epignōsis*), and salvation is aptly described as knowledge of God (1:2; cf. 1:3, 8; 2:20). God's love for his own is expressed in his election and calling of believers (1:10). Election refers to God's choosing believers unto salvation, and calling likely refers to the grace that secures a believing response to the message of the gospel. God's love is also expressed in his preservation of believers. Peter introduces the example of Noah and Lot (2:5–9) to underscore that God is able to preserve believers even when they live in environments that are remarkably hostile to righteous living. He concludes, "The Lord knows how to rescue the godly from trials" (2:9). God is not only a God of judgment but also one who grants grace and peace and salvation.

1 John

John reminds his readers, as an antidote to the false teachers who have left the church (2:19), that "God is light" (1:5). In the context of 1 John, he means by this that God is holy, for John goes on to say in the same verse that there is no darkness in God. God is radiantly and beautifully good and unstained by any moral defilement. Hence, anyone who claims to know God and yet practices evil contradicts the profession of allegiance to God.

The love of God shines out as a central theme in the letter. God displayed his love supremely in the gift of his Son, Jesus Christ, who died on behalf of sinners and atoned for their sins (1:7; 2:2; 3:16; 4:9–10). John announces that "God is light" (1:5), and he also proclaims that "God is love" (4:8, 16). For John, the love of God is displayed in the sending of Christ and his atonement on the cross. John particularly emphasizes that believers did not take the initiative in loving God. They did not demonstrate their devotion to God with their piety and thereby merit his love. One of the characteristic themes in John's Gospel is that the Father sent the Son. The same theme is found in

1 John, and in every instance the Father sent the Son to bring salvation. God sent his Son so that human beings would enjoy new life (4:9). God sent him as an atoning sacrifice as a satisfaction for sins (4:10). Those who know God's love personally are his dear children and have experienced the wonder and joy of being the children of God (3:1–2). God poured out his love on them first, and any love that believers express toward God is in response to his love (3:16; 4:10, 19). One of the fundamental themes of 1 John is that God's love takes the initiative, so that human love is an answering love.

Revelation

In Revelation, John addresses seven churches in Asia Minor to encourage and strengthen them in the face of Roman persecution and in the temptation to compromise with their surrounding social world. Revelation is radically God-centered. The message of the book could be summarized in the angel's directive "Worship God" (19:10; 22:9). Believers will serve in God's presence forever and experience the comfort of his sheltering love (7:15). One of the prime reasons that God is worshiped and adored in Revelation is his sovereignty. John's message to a persecuted and afflicted church is that God reigns. God is designated in Revelation as the one "who is and who was and who is to come" (1:4, 8; 4:8). Here we have clear allusion to Exod. 3:14, where God reveals himself to Moses as "I AM WHO I AM." God is also designated as "the Alpha and Omega" (Rev. 1:8; 21:6) and "the Almighty" (1:8; 4:8; 11:17; 15:3; 16:7, 14; 19:6, 15; 21:22). The words "Alpha and Omega" represent the first and last letters in the Greek alphabet, signifying that God reigns over all of history. No segment of history elapses apart from God's rule. The term "Almighty" (*pantokratōr*) underscores God's dominion over all things as well. It may seem that Rome exercises control over history, but God is working his purposes out as the Almighty One.

The churches that John addressed likely felt small and weak and perhaps were tempted to see themselves as victims of powers beyond their control. In response, John constantly emphasizes God's supremacy over all things. Thus he regularly uses the term "throne" to designate God's power and rule.[1]

One of the key chapters in Revelation is chapter 4, where John is granted a vision of God on his throne. The God revealed to him, however, is too glorious to be seen by human eyes. His glory is compared to priceless gems that radiate with beauty (4:3). Here we have a clear allusion to the vision of God in Ezek. 1:26–28, where Ezekiel sees the glory of the Lord and describes God in similar terms. Entering God's presence is fearsome because something like a massive thunderstorm blazes in his presence. The angels surrounding

1. Rev. 1:4; 3:21; 4:2, 3, 4, 5, 6, 9, 10; 5:1, 6, 7, 11, 13; 6:16; 7:9, 10, 11, 15, 17; 8:3; 12:5; 14:3; 16:17; 19:4, 5; 20:11, 12; 21:3, 5; 22:1, 3.

the throne echo the words of the seraphim in Isa. 6:3 with the words "Holy, holy, holy" (Rev. 4:8). The God on the throne is transcendent, terrible, and beautiful in his holiness. The holy and sovereign one is the creator of all that is (4:11). Indeed, he is the sovereign Lord precisely because he is the creator. The one who brought all things into existence also determines the course of human history. The destruction of Babylon by the beast and the ten kings is the work of God himself; he put it into their minds to destroy the great city (17:16–17). For John, none of this is abstract theology, for the vision of God on his throne tears back the curtain on reality. The four living creatures and twenty-four elders fall down and worship in God's presence as he rules from his throne (4:8–11). The worship given by the angels should be replicated by human beings. When humans see God in his holiness and recognize him as king, perceiving him in all his glory, they will be stunned into worshiping him as creator and Lord.

As we have noted already, one of the central themes of Revelation is that God should be worshiped. He deserves praise because salvation comes from him (7:10–12). He is worshiped because he will accomplish his kingdom promises (11:15–19), both in recompensing evil and in rewarding his servants. Another way of describing conversion is to say that when people are saved, they give glory to God (11:13; 14:7); they worship him as their creator and lord. Unbelievers worship the beast (13:15), but those who know God refuse to succumb to economic pressure to bow before the emperor (14:9–12). Those who know God sing the same song of worship hymned by Moses in Exod. 15, declaring that God deserves praise for his saving deeds, his unutterable beauty, his justice, and his goodness (Rev. 15:3–4).

One of the pervasive themes in Revelation is that God judges the wicked. The God who rules over all and is the creator of all will righteously requite those who practice evil and resist his authority. Rome and the Roman Empire, depicted as the new Babylon and the beast respectively, wreak havoc upon God's people. Revelation depicts the judgments that will be unleashed upon those who do not know God (6:1–17; 8:1–9:21; 14:14–20; 15:1–16:21; 17:1–19:4; 20:11–15). The God who inflicts judgment and is the holy one is full of wrath because of the evil of human beings (6:17; 11:18; 14:10, 19; 15:1, 7; 16:1, 19; 19:15).

Is God an arbitrary and unjust judge? Does he pour out his judgments with a vindictive fury that is unwarranted and excessive? John repeatedly emphasizes that people deserve the judgments they receive (16:6–7; 18:5–6; 19:2). Human beings are judged not by an arbitrary standard but in accord with the works that they have done (20:11–15). Before the bowl judgments are poured out, God is extolled as king because his ways are "just and true" (15:3). The punishment meted out fits with the extent of the crime. Indeed, the judgments were designed to provoke people to repent, but people stubbornly refuse to change their ways (9:20–21; 16:9, 11). Those who repent give glory to God, honoring his justice by admitting wrongdoing, but those who are recalcitrant reject and curse God (16:8–11), for they hate any intrusion by him into their lives. They do not repent, because they desire to worship their idols rather than God (9:20).

God's judgments, therefore, do not call into question his justice but rather express it. Therefore, the people of God respond to his judgments by praising and worshiping him (19:1, 3–4). The four living creatures join the chorus with the words "Amen! Hallelujah!" (19:4).

Conclusion

Our survey of "God" in the NT reveals that he is foundational for NT theology. The God of the NT is not a new God; he is the God of the OT—the Creator and Redeemer. The promise of universal blessing given to Abraham and his descendants in the OT is fulfilled by this God. He is a God of love and mercy, so that he fulfills his saving promises to bless the whole world. He is the God who has revealed himself in Jesus Christ and offers salvation to all through the crucified and risen one. He is the sovereign God, who rules over all of history, and hence the words that he has spoken are reliable and true. Because he is sovereign, he is able to fulfill his saving promises. At the same time, as the sovereign God, he judges those who practice evil, demonstrating that evil will not have the last word. All human beings are called upon to honor and worship the creator God. All their energy and strength are to be used to praise him, and God is particularly glorified when human beings trust him and therefore obey him.

Pastoral Reflection

All human beings are summoned to trust God for three reasons. First, as the sovereign God, he rules over all. Hence, he secures the future for those who give their lives to him. Nothing spins out of his control since he is the sovereign creator. Second, his love demonstrated in the sending of his Son reveals that he is worthy of trust, that he truly loves human beings. Because of his great love, God sent his Son to rescue us from his wrath. Third, failure to trust and obey him is disastrous, for he will judge the wicked.

3

The Centrality of Christ in the Gospels

In the preceding chapter we explored the centrality of God in NT writings. Here we consider the centrality of Jesus Christ. Does the pervasiveness of the Christ in the NT contradict or diminish God's supremacy? The NT writers regularly teach that God sent Jesus Christ to bring glory to himself. The coming of the Christ does not diminish God's glory but rather enhances it. The next several chapters will explore what the NT teaches about Jesus Christ. This is scarcely surprising since Jesus Christ is central in the NT witness. Virtually every book of the NT shines its spotlight on him, and so any NT theology that adheres to the text must devote considerable attention to Christology. Here the study of Christology is not confined to christological titles, though they are included. Indeed, the subsequent chapters also examine what Jesus Christ accomplished for his people.

The current chapter is devoted to the Christology of the Gospels. The Gospels communicate the significance of Jesus Christ in innumerable ways, portraying Jesus as the new Moses, the last and greatest prophet, the Messiah, the Son of Man, the Lord, the Son of God, the Logos, and God. Jesus is also the Servant of the Lord, who gave his life to secure forgiveness of sins. Indeed, these titles do not exhaust who Jesus Christ is, as we shall see.

In the ensuing chapters we shall examine the Christology of Acts, and two chapters are needed to set forth the Pauline teaching since his Christology is rich and detailed. A final chapter relative to Christology will consider the contributions of the remainder of the NT. The discussion of Christology here is not limited to the identity of Jesus; we shall also attend to what Jesus accomplished by his ministry, and especially his death and resurrection. When we consider the centrality of Jesus in the NT documents, both who he is and what he has accomplished, it is scarcely astonishing that Christology takes up more space in this book than any other topic.

Jesus as a Prophet and More than a Prophet

Jesus is a new and superior Moses. He ascends to the mount and teaches his disciples from there (Matt. 5:1), which is redolent of Moses receiving the Torah on Mount Sinai (cf. also 28:16–20). In what are often called "the antitheses," Jesus stands forth as the sovereign interpreter of the Mosaic law (5:17–48). Just as manna was given to the people in the wilderness in Moses' day, so also Jesus miraculously provided food for the people in the feeding of the five thousand (14:13–21). Perhaps Matthew also compares and contrasts Jesus with Moses in the transfiguration scene (17:1–9). We are told that Jesus' face shines, just as Moses' did (Exod. 34:29). Moses promised that a prophet would arise to replace him in the future (Deut. 18:15–22). We see a clear allusion to this text in the transfiguration scene, for Moses and Elijah appear and speak to Jesus, but Jesus is the focus of God's revelation. The divine voice enjoins the disciples present to listen to Jesus (Matt. 17:5; Mark 9:7; Luke 9:35).

Jesus' role as a prophet was acknowledged by some during his ministry and clearly was endorsed by the Synoptic writers (Matt. 13:53–58; 21:11, 46; Luke 7:11–17; 24:19). Jesus displays his prophetic authority by his predictions that come to pass (Matt. 16:21; 17:22–23; 20:17–19 par.; 26:34; John 13:38). He affirms the authority of his words, declaring that they will never pass away (Matt. 24:35). Jesus also demonstrated his prophetic stature in his ability to read the thoughts of others (9:2–5; 22:18; Luke 7:39–43). And his prophetic authority was evident when he entered the temple and expelled those selling and buying, enraged that God's house had been turned into a marketplace (Matt. 21:12–13). The same kind of authority manifests itself in Jesus' cursing of the fig tree (21:19–21; cf. Luke 13:6–7). The symbolism of the cleansing of the temple and the cursing of the fig tree recall prophetic symbolism and the judgments that the prophets threatened against Israel and Judah. The prediction that Jerusalem and the temple would be destroyed within a generation (Matt. 24) was highly significant, and the fulfillment of these prophecies verified Jesus' prophetic status.

The Synoptic Gospels feature Jesus' distinctiveness in his miracles, exorcisms, and raising of the dead. For instance, when a storm assailed the Sea of Galilee, Jesus exercised his authority over the recalcitrant wind and waves as well. He speaks the word, and the storm instantly subsides (Matt. 8:23–27). In the OT only Yahweh triumphs over a stormy sea (Pss. 65:7; 77:19; 107:23–32, esp. 29; cf. Job 9:8; Isa. 43:16; 51:9–10; Hab. 3:15). The disciples recognized the power of Jesus in quieting the storm and rightly exclaimed, "Who then is this, that even wind and sea obey him?" (Mark 4:41). A similar miracle takes place in Jesus' walking upon the sea (Matt. 14:25; Mark 6:48; cf. John 6:19). Again this hearkens back to Yahweh, who walks upon the sea (Job 9:8 LXX; cf. Ps. 77:19; Isa. 51:9–10; Hab. 3:15).

The stature of Jesus is indisputable in that he calls others to be his disciples, and in calling them he asserts his authority in a remarkable and distinctive way. Thus Jesus summons the disciples to follow him and does not merely say that they should be devoted to God. The available evidence indicates that rabbis did not summon others to follow them. Instead, would-be disciples sought rabbis out and asked to serve as their disciples. Jesus, however, took the initiative in calling others to be his disciples, and he did not ask if they wanted to follow him. He sovereignly and authoritatively called them to do so. He does not envision a time, as did the disciples of the rabbis, when they would graduate and, in turn, attract their own students.

Jesus must have supremacy even over one's family—a startling message for the culture of Jesus' day, for other rabbis did not require people to leave their families. Nor did others make the kind of shocking declarations that we find in Jesus' teaching (Matt. 10:37). Jesus' distinctiveness is evident because those who obey him are considered to be part of *his* family (12:46–50; Mark 3:31–35; cf. Luke 8:19–21; 11:27–28).

Jesus' authority is evident when he declares, "I came not to call the righteous, but sinners" (Matt. 9:13; Mark 2:17). Jesus does not merely speak in God's name; he himself summons human beings to renounce their sins, suggesting his unique role and stature as the one whom God sent. Jesus also insists that people must be willing to take up their cross in following him (Matt. 10:38–39), saying that those who give up their lives "for my sake, and for the sake of the gospel" (Mark 8:35 NRSV) will retrieve them in the end (Matt. 10:39; 16:25; Luke 9:24). Jesus does not envision himself, however, as displacing God, for the one who receives Jesus receives the Father, who appointed and sent Jesus (Matt. 10:40; cf. Luke 10:16; John 13:20). He does not shrink back from being invoked as "Lord, Lord" (Matt. 7:21–23), acknowledging that he has the authority to determine who will be included and who excluded from God's kingdom.

When believers gather to pray, Jesus says, he is present with them (Matt. 18:20). No prophet, king, or priest in Israel ever said anything remotely similar, and this fact demonstrates the astonishingly high Christology of Matthew's Gospel. The centrality and distinctiveness of Jesus is featured in his forgiveness of sins. The theme that Jesus forgives sins emerges in the account of the healing of the paralytic (9:2–8). Observe Jesus' response to the accusation that only

God can forgive sins. He could have protested that he was not forgiving sins by virtue of his own authority, and that he was only pronouncing forgiveness in God's name, like the prophets of old. Jesus goes out of his way, however, to demonstrate that he, as the Son of Man, possesses the authority to forgive sins, which is the prerogative of God alone. He heals the paralytic in order to demonstrate that he possesses the authority to forgive sinners. Jesus' healing of the paralytic and his claim to forgive represent divine actions, hearkening back to Ps. 103:3, where Yahweh is the one who forgives sins and heals diseases (cf. Isa. 33:24; cf. also Luke 7:36–50).

Mark 9:24 reports a prayer addressed to Jesus. The man with the demonized boy cries out to Jesus, "I believe; help my unbelief!" The most natural way of understanding his prayer is that he addresses Jesus himself, asking that Jesus grant him faith. But only God is able to beget faith in others, and hence, instinctively and without any reflection on the significance of what he was doing, the boy's father entreats Jesus as one entreats God. Mark includes this in his Gospel because the man's instincts were fitting and accorded with Jesus' stature.

The story in which Peter begs Jesus to depart because Peter is too sinful to be in his presence is illuminating. The text hearkens back to Isa. 6, where Isaiah was undone in the Lord's presence, and Peter has a similar reaction in Jesus' presence here. The account intimates that Jesus is like Yahweh, in whose presence a sinful person cannot abide, and hence the account places Jesus with God rather than with human beings.

In biblical thought a name often denotes the character and essence of a person (cf. Exod. 34:5–7), so that knowing God's name takes on great significance. "Misuse of God's name in magic or false oaths . . . is forbidden (Exod. 20:7), for the name of Yahweh is a gift of the revelation which is not at man's disposal" (Bietenhard 1976: 650). God's name is awesome because "whoever knows God's name knows God—or as much of God as he has revealed" (Hartman 1991: 520). Thus it is important to discern the significance of the name in relationship to Jesus in the Synoptic Gospels. Prophets are to prophesy not in their own name but in the name of the Lord (Jer. 11:21; 14:15; 23:25), but it is assumed that people will prophesy in Jesus' name (Matt. 7:22). Similarly, the Gentiles will put their hope in Jesus' name (12:21). The heavenly power of Jesus' name is indisputable, for the demons are subjected in his name (Luke 10:17). Perhaps even more astonishing, forgiveness is to be offered and repentance demanded in his name (24:47). Indeed, baptism is not restricted to God's name; the name of the Son and the Spirit are also included (Matt. 28:19). Jesus anticipates the people of God gathering in his name (18:20) and promises his presence in such meetings. Obviously, Jesus is not guaranteeing his physical presence, and it seems to follow that the divine ability to transcend spatial limitations is promised (28:20).

Messiah

The term "Messiah" simply means "anointed one." To call someone "Messiah," whether with the verbal or nominal form, does not mean that the person so-called is actually God, as many in popular circles think. It simply designates someone who is anointed by God for a particular task. Nor does the term "anointed one" necessarily mean that one is a king. In the OT, priests were anointed by God.[1] In fact, even inanimate objects could be anointed to set them apart for the holy, such as unleavened cakes (Exod. 29:2; Lev. 2:4; 7:12), the altar of burnt offering (Exod. 29:36), and so forth. It is not as common for prophets to be called "anointed," but the appellation does occur (1 Kings 19:16; Isa. 61:1; cf. 1 Chron. 16:22; Ps. 105:15). Kings often were anointed or designated as the Lord's anointed.[2]

Scholars have often noted that the OT says little about the coming of a future anointed one. Is the NT expectation for Messiah, then, fundamentally misconceived? What actually takes place, however, is quite understandable and accords with the OT. First, it should be observed that David and his heirs are often described as anointed ones.[3] Second, David and his heirs were not merely anointed as kings individually apart from God's larger saving purposes. Yahweh made a covenant with David in which he pledged that David's dynasty would never end, that one of his sons would always rule upon the throne.[4] Readers of the OT naturally combined the promises of the Davidic covenant with the fact that kings were anointed. No violence is done to the OT in saying that it promises the coming of a Messiah, for when we merge the promises of the Davidic covenant with the anointing of the Davidic king, it is legitimate to say that the OT looks forward to the coming of an anointed one in the line of David.[5]

The NT teaching on the Messiah flows from OT antecedents. Still, in the Gospels Jesus' reserve in identifying himself as the Messiah is quite striking. He did not publicly proclaim himself as the Messiah when his ministry commenced, nor did he regularly use the title. A turning point of his ministry occurred at Caesarea Philippi (Matt. 16:13–20). He privately asked his disciples to identify him, for people thought he was a prophet, John the Baptist, Jeremiah, or the like. Peter responded that Jesus is the Christ, the Messiah. In all the Synoptic

1. Exod. 28:41; 29:7; 30:30; 40:13, 15; Lev. 4:3, 5, 16; 6:20; 7:36; 8:12; 16:32; Num. 3:3; 35:25.

2. For example, Judg. 9:8, 15; 1 Sam. 2:10; 10:1; 15:1; 16:3, 6, 12, 13; 2 Sam. 2:4, 7; 3:39; 5:3, 17; 12:7; 19:10; 1 Kings 1:34, 39; Pss. 2:2; 45:7; 89:20; 132:10.

3. See 1 Sam. 16:12–13; 2 Sam. 2:4, 7; 3:39; 5:3, 17; 12:7; 1 Kings 1:34, 39, 45; 5:1; Pss. 89:20, 38, 51; 132:10, 17.

4. 2 Sam. 7:11–29; 1 Chron. 17:10–27; Pss. 89; 132; Isa. 9:6–7; 11:1, 10; 55:3–4; Jer. 23:5–6; Ezek. 34:23–24; Hos. 3:5; Mic. 5:2.

5. For views of the Messiah in Second Temple Judaism, see Schreiner 2008: 201–5.

accounts, the story concludes with the disciples being sternly warned not to disseminate to others what they now know.

The restriction cannot be explained by saying that Jesus did not truly believe that he was the Messiah. Jesus' hesitation to proclaim himself as the Messiah or to accept the title publicly is best explained by the explosive political implications of accepting the title. In all the Jewish traditions, the Messiah reigns as king, and one of his prime tasks is to expel Gentiles from Israel. This theme especially manifests itself in Pss. Sol. 17–18, but it is by no means limited to that text. If Jesus had identified himself as the Messiah, he would have concocted a political brew that would inevitably boil over. Most important, Jesus did not intend to fulfill the promises in the manner expected by his contemporaries. He would conquer not through military might and force but through suffering and death. The promises of the kingdom would come to pass through sacrificial love rather than at the point of a sword.

The Synoptics make it plain that none of the disciples grasped Jesus' mission. They concurred with Peter that he was the Messiah. But when Jesus articulated his vocation, which included suffering and death, Peter rebuked Jesus (Matt. 16:21–23). Jesus in turn called Peter's intervention and perspective satanic. If even Jesus' closest and most loyal followers could not grasp the nature of his messianic mission, we can scarcely doubt that the remainder of the people would have been completely baffled by the idea that the Messiah would suffer. Jesus could not use the title "Messiah" without imperiling his mission, since those whom he addressed would have concluded that he would be a conquering king. His reserve, therefore, does not indicate self-doubt about his messianic status; rather, it reflects a desire to forestall serious misconceptions on the part of his followers and the attending crowds.

On occasion Jesus did declare himself to be the Messiah (John 4:25–26), but he did so in situations where his claim would not arouse a political movement. The incident in which Nathaniel acclaimed Jesus as the king of Israel and the Son of God (1:49) may seem to contradict the argument here (cf. 1:41, 45). Did the disciples, then, from the beginning of Jesus' ministry know that Jesus was the Messiah and God's Son? It is likely that Nathaniel spoke better than he knew due to his enthusiasm. The disciples recognized Jesus as Messiah from the beginning, but they also had doubts because Jesus did not fit their conception of what the Messiah would do. We should not conceive of their view of Jesus as if they wrote down the right answer on a test. Their understanding of Jesus ebbed and flowed as they traveled with him and were taught by him. Sometimes they veered toward thinking that he was the Messiah, but on other occasions they were assailed with doubts about his identity.

Jesus was hailed publicly as David's son or the king of the Jews on a few occasions (e.g., Matt. 9:27; 20:30–31; 21:9). When asked at his trial whether or not he is the Messiah, Jesus agreed that he was (26:63–64; Mark 14:61–62; Luke 22:66–70). It appears that Jesus was more forthright about his identity as the cross drew near. So it is not that Jesus ever denied that he was the Messiah, but rather that the triumphant view of Messiah so popular in Judaism vied with his own conception of his messianic mission. Had he used the title "Messiah" openly, he was certain to have been misunderstood. Hence, he felt free to use the title openly near the end of his ministry, when his death was impending.

Some have interpreted Jesus' query to the Pharisees about the Messiah as Jesus denying that the Messiah was David's son (Matt. 22:41–46). Jesus appealed to the first verse of Ps. 110 to point out that the Messiah was David's lord. If taken in isolation, this passage could be understood as a refutation of the Davidic lineage of the Messiah. Another interpretation of what Jesus meant fits well with the narrative of the Gospels as a whole: Jesus understood the Messiah to be both the son of and the lord of David.

The importance of Jesus being identified as the Messiah is undeniable in the Gospel of John, for John explicitly informs the readers that he wrote so that Jesus would be confessed as Messiah and the Son of God (John 20:30–31). This passage serves as the purpose statement and the conclusion of this Gospel, and it echoes the prologue, where Jesus is identified as the Messiah (1:17). Indeed, eternal life is defined as knowing God and Jesus as Messiah.

Son of Man

One of the most important designations for Jesus in the Gospels is "Son of Man." Consequently, intense discussion over the meaning of the term has informed NT scholarship since critical study commenced. In Hebrew the expression "son of man" (*ben 'ādām*) is simply another way of saying "human being." This is clear from Hebrew poetic parallelism in a number of texts (Num. 23:19; Ps. 8:4; cf. Job 25:6; Ps. 80:17; Isa. 51:12; 56:2; Jer. 49:18, 33; 50:40; 51:43). In Ezekiel the term "son of man" is used ninety-three times (e.g., Ezek. 2:1, 3, 6, 8). In the context of Ezekiel, the emphasis is likely on Ezekiel's mortality and weakness in contrast to the glory and majesty of God.

The most controversial reference to "son of man" in the OT is in Dan. 7. Here "son of man" is in Aramaic, *bar 'ĕnāš* (7:13). Deciphering the meaning of "son of man" in Dan. 7 is discerned by its context. In Dan. 7 four different kingdoms are depicted as bestial animals: Babylon as a lion with eagle's wings; Medo-Persia as a bear; Greece as a leopard; Rome as an indescribably ferocious beast, a terrible combination of the beastly character of all the kingdoms. On the other hand, God's kingdom is given to a "son of man." We have seen above that "son of man" in the OT is merely a way of saying that one is a human being. Such an interpretation is reflected in the NRSV's translation of 7:13: "I saw one like a human being coming with the clouds of heaven." The kingdom is given to this son of man forever, so that all other

kingdoms are subjugated to the kingdom of a son of man. The kingdom of
a son of man will be humane and beneficent instead of bringing devastation,
as beastly kingdoms do.

What is particularly fascinating is the interpretation given to Daniel regarding his vision of the four beasts and the son of man. In 7:17 the beasts
are said to represent four kings. We can conclude that these kings function
as the representative heads of the various kingdoms. The kingdom given to
a son of man in the vision is explained in terms of the kingdom being given
to the saints: "But the saints of the Most High shall receive the kingdom and
possess the kingdom forever, forever and ever" (7:18). The saints who are
conquered are the Israelites who are oppressed and persecuted by this evil ruler
(7:22, 25, 27). Pagan nations will rule for a certain period of history, but they
will not ultimately triumph. God will intervene, judge the wicked, inaugurate
the kingdom, and give it to his people.

Nevertheless, the people of God—the saints of the Most High—are represented by an individual. We saw in Dan. 7:13–14 a focus on an individual, but
when the vision is explained, the son of man is identified as the saints. Just
as the four kingdoms are represented by the kings who rule over them, so too
"son of man" refers to Israel in terms of its representative king. Indeed, there
are hints of the divinity of the son of man. The Aramaic verb for "serve" (*plḥ*)
in 7:27 is used elsewhere of service and worship of God (3:12, 14, 17, 18, 28;
6:16, 20; 7:14). Further, coming on the clouds of heaven in 7:13 suggests deity,
for elsewhere in the OT only God rides on the clouds of heaven.

Son of Man in the Synoptic Gospels

One of the striking features about the term "Son of Man" is that the title
is reserved almost exclusively to the Gospels.[6] Matthew uses the expression
thirty times, Mark fourteen, Luke twenty-five, and John thirteen. Outside
the Gospels, the term is used with reference to Jesus only in Acts 7:56; Heb.
2:6; Rev. 1:13; 14:14.

The "Son of Man" sayings are often placed in three categories: (1) those that
refer to the Son of Man's work on earth; (2) those that refer to his suffering;
(3) those that refer to the future. We begin with what scholars typically call
the earthly sayings. The Son of Man is persecuted, and so he has nowhere to
lay his head (Matt. 8:20; Luke 9:58); detractors accuse him of excessive eating
and drinking (Matt. 11:19; Luke 7:34); the disciples are blessed if persecuted
for the sake of the Son of Man (Luke 6:22); he has the authority to forgive
sins (Matt. 9:6; Mark 2:10; Luke 5:24); he is Lord of the Sabbath (Matt. 12:8;
Mark 2:28; Luke 6:5); those who speak a word against him can be forgiven
(Matt. 12:32; Luke 12:10); he sows the good seed of God's word (Matt. 13:37);

---

6. For the use of Son of Man in Second Temple Judaism and for a more detailed discussion
of Son of Man in the Gospels, see Schreiner 2008: 216–29.

he has come to seek and save the lost (Luke 19:10). The authority of the Son of Man breathes through these sayings because he forgives sins, is sovereign over the Sabbath, speaks God's word, and has a mission from God to seek and to save those who are lost. The other sayings focus on persecution and could perhaps even be placed in the category of the suffering Son of Man.

The second category of sayings relates to suffering. Just as John the Baptist suffered at the hands of Herod, so the Son of Man will suffer (Matt. 17:12; Mark 9:12–13). In the passion predictions, Jesus said that the Son of Man would be handed over to authorities by the religious leaders in Judaism, be mistreated and persecuted, put to death, and raised on the third day.[7] In most of these texts the suffering of the Son of Man overlaps with his future triumph, for he will not only suffer but also be raised from the dead (see also Matt. 17:9; Mark 9:9). It is not as if Jesus will be sentenced to death inadvertently. As the Son of Man, he came to earth to serve and "to give his life as a ransom for many" (Matt. 20:28; Mark 10:45).

The last category includes sayings about the Son of Man that relate to the future. The disciples will not finish evangelizing Israel "before the Son of Man comes" (Matt. 10:23). The Son of Man will commission his angels to remove from his kingdom all the unrighteous (13:41–43). The Son of Man will come in the future and repay all people according to what they have done (16:27). On the day of judgment the Son of Man will be ashamed of those who are ashamed of Jesus (Mark 8:38; Luke 9:26). Similarly, those who acknowledge Jesus before others will be acknowledged by the Son of Man before God's angels (Luke 12:8).

Jesus asks whether people will continue to believe when the Son of Man comes (Luke 18:8). Disciples should stay vigilant to the end, praying that they will be able "to stand before the Son of Man" on the last day (21:36). Some of Jesus' disciples will not die before seeing "the Son of Man coming in his kingdom" (Matt. 16:28). In the coming world when the Son of Man sits on his throne, the twelve disciples will also sit on thrones, ruling the people of God (19:28). In the future the disciples will desire "to see one of the days of the Son of Man" (Luke 17:22). The Son of Man will come as clearly as lightning that blazes across the entire expanse of the sky (Matt. 24:27; Luke 17:24). People "will see the Son of Man coming on the clouds of heaven with power and great glory" (Matt. 24:30; Mark 13:26; Luke 21:27). People will be unprepared for the Son of Man's coming as they were unprepared for judgment during the days of Noah and Lot (Matt. 24:37–39; Luke 17:26–30). The Son of Man is coming at an hour that people do not expect (Matt. 24:44; Luke 12:40). He will come with brilliant glory and reign on his throne (Matt. 25:31). Jesus

7. (1) Matt. 16:21; Mark 8:31; Luke 9:22; (2) Matt. 17:22–23; Mark 9:31; Luke 9:44; (3) Matt. 20:18–19; Mark 10:33–34; Luke 18:31–33; (4) Matt. 26:2; (5) Matt. 26:45; Mark 14:41; (6) Luke 24:6–7.

tells the religious leaders at his trial, "You will see the Son of Man seated at the right hand of Power and coming on the clouds of heaven" (26:64; Mark 14:62; cf. Luke 22:69). The future sayings emphasize the glory of the Son of Man when he comes to the earth. He will reign and rule and determine the final destiny of those on earth.

Why did Jesus use the title "Son of Man" so often and in comparison, relatively speaking, the title "Messiah" so little? We have seen that the title "Messiah" was apt to be understood in militaristic and political terms, contrary to Jesus' mission. The term "Son of Man," on the other hand, was ambiguous. Even though the term was used in the OT, there was some uncertainty about its meaning. We see from John 12:34 that Jesus' contemporaries were perplexed and puzzled by his use of the term. By using this term, Jesus did not automatically arouse suspicion and antagonism, and he could slowly teach his followers the significance and meaning of "Son of Man." Their understanding of "Son of Man" could be reoriented as Jesus' teaching and ministry progressed.

Son of Man in the Gospel of John

The Son of Man in John fits with the exalted Christology of this Gospel as a whole and bears the distinctive stamp of Johannine theology. It would be a mistake, however, to drive too large of a wedge between the Son of Man in the Synoptics and in John. Borsch (1992: 142) remarks on the overlap between the Synoptics and John relative to the Son of Man: "What is, on any explanation, so remarkable about these sets of traditions is that they say many of the same things about the Son of Man in quite distinctive language." Jesus responded to Nathaniel's enthusiastic acclamation of his messiahship with the claim that he would see still greater things (1:50–51). The heavens would open and he would see angels "descending and ascending on the Son of man." The meaning of this verse is not easy to discern. John alludes to Gen. 28:12, where Jacob dreams at Bethel and sees a ladder, probably something like a ziggurat, reaching up to heaven, and angels ascending and descending upon the ladder. John replaces the ladder with Jesus as the Son of Man, teaching that access to God has become a reality through Jesus. Perhaps a connection also exists between 1:51 and 3:13 and 6:62. Jesus as the Son of Man is the one who has descended and ascended into heaven (3:13). Life is available to all because Jesus has come down from heaven and has returned to God's presence.

Perhaps Jesus' ascension (cf. 6:62) evokes Dan. 7:13–14, where he enters the presence of the Ancient of Days to receive a kingdom. If so, we would have an example of John's inaugurated eschatology. The saying about the Son of Man in John 6:62 occurs in a context in which even some of Jesus' disciples are scandalized over his teaching. Jesus emphasizes that the Spirit alone gives life and grants the ability to grasp what he teaches (6:63). If some of his so-called disciples are offended by his words, how would they respond if they saw him as the Son of Man ascending to heaven (6:62)? In Johannine theology, the ascension and Jesus' glorification occur via the cross. Jesus emphasized that their sense of being offended would not be removed even if they saw him return to God's presence, for the means by which he will be exalted as the Son of Man is the suffering of the cross.

John often emphasizes that the Son of Man will be lifted up (3:14; 8:28; 12:34) and glorified (12:23; 13:31). The lifting up and the glorification both refer to the cross. The positive terms used for Jesus' death indicate that it is the pathway to his exaltation and glorification. Jesus is exalted not despite the cross but precisely because of it. John coheres with the Synoptics in seeing a suffering and exalted Son of Man.

Son of God

If we begin with the plural "sons of God" in the OT, we find that the expression applies particularly to angels (Ps. 89:6). The singular, "son of God," refers to Israel, signifying God's special and covenantal relationship with his people. In Exod. 4:22 Israel is designated as God's "firstborn son" (cf. Jer. 31:9; Hos. 11:1). Although the terminology is not used often, God is also represented as the father of Israel (Deut. 32:6; Jer. 3:4) or with maternal imagery as the one who gave birth to his people (Deut. 32:18). The plural "sons" also denotes God's fatherly relation to Israel (Deut. 14:1; Isa. 43:6). The Davidic king is also specially related to God, via the Davidic covenant, and designated as son. God relates to the Davidic king as a father to a son, and he will never withdraw his covenantal love from the king (2 Sam. 7:14–15; 1 Chron. 17:13–14; 22:10; 28:6–7; Pss. 2:6–7; 89:26–27; Isa. 9:6).

If we open the Synoptic Gospels with the OT background in mind, the theme that Jesus is the true Son of God—the true Israel—emerges. Matthew suggests from Hos. 11:1 that Jesus is the true Israel, the Son of God. The title "Son of God," however, is not limited to the notion that Jesus is the true Israel. It also signifies that he fulfills the promises made to David as the king of Israel. When Jesus calms the storm, the disciples confess that he is God's Son (Matt. 14:33). Perhaps the disciples received a glimmer of Jesus' special relation to God, but they likely meant by this acclamation that Jesus was truly the Messiah, the one to whom the covenantal promises given to David pointed. The same conclusion should be drawn from 16:16: at a crucial juncture in the Gospel, Peter exclaims that Jesus is "the Christ, the Son of the living God." It is doubtful that at this stage in his thinking Peter grasped that Jesus was divine. The titles "Christ" and "Son of God" were synonyms, denoting that Jesus was the Messiah of Israel.

We have seen that the title "Son of God" means that Jesus is the true Israel
and the Messiah, the promised son of David. The Gospel writers, however, see
a deeper meaning in the appellation "Son of God." Jesus also shares a unique
and special relation with God. He even shares the prerogatives of deity. Indeed,
this last category is what the Gospel writers emphasize. Mark, for example,
introduces his Gospel with the proclamation that Jesus is the Christ, "the Son
of God" (Mark 1:1). The demons, as heavenly beings, understood who Jesus
is better than his Jewish contemporaries, recognizing him as God's unique
Son (Matt. 8:29; Mark 3:11; 5:7). The divine voice also acclaimed Jesus as the
Son of God at his baptism and transfiguration (Mark 1:11; 9:7). Mark's Gospel concludes with the same words on the lips of the centurion (15:39). The
centurion perceived that Jesus submitted to God in his death, and so he died
as God's obedient Son. Significantly, the centurion identified Jesus only after
his work on the cross was completed, suggesting that Jesus can be understood
rightly as God's Son only in light of the cross.

The distinctiveness of Jesus as God's Son emerges in Matt. 1:23, for Jesus
as the Son is Immanuel: "God with us." Such language is not merely symbolic
(cf. Luke 1:35), for Matthew concludes with the promise of Jesus' permanent
presence with his people (28:20). The uniqueness of Jesus' relation to God is
evident in 11:27. The Father and the Son know each other exclusively, mutually, and intimately. Only the Father truly knows the Son, and only the Son
truly knows the Father. The priority of the Father is maintained because he
has given to the Son all that he enjoys. And yet no person can come to know
the Father unless the Son desires to reveal the Father to that person. The
text clearly implies Jesus' divine status, for Jesus and the Father have mutual
knowledge, and the Son is the only one who knows the Father. Further, this
text makes clear that Jesus is part of the divine heavenly council and is thus
in a separate category from all human beings.

Jesus' uniqueness as God's Son stands out in the baptismal formula (Matt.
28:19). Baptism is to be applied in the name of the Father, the Son, and the
Spirit. There is one name, and yet three different entities that are to be invoked
during baptism. What is clear here is that the title "Son" represents divinity.
He is equal with the Father.

There is some evidence in John, as we saw in the Synoptics, that "Son of
God" is equivalent to "Messiah." I suggested earlier that when Nathaniel
exclaimed that Jesus was the "Son of God" and "the King of Israel" (John
1:49), he did not mean by "Son of God" that Jesus is divine. "Son of God"
in this instance is simply another way of saying that Jesus is the Messiah. We
probably can draw the same conclusion from Martha's confession in 11:27
(cf. 19:7).

When such statements are set against the backdrop of Johannine theology
as a whole, however, the point is that these people spoke better than they
knew. Jesus is God's Son in a way they never imagined. John's purpose in his

Gospel is to persuade readers to believe that Jesus is the Christ, God's Son (20:31). In this purpose statement the terms "Christ" and "Son of God" are not merely equivalent. "Christ" refers to Jesus being the Messiah, but "Son of God" also indicates Jesus' special relation to God—his divinity. That Jesus' sonship implies deity is clear from a number of texts. For instance, the Father and the Son know each other intimately and exclusively (10:15).

The stature of the Son blazes forth in one of the most remarkable statements in John: the Son must be honored in the same way as the Father (5:23; cf. 8:19). Indeed, those who fail to honor the Son also fail to honor the Father. It seems, then, that John is arguing that the Son must be worshiped in the same way as the Father, for the honor that belongs to the one and only God must also be given to the Son. In the monotheistic framework in which John writes, such honoring of the Son must mean that he is fully divine, for worshiping a creature or an angel was unthinkable in Judaism.

The stature of the Son is verified when we consider his glory. Jesus uniquely manifests the glory of God as the Son of the Father (John 1:14). The Son's glory cannot be limited to this life but transcends it, for he possessed glory before the world ever came into existence (17:5). Nor will his glory ever end, for the Son anticipates the future when believers will see his glory forever (17:24).

John maintains the priority of the Father. Jesus insists that the Father is greater than everything, even himself (10:29; 14:28). But at the same time he also teaches that the Son and the Father are equal (10:30). The equality in view cannot be limited to unity of purpose and aim, for the Jews took up stones to put Jesus to death for blasphemy (10:31–33). We think of John 5:17–18, where Jesus identified God as his Father and made himself equal to God, so that the Jews attempted to stone him for blasphemy (cf. 8:58–59). In John 10 as well, Jesus' subsequent words about humans being gods (10:34–35) do not nullify the statement on the Son's deity, for Jesus is arguing from greater to lesser. If even human beings can be called gods in a derivative sense, then Jesus is not blaspheming in calling himself the Son of God, since he was consecrated by the Father as such (10:36).

The "I Am" Sayings in John

Another dimension of John's Christology stands out in the "I am" statements that are sprinkled regularly throughout the Gospel. The words "I am" (*egō eimi*) draw on God's revelation of himself to Moses when he summoned him to liberate Israel from Egypt (Exod. 3:6, 14), but its closest antecedents are found in Isaiah, where Yahweh regularly uses "I am" in contrasting himself with idols, assuring Israel that he will free them in a second exodus (Isa. 41:4; 43:10, 25; 45:8, 18, 19, 22; 46:4, 9; 48:12, 17; 51:12; 52:6 LXX). The texts in

Isaiah occur in contexts where monotheism is taught emphatically and the creator God is contrasted with idols.

The words "I am" (*egō eimi*) do not necessarily or always hearken back to the OT revelation of Yahweh. In John 9:9 the man to whom Jesus restores sight identifies himself with the words "I am" (*egō eimi*), and he is certainly not claiming to be divine. Perhaps some of Jesus' "I am" statements in John's Gospel involve simple identification (4:26; 6:20), though even these probably have a greater significance.

Often the "I am" statements are tied to an event, so that discourse and event interpret one another. After Jesus fed the five thousand (6:1–15), he declared that "I am the bread of life" (6:35, 48; cf. 6:41, 51, 58). Jesus also announced, "I am the light of the world" (8:12). The event aligned with this declaration is the lighting festival that occurred at the Feast of Tabernacles (see *m. Sukkah* 4.1, 9–10; 5.2–4). It also accords with the restoration of sight to the blind man in John 9. Jesus is the true revelation of God and grants spiritual sight to the blind. In John 10 Jesus gave the "good shepherd" discourse (10:1–30) and identified himself as "the door" for the sheep (10:7, 9) and as "the good shepherd" (10:11, 14). Jesus stands in contrast to the false shepherds of Israel (Ezek. 34:1–6). Yahweh himself promises to become their shepherd (34:15–16). A few verses later we are informed that a coming David will shepherd the flock (34:23–24). Ezekiel's prophecy of Yahweh serving as the shepherd for the flock finds its fulfillment in Jesus as the good shepherd (cf. Ps. 23:1; Isa. 40:11).

Jesus also declared, "I am the resurrection and the life" (John 11:25). This declaration is followed by his raising Lazarus from the dead, so that it is closely linked with the sign performed. Jesus also said, "I am the true vine" (15:1). In the OT Israel is described as the Lord's vineyard (Ps. 80; Isa. 5:1–7; cf. Jer. 12:10), signifying that they are the elect people of the Lord. The allusions to the OT provide the necessary backdrop for interpreting John 15:1. When Jesus announced that he is the true vine, he taught that he is the true Israel. Jesus is the exclusive pathway to God, for he declared, "I am the way, and the truth, and the life. No one comes to the Father except through me" (14:6).

The most striking "I am" statement is in 8:58, where Jesus asserts, "Truly, truly, I say to you, before Abraham was, I am." The Jews believed these words were blasphemy, for they immediately took up stones to put him to death. Those who confess Jesus as Lord and God (20:28) belong to God. In honoring the Son, they also honor the Father (5:23).

The "I am" statements contribute significantly to Johannine Christology. They demonstrate that Jesus fulfills the OT hope for Israel. Jesus is the unique revelation of God: in Jesus, God himself has been manifested among his people. The one who has seen Jesus has seen the Father (14:9), for he has explicated the Father to human beings (1:18).

Logos

Another one of John's distinctive terms for Jesus is "Word" (*logos*). Scholars have debated whether the Logos theme reflects Hellenism or a Jewish background, but today most scholars think that the Jewish background is fundamental (see Schreiner 2008: 254–57). In the OT, God's word is effective, bringing into existence that which he says. The power of God's word is evident in Gen. 1, for whatever God says comes into existence. When God says, "Let there be light," light springs into existence (Gen. 1:3; cf. Pss. 33:6; 107:20; 147:18; Isa. 55:10–11). God's creative word, however, is also closely related to wisdom, as Prov. 8:22–26 attests (Sir. 24:1, 23; Wis. 9:1–2).

John's Gospel (1:1) commences with the same words that we find in Gen. 1:1: "In the beginning." In Gen. 1 all things come into existence by means of God's word, whereas in John's Gospel all of created life is ascribed to the Logos (1:3). John surely reflects on the beginning before the beginning, since "the Word was with God" (1:1) before the creation of the world. John also represents an advance over the OT and postbiblical Judaism because the Logos is personal and divine. John slides from the Logos in John 1:1 to "this one," or "he" (*houtos*), emphasizing again the personal identity of the Logos. The distinctiveness of the Gospel manifests itself with his assertion that "the Word became flesh and dwelt among us" (1:14). The personal "Word" that existed with God from all eternity took on flesh and became a human being. The Logos for John is not merely a personification but actually a person, not merely one who existed with God for all eternity but also one who has entered history as a human being. This shocking claim sets John's Gospel apart from any other previous writing about God's word.

The progression of thought in John 1:1 reaches a climax. First, the Word existed for all eternity. There is no beginning at which he is not present. Second, "the Word was with God." The Logos and God are not equivalent, for they can be distinguished. The Word existed with God for all eternity and had fellowship with God. Third, and most stunning, John tells us that "the Word was God." This sentence cannot be rendered as "the Word was a god." When the predicate nominative precedes the linking verb, the noun preceding this copula emphasizes quality. So the predicate "God" (*theos*) preceding "was" indicates that the Logos is divine. He is fully God. Could we conclude from this that John falls into modalism, so that God collapses, so to speak, into the Word? We can confidently rule out modalism, for in the preceding clause we are told that "the Word was with God." The Word and God both existed from all eternity and enjoyed fellowship with one another. We are at the brink here of the paradox of the Trinity, in which Jesus is fully God, and God is one, and yet Jesus is not God without remainder. The Father is God as well. We have the paradox of the Logos being with God and yet also being God.

The Gospel climaxes with Thomas's declaration to Jesus: "My Lord and my God!" (20:28). The disciples grasp who Jesus truly is when he is raised from the dead. The acclamation of Jesus' deity forms an inclusio with John 1:1, framing the entire Gospel. The same framing device exists in the prologue itself. The best textual reading of John 1:18 proclaims that Jesus is "the only God" (*monogenēs theos*).

Jesus' Saving Work in the Gospels

In the NT, Christology always serves soteriology. The NT writers betray no interest in Christology for its own sake. A decisive OT text on Jesus' work is the Servant of the Lord text in Isa. 52:13–53:12. Old Testament scholars have vigorously debated the Servant Songs in Isaiah, but our task here is to interpret them canonically, as they appear in the final form of Isaiah. Some have counted the servant as a king, a prophet, and a new Moses, but Isaiah clearly identifies Israel, the children of Abraham, as his chosen servant (41:8–9; 44:1–2; 45:4). Still, the servant is not always coterminous with Israel. A simple identification of the servant as Israel in Isa. 49:5–6 is precluded, for this servant also brings Jacob and Israel back to God. This servant not only will bring back Israel to Yahweh but will also function as "a light for the nations, that my salvation may reach to the end of the earth" (49:6; cf. 42:1).

The servant in Isa. 50 also transcends Israel. Unlike Israel, he is not rebellious (50:5). Even though human beings have humiliated him, he will be vindicated by God himself so that he will not be shamed (50:7–9). That the servant transcends Israel is confirmed by 50:10, for God's people are summoned to obey the voice of his servant. The Servant Songs reach their climax in 52:13–53:12. The servant cannot be identified as Israel, for he bears the griefs and sorrows of Israel (53:4–5), and the iniquity of Israel is laid on him (53:6, 8). The servant must be distinguished from Israel because as the innocent one, he atones for the sins of the people. He bears the sins of his people sacrificially (53:4, 11–12). He is wounded and crushed for the iniquities of his people, so that the Lord placed the sin of his people upon him (53:5–6).

The Synoptic Gospels do not directly address the question of whether Jesus is the fulfillment of the suffering servant of Isaiah. Yet it is clear from quotations, allusions, and hints that a positive identification was made. Further, we must never forget that the narrative of the Gospels culminates in the death and resurrection of Jesus, which the extended passion accounts demonstrate to be the climax of the story. In the Synoptics, Jesus regularly predicts his future suffering, death, and resurrection, teaching that his death and resurrection fulfill what the Scriptures predicted would happen (Matt. 26:54, 56; Mark 14:49; Luke 24:25–27, 44–46). In Luke 9:51 Jesus "set his face" to travel to Jerusalem and die. An allusion to Isa. 50:7 seems probable, for there the servant says that to endure suffering, "I have set my face like a flint."

A number of other details suggest that the Synoptic writers detected in Jesus' death a fulfillment of the suffering servant of Isa. 52:13–53:12. The approbation expressed in God's pleasure with Jesus at his baptism and trans-figuration (Matt. 3:17; 17:5) probably alludes to the Servant of the Lord in Isa. 42:1. Matthew (8:17) sees a fulfillment of Isa. 53:4 in Jesus' healing ministry. Luke (22:37) also cites Isa. 53:12 as Jesus anticipates his death.

When Jesus was prosecuted at his trial, he did not engage in self-defense but remained silent when interrogated (Matt. 26:62–63; 27:12–14). Such behavior fulfills Isa. 53:7, where the servant is led like a lamb to the slaughter and yet does not open his mouth in self-defense.

A crucial text for Jesus functioning as the servant is Mark 10:45: "For even the Son of Man came not to be served but to serve, and to give his life as a ransom for many" (cf. Matt. 20:28). The verse does not contain a quotation from Isa. 53, though the use of the word "many" (*polloi*) is a likely allusion (Isa. 52:14–15; 53:11–12). Further, the notion of the Son of Man coming to serve points to the Servant of the Lord. Finally, describing his life as a ransom for many reproduces well the notion of dying in place of and instead of others, which suffuses Isa. 53. A similar allusion probably exists in the statement at Jesus' final Passover meal: "This is my blood of the covenant, which is poured out for many" (Mark 14:24; cf. Matt. 26:28). The use of the term "many" (*polloi*) and the notion that Jesus' death secures forgiveness of sins resonates with the themes of Isa. 53. Here Jesus' death is viewed as a sacrifice that procures forgiveness, so that soteriological significance is ascribed to his death.

A suggestive allusion to the servant occurs in John's notion that Jesus' death consists of his being "lifted up" (3:14; 8:28; 12:32, 34),[8] for in Isa. 52:13 the servant will "be lifted up." John shares the thought world of Isaiah remarkably, for in both accounts the exaltation of the servant becomes a reality through suffering. John (12:38) cites Isa. 53:1 in a significant text in which he sums up Jesus' public ministry and explains why so many Jews failed to believe in him. Their unbelief should not surprise, for it was predicted all along that many would not believe the proclaimed word (John 12:40; Isa. 6:10).

In John, Jesus is "the Lamb of God, who takes away the sin of the world" (1:29; cf. 1:36). The statement must be interpreted in light of the Gospel as a whole, and the narrative climaxes with Jesus' death for his people. Hence, the background is to be sought in the OT, where lambs were offered in sacri-fice. It is difficult to discern whether the lamb refers to the Passover lamb, the lambs offered as part of the sacrificial cultus, or the lamb of Isa. 53:7. In any case, it seems that later in this Gospel, Jesus was sacrificed at the time that

---

8. John also implicitly refers to the cross in Jesus' "going to" the Father (see Schreiner 2008: 283).

the Passover lamb was slain (John 18:28; 19:14), suggesting that Jesus is the Passover lamb, but the reference is too uncertain to determine the meaning of Lamb of God in John 1. The vagueness of the reference to the Lamb of God invites us to see a reference to the sacrificial cultus, the Passover lamb, and the lamb of Isa. 53:7.

The significance of Jesus' death is conveyed also through the terms "hour" and "glorify" in John's Gospel. The term "hour" conveys the fulfillment of redemptive history through Jesus (4:21, 23; 5:25, 28). God's plan for history turns upon the death of Jesus. Hence, the hour in John often represents the time of his death (2:4; 7:30; 8:20; 12:23; 13:1, 31–32; 17:1). Jesus' hour also represents the time when he will be glorified (12:23, 27–28). According to John, Jesus' death represents not his humiliation but rather his glorification (13:31–32; 17:4–5), for it represents his undying love for his disciples (13:1). Jesus' death is also his glorification because it is the pathway by which he was exalted as the Son of God.

Jesus' saving work is communicated vividly in the "bread of life" discourse (6:22–59). The food necessary for eternal life is Jesus himself (6:27). Jesus is God's true bread, and he grants life to the world (6:32–33, 48). The only way one can live is by eating the bread that is Jesus (6:50–51). Jesus then clarified that "the bread that I will give for the life of the world is my flesh" (6:51). This is almost certainly a reference to Jesus' death on the cross. Jesus then proceeded to speak in vivid language of the need to eat his flesh and drink his blood in order to obtain eternal life (6:52–59). The language would have been shocking in the extreme to the Jews, for drinking blood violated OT purity laws. The offense of the cross is thereby communicated (6:61). The only way human beings can have life is to feed on Jesus as the crucified one. They must put their trust in him by relying on his body and blood as the only basis by which they can enjoy eternal life.

Conclusion

The Gospels answer a key question, "Who is Jesus, and what has he done for us?" He is the new Moses and God's final prophet, and yet he is more than a prophet since he exercises an unrivaled authority. Indeed, Jesus is the Messiah, the promised son of David. Jesus himself did not use the title often because it was liable to be misunderstood in the political milieu of first-century Palestinian Judaism, but Jesus' followers gradually came to realize that he was the Messiah. The misunderstanding that arose over the term "Messiah" explains why Jesus preferred the term "Son of Man." Jesus used this term to refer to his ministry on earth, his suffering, and his glorification in the future. Even the sayings about suffering anticipate glorification, for they promise a future resurrection. Hence, the authority and the rule of the Son of Man form the theme that pulls together all the references to the Son of Man. The title is not used merely to emphasize Jesus' humility. Even as a man on earth, Jesus had authority to forgive sins and was Lord of the Sabbath. Hence, the Gospels proclaim that Jesus is the Son of God. The term "Son of God" designates Jesus as the true Israel and the true son of David. But the title "Son of God" cannot be restricted to messiahship even in the Synoptics. The title also designates Jesus' special and intimate relationship with God—his deity. Certainly the deity of Jesus is evident in the "I am" sayings in John's Gospel. Finally, Jesus is God's word and message to human beings: the word become flesh. As God's Logos, he has existed with God from the beginning and is himself very God, so that he is the revelation of God to human beings and is confessed by Thomas as Lord and God.

The Gospel writers also identified Jesus as the Servant of the Lord from Isa. 53. He gave his life as a ransom for many, to save his people from their sins. At the Lord's Supper he explained that his blood was being poured out covenantally to secure forgiveness of sins. John teaches that Jesus is the Lamb of God, who sacrificially takes away the sins of the world. His death, Caiaphas declared in a prophecy, is for the sake of the nation as a whole, so that he died vicariously for his people (John 11:49–52). Jesus' body and blood were poured out for the life of the world. Human beings will live only if they eat Jesus' flesh and drink his blood—that is, if they put their faith in his atoning death.

Jesus' death does not save apart from the resurrection. The cross and resurrection together constitute the saving event. It is imperative to see that every Gospel narrative concludes with the resurrection, for the cross alone is insufficient to secure forgiveness of sins. John particularly emphasizes that the cross is the pathway to victory, for he describes it as a lifting up, as Jesus' glorification, and as his going to the Father. The cross, in other words, cannot be separated from Jesus' exaltation. Indeed, the cross is the very means by which Jesus is exalted and victorious over all. Jesus as the crucified and risen Lord saves because of who he is. His death and resurrection save because he is the Messiah, the Son of Man, the Son of God, the great I Am, and truly God.

Pastoral Reflection

Understanding Jesus' identity and the mission of his life is a historical question, but the Gospel writers insist that it is also a burning existential question. For if we do not honor Jesus as we honor the Father, we will not enjoy eternal life (John 5:23). He must be recognized as our prophet, Messiah, and God—as the one who gave his life so we can enjoy forgiveness of sins. He is the only way to God, and we know that we understand Jesus when we say with Peter, "Lord, to whom shall we go? You have the words of eternal life" (John 6:68).

4

Jesus' Saving Work in Acts

We saw in chapter 1 that the new age has dawned and God has fulfilled his covenantal promises in Jesus Christ. In chapter 3, the Christology of the Gospels was examined. The Acts of the Apostles sketches in a new period in salvation history—the period of time following Jesus' death and resurrection. Even though Acts reflects the period after Jesus' ministry, the identity of Jesus and what he has accomplished still play a significant role in the book, and it is natural to consider what Acts says about Jesus Christ after studying the Christology of the Gospels.

Christology of Acts

When we study the Christology of Acts, it is imperative to recall that Luke and Acts were written by the same author. Examining the Christology of Luke and Acts together, then, assists us in pulling together the strands of Luke's theology. In considering Christology, however, we investigated Luke along with Matthew and Mark because the agreements among the three Synoptic Gospels are so remarkable. Recalling that Luke and Acts were written by the same author, on the other hand, may forestall some interpretive missteps. In some ways, the Christology of Acts seems rather undeveloped, but it is quite unlikely that the Christology of Acts should be interpreted as a step down from the Christology of Luke. In our study of the Synoptics, we saw that Jesus is the exalted Son of Man and the unique Son of God, and he assumes divine prerogatives. The Christology of Acts presumably will fit with what we have found in Luke, even if some of the same themes are not featured to the same extent. In Acts, for instance, Jesus is identified as the Son of Man and the Son of God in only one text each, but the scarcity of these appellations does not yield the conclusion that Luke questions whether Jesus is the Son of Man or the Son of God. The purpose of Acts must be recalled in any study of its Christology. Luke did not write a theological treatise, nor did he try to sketch out his theology. In recent years scholars have rightly seen that Luke is a theologian, though some have unconvincingly concluded that since he is a theologian, he is not a historian. It is better to say that Luke is a historian who writes history from a theological point of view.[1]

Reading the book of Acts, we find an emphasis on Jesus as the exalted and resurrected Lord. Luke often includes accounts that scripturally and historically emphasize Jesus' resurrection. Jesus could not be the Messiah and Lord and the one through whom people receive forgiveness of sins if he remained in the grave. Luke speaks of "many proofs" relative to Christ's resurrection (Acts 1:3). Both Peter and Paul argued that Ps. 16 was not fulfilled in David's life, and hence the words recorded fit only with Christ's resurrection (Acts 2:24–31; 13:35–37). The Scriptures themselves point to Christ's death and his resurrection (13:31–33; 26:22–23). Whereas the Pharisees are the primary opponents in Luke, the Sadducees come to the forefront in Acts, particularly because the apostles preached the resurrection (4:1–2; cf. 5:17). The Sadducees, we know, rejected the notion of the resurrection (Matt. 22:23; Mark 12:18; Luke 20:27; Acts 23:8).

One of the central themes in Acts, then, is that Jesus is now the exalted Lord. The crucified one has been vindicated by God. Jesus' resurrection indicates that he is "the cornerstone" of the people of God (4:11). As the resurrected one, he is now "exalted" as "Leader" and "Savior" (5:31). Since Jesus was raised from the dead and exalted, he has been "glorified" by God himself (3:13). At Jesus' resurrection, God "made him both Lord and Christ" (2:36). We know from the Gospel of Luke that Jesus was the Christ during his earthly ministry, and therefore this verse does not teach that Jesus "became" Lord and Christ only when raised from the dead. The point of the verse is that Jesus became the exalted Lord and Christ only at his exaltation. He did not *reign* as Lord and Christ until he was raised from the dead and exalted to God's right hand.

As the resurrected Lord, Jesus is the one who pours out the Spirit on his people (2:33). As Lord, Jesus speaks words that are authoritative (20:35; 22:18). As Jervell (1996: 29) says, "Luke in some sense regarded Jesus as on a

---

1. In defense of the idea that Luke is both a historian and a theologian, see Marshall 1970. Cf. also Gasque 1989; Hemer 1989.

level with God." Further, in 22:18 the exalted Jesus spoke the words to Paul in a vision. The exalted Jesus appeared to Paul on the road to Damascus, and such an appearance and the resulting commission suggest his divinity (9:5, 17, 27; 22:8, 10; 26:15). One might object that angels appear to people and give instructions, but Acts has Peter designating Jesus as "Lord of all" (10:36), and such a description does not fit any angelic figure. In 18:9–10, as Buckwalter (1998: 117) remarks, "Jesus appears to Paul in a vision and encourages him in language reminiscent of OT theophany and prophetic calling."

Jesus as the exalted Lord will return on the day of the Lord (2:20, quoting Joel 2:31). This is a remarkable text, for the day of the Lord in the OT is the day of Yahweh, but the prerogative of Yahweh is now assigned to Jesus Christ at his coming. Even more extraordinary, as Hurtado (2003: 181–82) notes, is the announcement that "everyone who calls upon the name of the Lord shall be saved" (Acts 2:21, quoting Joel 2:32). In the OT, the Lord who is called upon for salvation is clearly Yahweh, but in Acts the Lord who is invoked for salvation is none other than Jesus Christ. Luke "implies that Jesus in his risen status has been made equal with Yahweh of the OT, for 'Lord' was used by Palestinian Jews in the last pre-Christian centuries as a title for Yahweh" (Fitzmyer 1998: 260).

As the resurrected and exalted one, but also the one who suffered for the forgiveness of sins (see below), Jesus is the Christ. The word "Christ" retains its titular significance in Acts. It does not merely become a last name (cf. 3:20; 5:42; 9:22; 17:3; 18:5, 28). The messiahship of Jesus is closely intertwined with his lordship. The truth that he has been made Lord and Christ at his resurrection is proclaimed (2:36).

In Acts, Luke clearly teaches that Jesus is the suffering servant of Isa. 53, confirming what was argued for the Gospel of Luke earlier. The Ethiopian eunuch just "happened" to be reading Isa. 53 when Philip was instructed to approach his chariot (Acts 8:28–34). The use of the word "servant" (*pais*) in Acts is disputed, but it probably hearkens back to the suffering servant of Isaiah. The glorification of the servant refers to his exaltation in accord with Isa. 52:13 (Acts 3:13). The reference to the servant is confirmed by the context of Acts 3, where Jesus is handed over as a criminal by his people and suffered, as was prophesied (3:13–18). In both Acts and Isaiah the context suggests that the glorification follows his suffering. The glorification of the servant implies his resurrection (3:13), and 3:26 says that "God . . . raised up his servant." We have an echo here of Isa. 53:11–12 (cf. 52:13), which implies the vindication of the servant after his suffering.

Since Jesus as the Christ is the exalted Lord, Acts emphasizes the name of Jesus, signifying his authority and his divinity. Hurtado (2003: 197) says that name theology "is derived directly from the Old Testament usage, where it functions as a technical expression designating prayer and sacrifice offered specifically to *Yahweh*." It is quite striking, then, to see that believers are bap-

tized in the name of Jesus Christ (2:38; 10:48). Baptism is clearly associated
with forgiveness of sins based on Christ's death (2:38). Peter healed a lame
man "in the name of Jesus Christ of Nazareth" (3:6), stressing that faith in
the name of Christ is the basis of this man's healing (3:16; 4:10; cf. 8:12; 9:34;
15:26; 16:18). Most significantly, those who are saved call upon Jesus' name
to experience salvation (2:21; 9:14, 21; 22:16). Indeed, his is the only name
that brings salvation (4:12), and hence a divine function is clearly attributed
to Jesus. Hurtado (2003: 198–99) concludes that such a use of name theology
in Acts demonstrates that "the name of 'Jesus' itself was reverenced and functioned in the devotional life of these believers." Thus Luke's name theology
points to Jesus' deity.

   In Acts the title "Son of God" is used only once (9:20; the variant at 8:37
is not original), and so it could be equivalent to "Messiah." But the usage
in Luke's Gospel suggests that "Son of God" does not only mean that Jesus
is the Christ. The title "Son of God" indicates that Jesus has a unique and
special relationship with God. Jesus' divine stature manifests itself in Acts,
for both Stephen (7:59–60) and Paul (22:19–20) prayed to Jesus, and pious
Jews would voice prayers only to God. The Lord who appeared to Paul in a
vision in Corinth was almost surely Jesus himself (18:9–10). The same divine
authority surfaces in Jesus' encounter with Ananias. Jesus appeared to him
in a vision, summoning him to visit Paul (9:10–16). Ananias's response to the
vision accords with Isaiah's response when he saw the Lord in a vision. Isaiah
cried out, "Here am I! Send me" (Isa. 6:8). Ananias responded to the vision
by saying, "Here I am, Lord" (Acts 9:10).

   What Luke says about Jesus' lordship clearly implies his divinity: he appears
to Paul as the exalted Lord, human beings put their faith in him, believers are
baptized in the name of the Lord Jesus, and Jesus is exalted as the Lord of
all. The theology of the name is also prominent, so that Jesus takes on divine
status in baptism, healing, and salvation. Jesus' divinity is evident because he
is the Son of God, and prayers are offered to him by believers. He is clearly the
Servant of the Lord predicted in Isa. 53, the one in whom and through whom
God fulfills his promise to secure the forgiveness of sins.

The Saving Work of Christ

Since Jesus is the Christ, the exalted Lord over all, the Son of God, the Prophet,
and the Servant of the Lord, he is to be preached and proclaimed to all (Acts
5:42; 8:5, 12; 9:22; 18:5, 28; 28:31). Because Jesus Christ is the universal Lord,
salvation is available only through him (4:12). He will judge the living and
the dead on the last day (10:42; 17:31). Hence, people receive forgiveness of
sins by believing in and trusting in Jesus Christ the Lord (11:17; 16:31; 19:4;
20:21; 24:24).

Luke does not explain in any detail how Jesus' death and resurrection are the basis for the forgiveness of sins. The connections drawn are primarily suggestive instead of didactic. Acts 2:38 indicates that forgiveness is based on Jesus' work as the crucified and risen Lord. Similarly, Peter summons the people to repent for the removal of their sins (3:19) immediately after he mentions Christ's suffering (3:18). Presumably, Christ's suffering is the basis of the forgiveness offered (cf. 26:18).

In 5:30 Peter indicted the religious leaders for putting Jesus to death (cf. 3:14–15; 4:10; 7:52; 10:39; 13:28), emphasizing that he was hung on a tree. The reference to the tree probably alludes to Deut. 21:23, so in the background we have the echo of his being cursed by God. The crucified Jesus was exalted by God himself (Acts 5:31), and hence repentance and forgiveness of sins are now available in Israel. Peter intimates that Jesus took God's curse upon himself, and that forgiveness is given on the basis of Jesus' work on the cross and his resurrection/exaltation.

A particularly striking verse for both Christology and soteriology is Acts 20:28. God obtained the church "with his own blood." The reference to "God's blood" is rather startling, but it fits with what we have seen elsewhere in NT Christology, in that Jesus is both divine and human. The text also establishes that the church is saved or rescued from judgment by Christ's death. The verb translated "obtained" signifies the acquiring of God's people (cf. Isa. 43:21 LXX; Luke 17:33; cf. Eph. 1:14; 1 Pet. 2:9). Christ's death secures forgiveness because his death represents the death of God himself.

Conclusion

In Acts the theme that Jesus is the Christ and has been exalted as Lord and Christ at his resurrection receives prominence. The evangelistic context explains the emphasis on the fulfillment of prophecy and the forgiveness of sins available through Jesus. And yet there are also many indications that Jesus has divine stature: Jesus is the Lord of all, human beings pray to Jesus, believers are baptized in his name, salvation comes through believing in and turning to the Lord Jesus, and believers call on Jesus for salvation, whereas in the OT text cited, Yahweh is the one called upon (Joel 2:32). Luke does not reflect deeply on the ontological dimensions of Christology, but the material contained here fits with early Palestinian Christianity and cannot be dismissed as a low Christology.

It has often been remarked that Luke lacks an in-depth theology of the atonement, and such a judgment can be conceded if he is measured against the fuller statements found in Paul. Yet all of Acts emphasizes that salvation comes through the Lord Jesus Christ and him alone, showing that Luke ties forgiveness of sins to the death and resurrection of Jesus Christ. The gracious character of salvation is communicated, for forgiveness of sins is obtained through faith and repentance, not by living a noble life. The death of Jesus secures forgiveness of sins, and forgiveness comes only in Jesus' name. Luke does not explain in detail the basis for forgiveness of sins, but this is not surprising since the speeches in Acts are evangelistic in nature, and they also represent compressed summaries of what was said. The fundamental point is that forgiveness is secured through the death and resurrection of Jesus Christ, and it is left to other NT writers to provide a more detailed explanation of how this is so.

Pastoral Reflection

The evangelistic message of Acts cannot be separated from Christology. The message that must be proclaimed to the ends of the earth focuses on Jesus Christ. He is the Lord of all, and the Savior of all who call upon him for forgiveness of sins. Forgiveness is anchored, according to Luke, in the death, resurrection, and exaltation of Jesus Christ. Acts pulsates with the excitement and joy that forgiveness is available through Christ, and hence human beings can be freed from the sin and futility that binds them. Human life has meaning and significance, and those who are forgiven of their sins are so filled with joy that they long to share this same message with others who are destined for death.

5

The Christology of Paul

s we turn to the apostle Paul, we now see Christology worked out in epistolary literature. We need to take into account where Paul stands in salvation history. The Gospels, in contrast to the Pauline writings, rehearse the life of Jesus, which culminates with the cross and resurrection. The Acts of the Apostles sketches in the period from Jesus' death until Paul's Roman imprisonment in the 60s. The Pauline Letters reflect in more detail on the significance of what Jesus accomplished. In Paul's case we have the advantage of possessing thirteen letters addressed to a variety of situations, and so we are more confident of having a relatively complete picture of his Christology. In this chapter the identity of Jesus in the Pauline corpus is explored; in the next we consider what Jesus accomplished in his ministry.

Union with Christ

One of the most significant elements of Paul's Christology is his teaching about being "in Christ." Union with Christ or participation with Christ is surely one of the fundamental themes of his theology. Believers who were in the old Adam and the old age are now members of the new age inaugurated in Christ, and they are in Christ rather than in Adam. The phrase "in Christ" is used in a variety of ways and does not invariably denote union with Christ, though in many instances it does focus on participation in Christ. For instance, union with Christ dominates the Epistle to the Ephesians. Believers enjoy "every spiritual blessing" in Christ (1:3). They are chosen "in him" and adopted "through" him (1:4–5). Redemption is accomplished in him, as is the revelation of the mystery of his will, so that God's purpose is "to unite all things in him" (1:7–10). Believers enjoy an inheritance in him (1:11) and also were sealed with the Spirit in him (1:13). In Christ there is one new person (2:15). The church is God's holy temple in Christ (2:21), and in union with him as a "dwelling place for God by the Spirit" (2:22).

The notion of union with Christ points to a high Christology, for every spiritual blessing belongs to believers because of their participation in Christ. The nature of the blessings (new creation, redemption, election, and righteousness) suggests that Jesus Christ shares the same status with God. Otherwise it is difficult to explain how salvation and all its attendant blessings could be secured through union with Christ.

Messiah

Paul does not often speak of Jesus as David's descendant (Rom. 1:3; 15:12; 2 Tim. 2:8). Some have inferred from this that the Davidic descent of Jesus was unimportant in Pauline theology. A different conclusion is preferable. It seems probable that Jesus' Davidic lineage was proclaimed when Paul established the churches during his missionary preaching (Acts 13:22–23, 34–37). The messianic line of Jesus is not addressed often in the Pauline Letters because they are occasional in nature, and apparently the Davidic pedigree of Jesus remained uncontroversial. Interestingly, Paul in Romans does emphasize that Jesus descends from David (Rom. 1:3; 15:12), addressing a church that he did not establish.

When Paul identifies Jesus as the Christ, presumably he assumes Jesus' Davidic background. He often refers to "Jesus Christ" (80 times) or "Christ Jesus" (89 times). It is frequently said that the term "Christ" in Paul has lost its titular sense, so that it has become a formulaic name. Such a conclusion seems unlikely, given Paul's Jewish background. The title appears regularly because Jesus' messianic status was a given for Paul. Defending such a claim was superfluous since the title did not engender controversy in his churches.

Savior and Son

The use of the term "Savior" also suggests Jesus' equality with God. Lau (1996: 122) says that "it unequivocally declares the unity of God and of Christ (the Saviour) in the enactment of the saving plan." The word "Savior" appears especially often in the Pastoral Epistles, referring to God the Father on six occasions (1 Tim. 1:1; 2:3; 4:10; Titus 1:3; 2:10; 3:4), perhaps in response to the imperial cult or to the false teaching of the opponents. In any case, it is quite striking that the title "Savior" is applied also to Christ on four occasions in the Pastorals (2 Tim. 1:10; Titus 1:4; 2:13; 3:6), as also in Philippians (3:20) and Ephesians (5:23). The usage in Titus is especially interesting because on three different occasions Paul alternates between "God our Savior" (1:3; 2:10; 3:4) and Jesus Christ as Savior (1:4; 2:13; 3:6). In every instance, almost immediately after God is identified as Savior, Christ is also said to be Savior. God and Christ have rescued believers from the peril of sin. The close equivalency between God and Christ suggests that Jesus shares the same status with God.

The term "Son of God" (or simply "Son") also designates Jesus as the unique Son of the Father. Paul does not use this term often—only seventeen times in his thirteen letters. The gospel centers on God's Son (Rom. 1:3), and at the resurrection Jesus Christ was "appointed Son of God in power" (1:4 AT). The text is wrongly rendered "declared" instead of "appointed" by some versions (e.g., ESV, NRSV). The verb *horizō* never means "declare," and it is likely that versions opt for this because of fear of adoptionistic Christology. But the text makes a distinction between God's Son and Jesus' appointment as Son of God "in power." God's Son preexisted, before Jesus' ministry on earth, in accord with Rom. 1:3. His appointment as "Son of God in power" occurred at the resurrection, when he was exalted; he now reigns at God's right hand as king.

God's reconciling work occurred "by the death of his Son" (Rom. 5:10). The death of Jesus for sinners took place at the initiative of God himself. He "sent" his Son as an atonement for sin to free people from the bondage of sin (8:3; Gal. 4:4; cf. Rom. 8:32). Those who believe put their faith and trust "in the Son of God, who loved me and gave himself for me" (Gal. 2:20). As a result of Christ's work on the cross, God "sent the Spirit of his Son" into the lives of his children (4:6), so that they would "be conformed to the image of his Son" (Rom. 8:29). Those who have the Spirit have been "called into the fellowship of his Son" (1 Cor. 1:9).

From the foregoing texts we observe that "Son" is often used to designate the atoning and saving work of Jesus. In addition, the word "Son" is used where personal relations are in view, so that Paul speaks of fellowship with the Son, "knowledge of the Son" (Eph. 4:13), and God's love in sending the Son to die. It is also likely, given the exalted nature of the title "Son of God," that the title implies Jesus' preexistence. Especially the two texts that refer to God "sending" his Son support a reference to preexistence (Rom. 8:3; Gal. 4:4).

Philippians 2:6–11

The lordship of Jesus is a common feature of Pauline theology (ca. 180 times) and is communicated powerfully in the Philippian hymn (2:6–11). The hymn can be split into two sections, the first recounting Jesus' humiliation (2:6–8), and the second his exaltation (2:9–11). The stature of Jesus comes to the forefront in Phil. 2:6: he "was in the form of God." The word "form" (*morphē*) does not mean that Jesus was outwardly in the form of God but lacked the inner qualities of deity. The same word occurs in Phil. 2:7, where Paul says that Jesus took "the form of a servant." The text does not mean that he appeared to be a servant but in reality was not. Jesus truly became a servant, which was manifested in the taking on of humanity. Hence, to say that Jesus "was in the form of God" is another way of saying that he was divine.

The divinity of Jesus is confirmed by the phrase "equality with God" in 2:6, for Jesus' equality with God is another way of speaking of the "form of God." The NRSV rightly translates the last phrase in 2:6: Jesus "did not regard equality with God as something to be exploited" (cf. HCSB). We must pause here to note the significance of such a translation. Paul *assumes* that Jesus is equal with God. The verse does not teach that Jesus ceased trying to attain equality with God. Rather, Paul emphasizes that Jesus did not take advantage of or exploit the equality with God that he already possessed. Furthermore, saying that Jesus emptied himself implies a self-conscious decision on his part to do so, and such a decision is possible only for one who has consciousness and existence. It follows, then, that this hymn teaches the preexistence of Jesus. He shared the divine nature before he took humanity upon himself.

Nor does 2:7 indicate that Jesus surrendered his deity in becoming a human being. If we attend to the Greek participles in the text, it becomes clear that Jesus emptied himself by becoming a slave, by taking on humanity. The emptying consisted not in the removal of Christ's deity but rather in the addition of his humanity. Paul utilizes paradoxical language by describing Christ's emptying in terms of adding. Certainly the Philippian hymn witnesses to Jesus' humanity. The deity of Christ was veiled by his humanity, and some of his divine powers were not exercised, but this is not to be equated with relinquishing his deity.

For the Son of God to become a man is to humble himself. The humiliation, as 2:8 demonstrates, did not cease with the incarnation. Presumably, Jesus could have been feted as a king and could have chosen not to die. Not only did he consent to become a human being; he also was willing to undergo the agony of death for the sake of others. Not only did he consent to die; he also subjected himself to the most degrading and humiliating and excruciatingly painful death in the Greco-Roman world: death on a cross.

Philippians 2:9–11 explains that Jesus is now exalted as Lord because of his humiliation. As the preexistent Son of God, he reigned with the Father eternally, but Jesus of Nazareth, the God-man, was exalted as Lord only at the resurrection. Every knee will bend and every tongue will acknowledge the lordship of Jesus. The lordship of Jesus does not diminish the Father's glory but rather enhances it because Jesus' humiliation and exaltation are "to the glory of God the Father" (2:11).

Philippians 2:9–11 clearly alludes to Isa. 45:20–25. The text in Isaiah engages in a polemic against idolatry, insisting emphatically that the God of Israel is the only true God (45:21–22). Yahweh then declares, "By myself I have sworn; from my mouth has gone out in righteousness a word that shall not return: 'To me every knee shall bow, every tongue shall swear allegiance'" (45:23). If we consider together the themes assembled, we see something astonishing. Along with Isaiah, Paul confesses that there is only one God. Yet, he applies to Jesus what Isaiah attributes to Yahweh—every knee bending and every tongue confessing. Clearly, Paul teaches that Jesus shares the same divine nature as Yahweh himself, but Paul does this without denying monotheism or the distinctions between the Father and the Son.

Colossians 1:15–20

Another remarkable hymn to Christ is found in Col. 1:15–20. This hymn likewise can be divided into two stanzas, in which Jesus is the Lord of creation (1:15–17) and the Lord of the church (1:18–20). The divine nature of Jesus is suggested by the claim that he is "the image of the invisible God" (1:15; cf. 2 Cor. 4:4). Adam and Eve were created "in" God's image (Gen. 1:26–27), but Jesus is *uniquely* the image of the invisible God. The "firstborn of all creation" might suggest on first glance that Jesus is the first creature. The term "firstborn," however, derives from the OT, where the firstborn has the right of primogeniture. Israel is God's "firstborn" son (Exod. 4:22), receiving the same mandate given to Adam, which is to rule the world for God. The Davidic king representatively carries out this rule on behalf of God's people. Hence, we read about God's promise to David: "I will make him the firstborn, the highest of the kings of the earth" (Ps. 89:27). David was not the first Israelite king. That privilege belonged to Saul. Nor was David the oldest in his family. In fact, he was the youngest. Designating him as the "firstborn" signals his sovereignty, and this is confirmed by Hebrew parallelism.

When we apply the OT meaning of the term "firstborn" to the Colossians text, it becomes clear that identifying Jesus as the firstborn does not designate him as a creature. Rather, he is the sovereign one, the ruler and Lord of all. Indeed, Jesus cannot be a creature, since Col. 1:16 declares that all of creation was brought into being by Christ's agency. Not only were all things created "through him"; they also were created "for him." Jesus is the goal as well as the agent of all creation. The glory that belongs to the one true God also belongs to Jesus as creator and Lord.

The word "firstborn" probably has the notion of Jesus' temporal priority in addition to sovereignty. There is no notion, however, of his being a created being. He existed eternally before the world was created. Despite the reservations of some, this text clearly teaches preexistence. Paul draws on wisdom traditions in elucidating Christ's role in creation (Prov. 8:22–31; Wis. 7:25–27). Wisdom language in the OT and in Second Temple literature is an example of personification, and hence wisdom does not point to an independent being. Even though wisdom traditions inform Christology in Colossians, the antecedents do not dictate the significance of the fulfillment. Jesus transcends wisdom because he is a person, and hence to attribute creation to him implies preexistence. When Paul says that "he [Christ] is before all things" (Col. 1:17), this confessional statement refers both to Jesus' sovereignty and to his temporal priority. He has always existed, and he is the Lord of the universe. Such a reading fits the Jewish background nicely because typically the oldest son in the family enjoyed the benefits of the firstborn. Jesus' lordship over creation is expressed also by the coherence of all creation in him: "in him all things hold together" (1:17). The physical world does not "run on its own" as if it has an internal mechanism by which it sustains itself. The world is sustained and upheld by Jesus Christ.

Colossians 1:18–20 explicates Jesus' lordship over the church. He is not only the Lord of the universe but also the sovereign over God's people. Jesus is the fountainhead and origin of the new people of God because he is "the firstborn from the dead." Jesus rules over death because he was the first to conquer death. The risen Lord is the head of the church and was raised from the dead so that he would be "preeminent" in all things. Jesus' lordship is grounded in his divinity and his reconciling work (1:19–20). It is grounded in his divinity, for all of God's "fullness" dwelt in Jesus, just as God's glory dwelt in the tabernacle and temple (cf. 2:9). In other words, Jesus is fully divine because God dwells in him completely. Further, Jesus is Lord because his reconciling work embraces the whole universe.

Jesus' Lordship

Jesus' lordship pervades Paul's theology, and Jesus is regularly acclaimed and proclaimed as the risen Lord (2 Cor. 4:5). God raised Jesus from the dead and seated him at his right hand (Eph. 1:20–23), and the divine session at the right hand accords with Ps. 110:1. Jesus is enthroned above all demonic powers (Eph. 1:21; cf. Col. 1:16) and rules as head over the church (Eph. 1:22; cf. 5:23; Col. 2:10, 19). The church, then, expresses the fullness of Christ (Eph. 1:23). He is the ascended Lord, who has triumphed over his enemies and granted gifts to those in the church (4:8). Jesus' ascension on high presumes his previous descent and incarnation (4:9–10; cf. Rom. 4:24), as we saw in Phil. 2:6–11. Now, as the ascended Lord, he fills "all things" (Eph. 4:10; cf. Rom. 10:12).

The Father is confessed as the one God and the creator and source of all things; Jesus Christ is confessed as Lord and as the agent by whom all things came into existence (1 Cor. 8:6). One can truly and genuinely acknowledge that "Jesus is Lord" only by the work of the Holy Spirit (12:3). Those who have come to faith began their new life by receiving "Christ Jesus" as Lord (Col. 2:6). And only those who confess him as Lord will be saved (Rom. 10:9), for they acknowledge him as the only Lord (Eph. 4:5). Christians all over the world are characterized by a common affirmation of Jesus' lordship (1 Cor. 1:2). They live to please him (7:32–34; cf. 6:13). They see what was hidden from "the rulers of this age": Jesus, as the crucified one, is "the Lord of glory" (2:6, 8).

Paul often uses the term "Lord" in his Letters.[1] When he alludes to or quotes from the OT, "Lord" usually translates the divine name "Yahweh" (Rom. 4:7–8; 9:27–29; 11:34; 15:9–11; 1 Cor. 3:20; 2 Cor. 6:18). More significantly, in a number of texts Paul identifies the "Lord" as Jesus Christ, even though the OT allusion or quotation clearly refers to Yahweh (Rom. 10:13; 14:11; 1 Cor. 1:31; 2:16; 10:22, 26; 2 Cor. 10:17; Phil. 2:10–11; 1 Thess. 3:13; 4:6; 2 Thess. 1:7–8; 2 Tim. 2:19). Some of the texts noted here might possibly refer to God, but most of these clearly have Christ in view. Hence, there is no doubt that texts that referred to Yahweh in the OT are applied to Jesus Christ. The significance of such a move is staggering because Paul, as a Jew and a Pharisee, was nurtured in Jewish monotheism. He knew that he was identifying Jesus himself as God in assigning Yahweh texts to him.

Capes (1992: 164) rightly summarizes the significance of Jesus' lordship in six statements.

1. Jesus Christ was the object of devotion in creedal statements (Rom. 1:3–4; 10:9–10).
2. Believers prayed for Christ's return (1 Cor. 16:22) and identified themselves as those who "call upon the name of the Lord Jesus Christ" (1:2).
3. Hymns focusing on the person and work of Christ were composed (Phil. 2:6–11; Col. 1:15–20).
4. During worship, early Christians gathered in Jesus' name (1 Cor. 5:4).
5. New believers were baptized in Jesus' name (Rom. 6:3; Gal. 3:27).
6. Early Christians honored Jesus by celebrating a meal called "the Lord's Supper" (1 Cor. 11:20).

Thus Capes (1992: 164) is correct in concluding that Jesus' lordship involved worship and necessarily implies that Paul and early Christians thought of Jesus "in the way that one thinks of God." And yet God the Father is still distinct from Jesus, and Paul retains his belief in monotheism (1 Cor. 8:6). Apparently

---

1. For this section, I am dependent on Capes 1992.

Paul did not believe that honoring and worshiping Jesus as God compromised his monotheistic belief, but neither did he collapse God and Jesus together into a kind of modalism.

Jesus' Divine Status

Stettler (1998: 333) amasses significant evidence in the Pastoral Epistles for Christ's divinity: his patience (1 Tim. 1:16); the need to put faith in Jesus (3:16); his glory (Titus 2:13); his kingdom (2 Tim. 4:1, 18); prayer is offered to him (4:22); a doxology is offered to him (4:18); Jesus is thanked (1 Tim. 1:12) just as God is thanked (2 Tim. 1:3); the saving work attributed to God in the OT is ascribed to Jesus (4:17; Titus 2:14); he alone is the final judge (2 Tim. 4:1, 8).

According to Paul, Jesus shares divine status since prayers are offered to him. For instance, Paul concludes 1 Corinthians with the invocation "Our Lord, come!" (16:22). He does not entreat God to send Jesus but rather asks the Lord himself to return. Another example surfaces in the account about the thorn in the flesh. Three times Paul entreats "the Lord" to remove the thorn, but the Lord informs him that he will not take away the thorn, so that his power can be maximized in Paul's life (2 Cor. 12:8–9). But what is the identity of this Lord with whom Paul pleads? The context reveals that the "Lord" is Christ himself. He replies to Paul's supplication with the words "*My power* is made perfect in weakness" (12:9, stress added). Paul proceeds to say that he will boast of his difficulties "so that the *power of Christ* may rest upon me" (12:9, stress added). The italicized words demonstrate that the person addressed by Paul's prayer is Christ himself (cf. 1 Thess. 3:11–13; 2 Thess. 2:16–17).

The parallels between God and Christ would likely seem more astonishing if they were not so common: the Holy Spirit as the Spirit of God and the Spirit of Christ (Rom. 8:9), the church as the church of God and the churches of Christ (1 Cor. 1:2; Rom. 16:16), grace and love as coming from God and Christ (Rom. 5:15; 2 Cor. 8:9/Rom. 8:39; Rom. 8:35), the day of God and the day of Christ (Rom. 2:5; 1 Cor. 1:8), the judgment seat of God and the judgment seat of Christ (Rom. 14:10; 2 Cor. 5:10), faith in God and faith in Christ (Rom. 3:22; 4:24), God and Christ functioning as the end-time judge (2:16; 1 Cor. 4:4–5), Christians living for God but also living for Christ (Rom. 6:11; 2 Cor. 5:15), believers serving God but also serving Christ (1 Thess. 1:9; Rom. 14:18), and Paul being appointed as an apostle by God and Christ (Gal. 1:15–16; Rom. 1:5). It is difficult to imagine these collocations unless Paul views Jesus Christ as divine.

A trinitarian statement emerges in the discussion of spiritual gifts (1 Cor. 12:4–6). It is difficult to escape the conclusion that the Spirit, the Lord Jesus Christ, and God share the same status here. We see a similar phenomenon in 2 Cor. 13:14. In Eph. 4:4–6, Paul refers to "one Spirit," "one Lord," "one God and

Father of all." This statement stands out because monotheism is affirmed, while at the same time the Spirit and Christ share divine status with the Father.

The trinitarian nature of Paul's theology peeps through in a variety of other texts as well. In Eph. 1:3–14 God elects and predestines in Christ and gives his Spirit as a seal and down payment. In the same way, in 2 Cor. 1:21–22 God confirms and anoints Paul and his coworkers "in Christ" and grants the Spirit as a seal and down payment. In Rom. 5:5–11 God pours out his love through the Holy Spirit, and the love given through the Spirit is anchored in the self-giving love of Christ on the cross. The Spirit is identified as both the "Spirit of God" and the "Spirit of Christ" (8:9). Further, the resurrection of Jesus is accomplished by the Father through the Spirit (8:11). Believers are heirs of God and coheirs with Christ, and the Spirit bears witness that believers are God's children (8:14–17; cf. Gal. 4:6). The collocation of the Father, the Spirit, and the Son is quite remarkable.

The issue of whether Jesus is specifically called "God" (*theos*) in Paul involves two texts, Rom. 9:5 and Titus 2:13. In Rom. 9:4–5 Paul itemizes the blessings of the Jewish people, culminating with the truth that the Messiah comes from them. He concludes with the words "the one who is over all, God blessed for the ages, Amen" (AT). This last phrase is the subject of ongoing controversy, for scholars debate whether Jesus or the Father is called "God" in this verse. There are several reasons for thinking that Paul departs from his normal practice and refers to Christ as "God" here: (1) The phrase "according to the flesh," even though it does not require an explicit contrasting phrase, fits more smoothly if a contrasting phrase is included. The series of benefits belonging to Israel comes to a stunning conclusion, for though Christ descended from Israel ethnically, he transcends that identity because he also shares the divine nature. (2) The natural antecedent to *ho ōn* (the one who is) is "Christ," for doxologies are almost always attached to the immediate antecedent (cf. 2 Cor. 11:31). (3) If this were an independent doxology to God the Father, the word "blessed" would occur first as it does in every other instance in the LXX and the NT. (4) To break off and utter praise to God in a context in which Paul grieves over Israel fits awkwardly in the context. Ascribing blessedness to Christ after identifying him with God fits more naturally because the Messiah sharing the divine nature is the consummation of Israel's privileges. (5) That Paul would call Christ "God" is not totally surprising in light of the other texts noted above that have a high Christology.

The attribution in Titus 2:13 is similarly disputed, so that scholars debate whether *theos* refers to God or to Christ. The relevant part of the verse reads, literally, "appearance of the glory of the great God and our Savior, Jesus Christ" (AT). Grammatically, the strongest arguments favor the claim that Jesus Christ is called "the great God." I will not reduplicate, however, the detailed arguments for this view by Harris (1992: 173–85), whom readers should consult for a thorough discussion of the possible alternatives. Two reasons adduced by Harris indicate that Paul designates Jesus Christ as God here. First, the phrase "God and Savior" (*theos kai sōtēr*) was a common formula in the Greco-Roman world, and it regularly refers to one deity in such formulas. There is no reason to think that Paul departs from standard practice here, and thus the most natural way to take the expression is to conclude that Paul identifies Jesus Christ as God. Second, the one article *tou* (the) is best explained as introducing both the nouns "God" and "Savior" (*theou* and *sōtēros*).[2] If Paul had wanted to distinguish "God" and "Savior," he probably would have inserted a second definite article before the noun "Savior." By omitting the article before the second noun, Paul indicates that both nouns refer to the same person, Jesus Christ.

Conclusion

It is hardly controversial to say that Jesus Christ is central in Pauline theology. Nor is his centrality abstracted from everyday life, for the lordship of Christ pulsates throughout every aspect of Paul's thought, whether Paul speaks of eating or drinking or of how husbands and wives relate to one another. Paul teaches that Jesus was the Messiah of Israel, but he is also the Son of God, who was exalted to God's right hand at the resurrection. God's promises of rule for Israel have been fulfilled with Jesus being crowned as Lord. Jesus' lordship also signals his divinity. In a multitude of ways, Paul communicates that Jesus shares equal stature with God. Despite some unique features in his thinking, Paul remarkably shares with the Gospel writers and Acts the supremacy of Jesus. Hence, any Christian faith that is worthy of the name will exalt Jesus Christ as Lord and Savior.

Pastoral Reflection

The supremacy of Jesus is reflected in the everyday lives of believers. When we trust in him and obey him and treasure him, we show that he is indeed supreme in our lives. The centrality of Christ, according to Paul, cannot be limited to the intellect. Those who truly "understand" the supremacy of Christ say with Paul that "to live is Christ, and to die is gain" (Phil. 1:21). In everything they do, they give thanks to Jesus as Lord (Col. 3:17). The gifts we have are carried out under the lordship of Christ (1 Cor. 12:3). We confess with Paul that Christ is our life (Col. 3:4), and whether we live or die we recognize that our lives belong to him (Rom. 14:7–9). Hence, we ask ourselves how we can spend our lives in a way that pleases Jesus as Lord.

2. This is the famous Granville Sharp rule. For the best contemporary explanation, see Wallace 1996: 270–90.

6

The Saving Work of God and Christ according to Paul

The previous chapter explored the identity of Jesus in Pauline theology. In this chapter we consider what Christ accomplished according to Paul. The richness and depth of Christ's work cannot be exhausted by a single category. We actually begin with God's work of foreknowing, electing, and calling his people in Pauline thought. God's election is secured in Christ. Those whom God has chosen are justified, saved, reconciled, adopted, redeemed, and sanctified and will be glorified. God's saving work for his people has all been accomplished in and through Christ, and it is the burden of this chapter to unpack these themes.

Foreknowledge, Election, and Calling

We begin where Paul does, in Rom. 8:29. From the beginning, God foreknew whom he would predestine to be like his Son, Jesus Christ. The term "foreknow" means that God knew from the beginning those who would belong to Jesus Christ (cf. Acts 26:5; 2 Pet. 3:17; Wis. 8:8; 18:6). It is likely, however, that the term means even more than this when attributed to God. God's knowledge of his people in the OT refers to his covenantal love, by which he set his affection on his people (Gen. 18:19; Jer. 1:5; Amos 3:2). The OT background assists us in interpreting Rom. 8:29. Notice that the object of the verb "foreknew" is personal. God foreknew "those whom" (*hous*) would become like Christ. He placed his covenantal affection on certain ones according to the mystery of his grace. In 11:2 Paul discusses whether God has abandoned Israel as his people. He asserts, "God has not rejected his people whom he foreknew." The words "rejected" and "foreknew" function as antonyms in the verse.

Paul refers to the conversion of the Galatian Christians in Gal. 4:9, designating it as their coming to know God. But he immediately qualifies his statement, remarking that it is not fundamentally that they have come to know God but rather that they are "known by God." Conversion is not primarily a matter of the human will choosing to know God but rather of God's knowing of human beings (cf. 1 Cor. 8:3).

In Paul, God's love is often connected to his election or calling of his people (Rom. 1:7). Those who are elected in Thessalonica are also said to be "loved by God" (1 Thess. 1:4; cf. Col. 3:12; 2 Thess. 2:13). The new life granted to believers when they were dead in sins is traced back to God's mercy and "the great love with which he loved us" (Eph. 2:4–5). Since God's election and love are often closely allied in Scripture, it is likely that the phrase "in love" in Eph. 1:4–5 should be joined to the clause that follows it rather than to the one that precedes it and so be rendered "in love he predestined us for adoption" instead of "that we should be holy and blameless before him in love." God's choice can be portrayed in terms of his love, as in the text "Jacob I loved, but Esau I hated" (Rom. 9:13).

Just as God's election and calling are often attributed to his love, they are also ascribed to his mercy (Exod. 33:19; Rom. 9:15, 18, 23). According to Rom. 11:30–32, God has constructed salvation history in such a way that he bestows his mercy upon both Jews and Gentiles. Paul ascribes his own salvation to God's mercy, for he was the "foremost" of sinners (1 Tim. 1:13–16; cf. Titus 3:5).

God's choice of some rather than others is never fully explained by Paul. Nor does he attempt a resolution to the problem of evil. The emphasis on God's mercy and love in election, however, demonstrates that the choice of any was undeserved, that the reception of salvation is a stunning gift. Sinners merit judgment and punishment, but Paul is astonished and grateful at the merciful and kind love of God, which reaches out and saves some. At the same time, he asserts that those who fail to believe are fully responsible for their cold and resistant hearts. They have every reason to respond in faith and obedience but refuse to do so. Paul does not provide a philosophical resolution to this issue. Perhaps we should not be too surprised, since even in science we have not resolved why electrons behave sometimes like waves and sometimes like particles, nor do we fully grasp how the human body and soul interact. The most profound realities in the universe seem to exceed our rational capacities.

According to Eph. 1:4 God chose believers before the world began so that they would live holy and godly lives. The theme of election is introduced as one of the blessings that believers have received (1:3), so that they would in turn bless God. Three times Paul insists that God's redeeming work, which includes his election, should lead believers to praise God (1:6, 12, 14). Some scholars argue that the election in Eph. 1:4 is corporate, referring to the church and not individuals. Surely corporate election is in view, especially in Ephesians, where the focus is on the church of Jesus Christ; yet on the other hand, we should not drive a wedge between the corporate and individual—both are intended. It is scarcely the case that redemption, the forgiveness of sins, trust in Christ, and the sealing of the Spirit, all of which are mentioned in a very long sentence (1:3–14), are only corporate and not individual. Nor will it do to say that the point of the verse is that God chose Christ or the church, and then human beings choose to belong to Christ or the church. The text specifically says that God chose human beings (1:4).

In Rom. 9 Paul emphasizes that the salvation of Isaac and Jacob was due to God's special love and calling. Paul excludes the notion that God selected Jacob rather than Esau because the former lived a more virtuous life. His choice of Jacob rested on his purpose alone. God's choice of Jacob rather than Esau is not unjust, because the selection of any is due to his mercy (9:14–18). Furthermore, God as the sovereign potter has the right to show mercy to whom he wishes (9:19–23), so that his mercy will shine against the backdrop of his wrath.

Some have argued that Paul does not have in mind election unto salvation in Rom. 9, but that he discusses the historical destiny of Israel and the nations. Hence, he thinks of the place of the sons of Ishmael and Esau in history. The reference to Pharaoh also demonstrates, according to many, that the destiny of nations is in view (9:17). Paul does reflect on the destiny of peoples in these chapters, but such a destiny cannot be separated from salvation, for Paul grieves over Israel because it is unsaved (9:1–5; 10:1). He does not veer away from salvation and discuss historical destiny alone in the subsequent verses. All three chapters focus on the salvation of Israel and the Gentiles.

Another common view is that Rom. 9–11 refers to corporate but not individual election. It is clear that corporate election is in view in these chapters because Paul refers to Jews and Gentiles as a whole. Nevertheless, Paul's emphasis on corporate groups does not exclude individuals. Both corporate and individual election are in view for the following reasons: (1) Singulars, not plurals, are used in 9:16, 18. (2) Israel is indicted for lack of faith in 9:30–10:21, but failure to believe cannot be limited to Israel as a corporate entity; it is also the individual fault of those who disbelieved. (3) The emphasis on the remnant indicates that there are individuals within the larger group who believed

(11:1–6). (4) Corporate groups are made up of individuals, so that the former could not exist without the latter.

Paul's theology of election should not be considered in the abstract. God's choice of a remnant guarantees that salvation is by God's grace (11:1–6). If we remove election from its soteriological context, the Pauline teaching may communicate a distant God. In Paul's view, however, election supported his teaching on the freedom of God and the grace of the gospel.

The theme of God's "call" is common in Paul. Several verses establish a definition. The gospel is proclaimed and heralded (*kēryssō*) to all, whether Jews or Greeks (1 Cor. 1:22–23), but only some among all those who hear the message are "called" (*klētos*; 1:24). Indeed, in subsequent verses the term "called" is explicated in terms of those whom God "chose" (*eklegomai*; 1:26–28). Calling occurs through the proclaimed word (2 Thess. 2:13–14), and yet calling is not absolutely coterminous with the word proclaimed, since only some of those who hear the word are called. Calling, then, cannot be the same thing as being invited to be saved, for all those who hear the word preached are summoned to faith and obedience. The word calling, then, refers to God's effective work in bringing some who hear the gospel to saving faith.

The foregoing definition is confirmed in Rom. 8:30: "Those whom he called he also justified." Romans 5:1 asserts that people are justified by faith, and yet Paul declares that those called are justified. It must follow, then, that calling creates faith (cf. 4:17), so that all those called are justified. The term "called" cannot merely mean invited and summoned to faith, for it is patently obvious that not all those invited to repent actually believe.

Justification

In Rom. 8:30 justification follows calling. Justification has long been debated by Pauline scholars. Wrede (1962: 122–23) identified it as a polemical doctrine in which Paul responds to his opponents, and he noted that it appears infrequently in nonpolemical contexts. Schweitzer (1931: 225) doubted whether justification serves as a foundation for ethics and life in the Spirit and subordinated it to Paul's "in Christ" theology, seeing justification as a "subsidiary crater" to the main crater of being in Christ. Participation with Christ, rather than the juridical doctrine of justification, is trumpeted by Sanders (1977: 502–8) as the center of Paul's thought. Dunn (1992: 2) maintains that Luther misunderstood Paul in formulating his view of justification. It is not my purpose here to arbitrate the debate on the status of justification in Paul. It seems, however, that those who doubt its centrality overstate their case (rightly Seifrid 2000).

Some scholars limit justification to God's saving righteousness and exclude any notion of retributive punishment. Such a view does not handle the evidence adequately, for in Rom. 3:5 righteousness refers to God's justice in judging sinners. The link between God's righteousness and wrath in 1:17–18 points in the same direction, and 2:5 specifically includes the idea of God's "righteous judgment." Those who emphasize that righteousness is always relational tend to minimize the external standards to which a relationship must conform (cf. 3:25–26).

Justification refers to God's verdict of not guilty on the day of judgment (2:13). God's eschatological verdict has now been announced in advance for those who believe in Jesus Christ. Those who have been justified by the blood of Christ will be saved from God's wrath at the eschaton (5:9). God will announce publicly to the world the verdict of not guilty on the last day, though this verdict already stands for those who belong to Christ Jesus. The forensic and legal character of the term "justify" (*dikaioō*) derives from the verbal form of *ṣdq* in the OT. Judges are to declare the righteous innocent and condemn the wicked (Deut. 25:1; cf. 2 Sam. 15:4; 1 Kings 8:31–32; 2 Chron. 6:23; Prov. 17:15; Isa. 5:23). Judges do not "make" anyone righteous. They pronounce on what is in fact the case—if they are righteous judges. In other words, the verbal form belongs in the forensic realm. For example, God will pass judgment on whether Paul is acquitted before the Lord on judgment day (1 Cor. 4:4). When Paul says that the doers of the law will be justified (Rom. 2:13), a declaration of righteousness is intended. God will pass judgment as to whether people are righteous, whether they have done what is right and good. The uniqueness of the Pauline gospel surfaces in the truth that God declares those who are sinners to be in the right before him if they trust in Jesus Christ for their salvation.

Scholars have continued to argue about the meaning of righteousness and justification in Paul.[1] Some of them have argued that God's righteousness should be defined as his faithfulness to the covenant. The OT background plays a vital role here, for in the OT righteousness often occurs in Hebrew parallelism with God's truth, mercy, and salvation (Pss. 31:1; 36:10; 40:10; 71:2; 88:10–12; 98:2–3; 143:1; Isa. 46:13; 51:5–8). God's saving actions *fulfill* his covenantal promises made to Abraham; however, evidence is lacking that righteousness should be *defined* as covenantal faithfulness. The Hebrew parallelism does not establish, for example, that "mercy" means "truth," and that "salvation" and "righteousness" have precisely the same definition. If every term is assigned the same meaning as the other terms with which it appears in parallelism, then we are perilously close to saying that every word has the same meaning, which verges on saying that everything means nothing.

Others have maintained that God's righteousness refers to his transforming righteousness. They defend this view with a number of arguments: (1) God's righteousness is said to be "revealed" (Rom. 1:17) and "manifested" (3:21). Hence, God's righteousness is an apocalyptic and effective work of God that

---

1. For a more detailed discussion of this matter, see Schreiner 2008: 351–62.

cannot be limited to a mere declaration; it includes the entire creation and not just the individual. (2) The parallelism apparent between the "power" (1:16), "righteousness" (1:17), and "wrath" (1:18) of God. (3) The transformative view points to the same evidence noted above in support of covenantal faithfulness. God's righteousness in the OT is often parallel to his salvation, truth, and mercy. The background demonstrates that God's righteousness is his saving action on behalf of his people, and it should not be limited to his forensic declaration since God's gift and God's power cannot be separated from one another. (4) In 3:24 God's righteousness is "through the redemption that is in Christ Jesus." Redemption signifies the freedom and liberation of sin through Jesus Christ, finding its antecedent in God's liberation of his people from Egypt. If righteousness becomes ours through the liberation of sin effected by Jesus Christ, then righteousness must include the idea of freedom from sin. (5) Scholars have too rigidly separated justification and sanctification. This is apparent from 6:7: "For the one who has died has been justified from sin" (AT), which is interpreted to say that those who have died with Christ have been freed from sin's power. (6) Paul speaks of grace reigning through righteousness (5:21), of the service of righteousness (6:18–19; 2 Cor. 3:9), and of submitting to God's righteousness (Rom. 10:3). The same point is argued from 2 Cor. 3:8–9. Those who benefit from the "ministry of righteousness" also enjoy the "ministry of the Spirit." The effective work of the Spirit is part and parcel of the righteousness of God.

Despite some valid insights in the notion that righteousness is transformative, the case for such a view is overstated, and righteousness and justification in Paul should be understood as forensic.

1. We noted above that the verbal form in the OT (*ṣdq*) should be understood in terms of God's declaration. The legal character of the term is apparent in a number of other OT texts as well (Job 4:17; 9:2, 14–15, 20; 13:18; Ps. 51:4; Isa. 43:9, 26).
2. The verbal form "justify" (*dikaioō*) in Paul almost invariably refers to God's declaration and is used forensically (Rom. 2:13; 1 Cor. 4:4). The lawcourt background of "justify" is perhaps clearest in Rom. 8:33: "Who shall bring any charge against God's elect? It is God who justifies." On the last day some may bring charges before God's chosen at the divine tribunal, but all charges will be dismissed because God has declared his people to be in the right before him.
3. Paul often says that human beings are righteous by faith (e.g., Rom. 1:17; 3:22, 26; 4:3, 5, 9, 13; 9:30; 10:4; Gal. 2:16; 3:6, 11; 5:5; Phil. 3:9). In such contexts Paul contrasts righteousness by faith with righteousness by works. Paul maintains that it is not those who work but those who believe who are righteous before God (Rom. 4:4–5). Indeed, no one can be righteous by works before God, for all have fallen short of what he

requires (3:23). Righteousness by faith, then, must refer to the *gift* of righteousness given to human beings by God. Human beings are justified not on the basis of doing but of believing. Nor does Paul view faith as a "work" that merits the declaration of righteousness. Faith saves because it looks entirely to what God has done for believers in Christ. It rests on Christ's death for forgiveness of sins and his resurrection for the sake of their justification (3:21–26; 4:25). The righteousness given to believers, then, is alien because it is not based on anything they have done but rather on God's work in Christ.

4. That righteousness is a forensic declaration is supported also by the link between righteousness and forgiveness. We have already seen the connection between righteousness and forgiveness in 4:25 and 8:33. Paul slides easily from justification to forgiveness in 4:1–8. David's forgiveness of sins is nothing less than his justification, his being in the right before God (4:6–8).

5. The idea that righteousness is counted (*logizomai*) to believers indicates that righteousness is not native to believers, that it is granted to them by God (3:28; 4:3–6, 8–11, 22–24; 9:8; Gal. 3:6). This argument is strengthened when we add that righteousness is counted to those who believe, not to those who work. God does not "count" sins against those who have put their faith in Christ (2 Cor. 5:19). This is a strange reckoning or counting indeed when those who have done evil are considered to be righteous. This fits with the notion, however, that believers have received "the free gift of righteousness" (Rom. 5:17).

6. Should "the righteousness of God" also be understood as forensic (esp. 1:17; 3:21–22; 10:3; 2 Cor. 5:21)? Some scholars have maintained that Rom. 3:5, where righteousness is parallel to God's "faithfulness" and truth, supports covenantal faithfulness as the interpretation. Such an interpretation is scarcely clear in 3:1–8, for it seems that God's righteousness here refers to his judgment of sinners.

That the "righteousness of God" refers to a divine gift is clear from Phil. 3:9, where Paul speaks of "the righteousness from God" (*tēn ek theou dikaiosynēn*). The righteousness is not Paul's own, deriving from his observance of the law. It is a righteousness from God himself, obtained by faith in Jesus Christ. Philippians 3:9, then, provides an important clue as to how we should interpret God's righteousness in Rom. 1:17 and 3:21–22. It refers to God's saving righteousness, given as a gift to those who believe. The lack of the preposition "from" (*ek*) in the texts in Romans is not decisive, for in both instances the same subject is treated: the saving righteousness of God that is given to those who believe. It is unlikely that Paul would use a different definition of the word "righteousness" in texts that are so similar. Yet some argue that righteousness is transformative in 1:17 because it is parallel to God's power and wrath. It is

correct to say that each of the genitives (*theou*) should be identified as a genitive of source. God's wrath and power and righteousness all come from him.
Yet it does not follow from the collocation of terms that the words all refer to
a divine activity, if by that one concludes that God's righteousness must be a
transforming one. The words "power," "wrath," and "righteousness" do not
all have the same meaning. The phrase "righteousness of God" makes perfect
sense if it designates the gift of God's righteousness.

A powerful argument supporting this view flags the numerous parallels
between Rom. 10:1–5 and Phil. 3:2–9. The following parallels exist: (1) a reference to God's righteousness; (2) the contrast between righteousness by law
and righteousness by faith; (3) the parallel between Israel's quest to establish
its own righteousness and Paul's quest to do the same; (4) in particular, Paul's
emphasis on "not having a righteousness of my own that comes from the law"
(Phil. 3:9) and Israel's attempt to establish its own righteousness (Rom. 10:3),
a "righteousness that is based on the law" (10:5). The point is that the parallel
contexts indicate that righteousness in Rom. 10 cannot have a different definition from what we see in Phil. 3. In the latter text, righteousness clearly is a
gift given to sinners: a declaration that those who have failed to keep the law
but who have trusted in Jesus Christ stand in the right before God. The same
gift character of righteousness, therefore, is in view in Rom. 10.

We can go further. If such is the meaning in Rom. 10, it is highly unlikely
that Paul means anything different in 1:17; 3:21–22. When he speaks of God's
righteousness in declaring sinners to be in the right before him by faith in
Christ, he has in mind the gift of righteousness—God's declaration of "not
guilty." Paul would confuse the readers if in some instances he used the term
"righteousness of God" to refer to a gift of a righteous status from God and in
others of a divine activity that transforms believers. He would need to explain
much more clearly that he operates with such a distinction. That he refers to
the gift of righteousness is also clear from 2 Cor. 5:21. God made Christ to
be sin, even though he was without sin, so that believers would "become the
righteousness of God." The meaning of God's righteousness is explicated
by 5:19, which refers to forgiveness of sins. The verse also explains how God
could grant the gift of righteousness to those who are sinners. The gift of righteousness is secured through Christ's death on the cross. God "made him to
be sin" so that those who are wicked could become righteous. An interchange
between Christ and sinners is posited here.

Romans 3:21–26 is a key text and remarkably parallel to 2 Cor. 5:21. This
paragraph functions as the hinge for the Letter to the Romans and is one of
the most important, if not the most important, in the letter. The placement
of the text in the letter should be observed. Paul has finished arguing that all
people sin and deserve judgment (1:18–3:20). He summarizes this truth in
3:23: "For all have sinned and fall short of the glory of God." God demands
perfect obedience, and all fall short of his standard. How, then, will people

become right with God? Paul argues in 3:21–22 that a right relation with God is obtained not by keeping the law but rather through faith in Jesus Christ. All people who trust in Christ are justified by God because of the redemption accomplished by Christ Jesus (3:24).

Romans 3:25–26 is of particular importance for our subject. God set forth Christ as a propitiatory sacrifice by virtue of Jesus' bloody death. The terms "propitiation" and "blood" point back to the OT cultus and sacrificial system. Discussion has centered on the meaning of the term *hilastērion*, whether it should be rendered as "expiation" or "propitiation." Those who defend the notion of propitiation have had the better of the argument, for the term includes the sense of averting God's wrath—the appeasement or satisfaction of his righteousness. This fits nicely with 1:18, where the wrath of God against sin is announced, and 2:5, where the final judgment is described as the day of God's wrath. The line of argument in 1:18–3:20 provokes the reader to ask how God's wrath can be averted. The answer in 3:25 is that God's wrath has been satisfied or appeased in the death of Christ.

The words following "propitiation" substantiate the interpretation offered here. Paul explains that Christ was set forth as a mercy seat to demonstrate God's righteousness. The context reveals that by "righteousness" Paul refers to God's holiness or justice, for Paul immediately mentions the sins that God passed over in previous eras. By God's "passing over sins," Paul means that sins committed previously in history did not receive the full punishment deserved. Hence, God's failure to act calls into question his justice. Paul's solution is that God looked ahead to the cross of Christ, where his wrath would be appeased and justice would be satisfied. Christ as the substitute would absorb the full payment for sin.

The foregoing interpretation is also confirmed by 3:26: "It was to show his righteousness at the present time, so that he might be just and the justifier of the one who has faith in Jesus." Thereby God is both "just and the justifier" of those who put their faith in Christ. God's justice is satisfied because Christ bore the full payment for sin. But God is also the justifier, because on the basis of the cross of Christ, sinners receive forgiveness through faith in Jesus.

The argument of Gal. 3:10–14 is remarkably similar to Rom. 3:21–26. Galatians 3:10 teaches that God's curse stands upon all those who fail to keep God's law perfectly. How can such a curse be removed? Galatians 3:13 answers the question: "Christ redeemed us from the curse of the law by becoming a curse for [*hyper*] us—for it is written, 'Cursed is everyone who is hanged on a tree.'" The curse that humans deserve was borne by Christ. He died in the place of sinners. The sinless one took upon himself the curse of God.

Some of the arguments supporting transformative righteousness have been answered in the course of the discussion, but we need to pause for comments on a few that have not been examined thus far. To say that those who have died with Christ "are justified of sin" (Rom. 6:7) seems at first glance to be a compelling argument for the transformative view. On the other hand, virtually all scholars agree that in the vast majority of cases the verb "justify" (*dikaioō*) is forensic. Hence, to posit a different definition here is antecedently unlikely.[2] Furthermore, it is not as if Paul puts God's declaration of righteousness and a changed life into two discrete compartments. He believes that the two are related to one another without saying that they are precisely the same thing. God's declaration that sinners are in the right before him is the foundation for a changed life. A similar argument can be made regarding the collocation of the "ministry of righteousness" and the "ministry of the Spirit" in 2 Cor. 3:8–9. Paul never imagined that one could be righteous in God's sight without being transformed by the Spirit. And yet it does not follow that the transforming power of the Spirit and righteousness are precisely the same. Too many of those who defend the transformative view argue for identity of meaning from parallelism of terms. Such an approach is flawed, for it collapses the meaning of words so that they become virtually indistinguishable.

Believers are justified, therefore, on the basis of Christ's work. Justification does not describe the ongoing work of the Spirit in believers. By virtue of union with Christ, believers already enjoy justification in this present evil age. The ground of justification is not the moral transformation of believers, even though the transforming work of the Spirit is necessary to receive eternal life.

Salvation, Reconciliation, and Adoption

Salvation or deliverance in Paul centers on deliverance from God's wrath on the day of judgment. This is evident from 1 Thess. 1:10, where "Jesus . . . delivers us from the wrath to come," and "God has not destined us for wrath, but to obtain salvation through our Lord Jesus Christ" (5:9). Also, salvation is fundamentally eschatological. God's wrath will be poured out on the last day. Those who are justified through Jesus' blood will be saved from God's wrath on that day (Rom. 5:9). Similarly, those reconciled by Jesus' death "shall . . . be saved by his life" (5:10). The eschatological character of salvation is thus apparent: "Salvation is nearer to us now than when we first believed" (13:11).

Even though salvation is an end-time gift, it is the possession of believers now. Believers have been saved by God's grace through faith (Eph. 2:5, 8). They have been saved not by virtue of their works but on account of God's mercy (Titus 3:5). Similarly, Paul remarks in 2 Tim. 1:9 that salvation is realized because of God's purpose and intention before history began; hence, the salvation enjoyed by believers cannot be attributed to the works of believers. God has "delivered" believers from the domain of darkness and inducted

---

2. Even if Paul speaks of freedom from sin here, it does not follow that the term should be explained in such a way in other Pauline contexts.

them into the kingdom of his Son (Col. 1:13). Salvation is not only future and past but also has a present dimension. Believers "are being saved" because of God's power (1 Cor. 1:18).

Reconciliation presupposes a previous enmity that has been overcome (cf. Matt. 5:23–24; Acts 7:25–26; 1 Cor. 7:11). The breach between human beings and God is due to human transgression (2 Cor. 5:19; Col. 1:21). Human beings are God's enemies (Rom. 5:10), and the context clarifies that they are God's enemies because of their ungodliness and sin (5:6–8). God's wrath hovers over them because of their unrighteousness (5:9).

The situation in Ephesians is more complex. Gentiles are "far off" from God because they are separated from Israel (2:11–13). Hostility exists between Jews and Gentiles because the latter are not part of the covenant. The hostility is clearly sociological in Eph. 2 inasmuch as a cultural breach exists between Jews and Gentiles. Still, the hostility cannot be accounted for solely on the basis of sociological and cultural tension. Both Jews and Gentiles also need to be reconciled to God, and Paul locates their enmity to "the law of commandments expressed in ordinances" (2:15), which likely refers to their failure to keep God's law. Nor is the need for repentance limited to Gentiles, for the message of peace is also proclaimed to Jews, who are "near" (2:17).

Reconciliation between God and human beings is accomplished through the cross of Christ. The whole process of reconciliation was initiated and carried out by God himself (2 Cor. 5:18). Reconciliation is accomplished through the cross of Christ, whereby God no longer counts the sins of believers against them (5:19; Col. 1:20). Their sins have been placed on Christ, whom God has made to be sin (2 Cor. 5:21). It is evident, therefore, that justification and reconciliation are closely related (cf. Rom. 5:9–10). Those whom God has declared to be in the right with him are also considered to be friends and beloved by him.

Since believers are friends with God, they are his children and adopted. Those who enjoy the gift of the Spirit are led by the same Spirit and are God's "sons" and daughters (Rom. 8:14; cf. Gal. 3:26; 4:5). Those who are adopted as God's children no longer live in slavery to sin (Rom. 8:15), and this is witnessed by the fact that they love God as their dear Father. The Spirit confirms to believers that they are truly the "children" of God (Rom. 8:16; Gal. 4:6). And since believers are children now, they are assured of a future inheritance (Rom. 8:17).

Redemption and Triumph over Evil Powers

Christ's work of freeing believers from sin (redemption) is fundamentally eschatological. He "gave himself for our sins to deliver us from the present evil age" (Gal. 1:4). In both Eph. 1:7 and Col. 1:14 redemption is defined in terms of forgiveness of sins. The same emphasis on forgiveness of sins is likely present in Rom. 3:24. In Gal. 3:10 Paul argues that every human being is under a curse because of a failure to keep God's law. Christ Jesus liberates from the curse those who trust him because he became a curse in their place (3:13). The fundamental liberation needed by human beings, therefore, is forgiveness of sins.

The freedom of believers has been achieved through the cross of Christ. Those who were enslaved to sin under the law have been freed from their subjugation to sin through the death of Christ (4:4–5). Redemption cannot be traced to anything that believers have done. It has been accomplished by Christ Jesus alone (1 Cor. 1:30). Believers are free from sin and now are enslaved to righteousness (Rom. 6:18; cf. 6:22). Slavery to righteousness is no burden, for a constant desire to do what is right is actually freedom (Gal. 5:13). Those who are in Christ no longer live under condemnation (Rom. 8:1). They are free from the penalty and guilt of sin. Freedom from sin by the power of the Spirit functions as evidence that Christ has paid the penalty for sin (8:2–3) and has condemned sin in the flesh. We see another piece of evidence that God's justifying work in Christ is the basis for the new life of believers. The redemption accomplished by Jesus frees believers from "lawlessness" and animates them to be "zealous for good works" (Titus 2:14). Yet the fullness of this freedom will belong to believers only on the day of final redemption (Rom. 8:21).

On occasion Paul uses the word "redemption" to refer to the consummation of God's work in believers. The Spirit seals believers "for the day of redemption" (Eph. 4:30). At the conclusion of history, the bodies of believers will be redeemed (Rom. 8:23). God's saving work will be completed, and the fullness of redemption will then be the portion of those who have put their faith in Christ.

Do the terms used for redemption include the cost of redemption, so that the price at which redemption is gained is also in view? In some instances the price at which redemption is gained certainly is in view. Paul declares that believers "were bought with a price" (1 Cor. 6:20; 7:23). In other texts redemption is specifically ascribed to the shedding of Christ's blood (Eph. 1:7), although the parallel text in Colossians omits the reference to Christ's blood (Col. 1:14). The absence of reference to blood does not necessarily suggest that a price is excluded. Romans 3:24 is a case in point. Justification occurs "through redemption." Nothing is said about the price of redemption. Still, in this verse Paul emphasizes that justification is free, implying that it comes to believers at no cost. In the next verse Christ's blood propitiates God's anger (3:25). The reference to "blood" in 3:25 and the freedom of his grace in 3:24 imply that redemption is procured at the cost of Christ's blood.

Other texts are less clear. Nothing is said about the price of redemption in Gal. 3:13 or 4:5. Still, it is obvious in context that the death of Christ is the means by which people are freed from the curse and the enslavement that exists under law. In 1 Cor. 1:30 Paul affirms, among other things, that Christ

Jesus is "our ... redemption" (AT). One could argue that nothing is said about the cross in this verse. Such a claim would fail, however, to consult the surrounding context, where Christ crucified represents the wisdom and power of God (1:17–25; 2:2, 6, 8). Clearly wisdom, righteousness, sanctification, and redemption (1:30) are given to believers by virtue of Christ's work on the cross. Titus 2:14 is quite similar in this respect. The text fails to mention the blood of Christ as the cost of redemption, and yet the cost is implicit in his self-giving, in the life that he gave on behalf of others.

The two texts that speak of the consummation of redemption (Rom. 8:23; Eph. 4:30) are silent about the price of redemption, and they do not even mention the death of Christ. We could easily draw unwarranted conclusions from the absence of certain themes in these texts. Paul fixes attention on the completion of God's redeeming work, and he did not feel the need to explicate every dimension of redemption each time he uses the term. He assumes that the readers are well acquainted with the saving work of Christ from what he has said earlier in Romans and Ephesians.

To conclude, redemption in Paul refers to the liberation from sin that has come by means of the work of Christ. Fundamentally, this liberation belongs to believers by means of the forgiveness of their sins. Those who are redeemed, however, now have the power to live a new life that is marked by holiness and godliness. In every instance redemption focuses on the deliverance accomplished by God in Christ for believers. It also seems likely that the price of such redemption is implicit, even when it remains unstated, for the redemption that believers enjoy has come at the cost of Jesus' life and the shedding of his blood.

Christ's work on the cross not only broke the power of sin but also spelled the defeat of evil and demonic powers. The notion of God triumphing in battle recalls the exodus, in which Yahweh the warrior vanquished the Egyptians (Exod. 15:3). And the prophets often proclaim the day of the Lord, in which all of Yahweh's enemies will be defeated and his reign of peace will arrive for Israel (e.g., Isa. 13:6, 9; Ezek. 30:3; Joel 2:1, 11, 31; 3:14; Amos 5:18, 20; Obad. 15; Zeph. 1:7, 14; Mal. 4:5).

An important text on Christ's victory over evil powers is Col. 2:15. However the details of this verse are interpreted, the subjugation of these enemies was accomplished in the cross and resurrection of Christ (2:11–15). Believers share in Christ's triumph because their sins have been forgiven, their certificate of debt has been erased, and their sins have been decisively and finally nailed to the cross.

Sanctification and the Final Inheritance

The term "sanctification" derives from the cultic sphere, signifying that which is set aside for the realm of the holy (e.g., 1 Tim. 4:5; 1 Cor. 7:12–16). Paul generally uses the term to refer to God's definitive work of placing believers at conversion into the realm of the holy. This is apparent from 1 Cor. 1:2, where the Corinthians are said to be "sanctified in Christ Jesus." Paul could scarcely be referring to their notable progress in holiness, given the remainder of the letter. Nevertheless, the Corinthians were sanctified by virtue of their conversion. Since they are in Christ, they belong to the realm of the holy. They are sanctified definitively or positionally, even though they are not fully sanctified in terms of personal behavior (cf. Col. 3:12).

We should interpret 1 Cor. 6:11 within the same frame of reference: "You were washed, you were sanctified, you were justified in the name of the Lord Jesus Christ and by the Spirit of our God." The order of the verbs is remarkable here. If sanctification referred to progressive growth in the Christian life, Paul almost certainly would have placed sanctification after justification. Placing sanctification before justification indicates that definitive sanctification is in view, the sanctification that belongs to believers because they are in Christ and in the Spirit (cf. 2 Thess. 2:13).

Thus far we have seen that believers are definitively placed into the sphere of the holy at conversion, and that they will be sanctified entirely on the last day. Paul also emphasizes that believers must live in a way that pleases God in the interval between their conversion and the consummation. Here we could include virtually all the paraenesis in Paul's Letters, in which he exhorts believers to live worthily of their calling (cf. Eph. 4:1; Phil. 1:27). Those who have been liberated from slavery to sin and have become slaves of righteousness should live in a holy way (Rom. 6:19, 22). The metaphors of washing and holiness converge in 2 Cor. 7:1, where believers are exhorted to "cleanse [themselves] from every defilement of body and spirit, bringing holiness to completion in the fear of God." Clearly, Paul expects believers to live in a new way, indicating that they are truly consecrated to God (cf. 1 Thess. 4:3–8).

For Paul, then, sanctification usually refers to the definitive work by which God has set apart believers in the realm of the holy in Christ Jesus. This eschatological work is accomplished at conversion, so that believers can be said to be holy or sanctified in God's presence. Still, Paul recognizes the need for growth in holiness and that transformation is a process (cf. 2 Cor. 3:18), since complete sanctification and holiness will not be granted until Christ returns. Believers are already holy in Christ, and yet the fullness of that holiness will not be theirs until the day of redemption.

The final reward of believers can be designated by the terms "inheritance" and "glorification." The term "inheritance" refers most often to the future reward promised to believers. Paul warns that those who continue to practice sin will not receive the eschatological inheritance (Eph. 5:5). Conversely, slaves who serve Christ will receive an inheritance on the last day (Col. 3:24). In Galatians, Paul emphasizes that the inheritance is received by grace rather than being secured through the law (cf. 3:18, 29; 4:7; Titus 3:7). The inheritance, then, is obtained not through doing but rather by believing. It is a promise received, not the result of something earned. It is tied irretrievably to justification by faith (Titus 3:7), and hence it is a gift of grace and a certain reward for believers. Those who belong to Christ are coheirs with Christ (Rom. 8:17). In other words, all those who are God's children will certainly receive an inheritance (Rom. 8:17; Gal. 4:7). The gift of the Spirit, which clearly is the result of God's gracious work in Eph. 1:3–14, guarantees that believers will receive the final inheritance and be freed from their mortal bodies (1:14).

The eschatological glorification of believers is the hope that animates them in their everyday lives as they live in the interval between the already and the not yet (Rom. 5:2; Col. 1:27; cf. 2 Tim. 2:10), in that it gives them confidence that God will complete the salvation he has begun in them (cf. Phil. 1:6). The glorification of believers will occur when Christ returns in his glory (Col. 3:4; cf. Rom. 8:17). The hope of glory animates believers because what awaits them is incomparably beautiful and far exceeds what they can imagine (Rom. 8:18). Paul contrasts the "eternal weight of glory" destined for believers (2 Cor. 4:17–18) with what is now visible and observable. Glory will belong to believers with the coming of the new creation (Rom. 8:18–25). The body that is now marked by weakness and corruptibility will be free from corruption (1 Cor. 15:43; cf. Phil. 3:21).

Believers receive comfort because the hope of glory represents a sure confidence that God will complete the saving work that he has begun (Rom. 8:30). All those whom God has foreknown, predestined, called, and justified will certainly be glorified. Believers are full of confidence since the God who has effectually called them will see to it that they inherit the kingdom (1 Thess. 2:12; 2 Thess. 2:14).

Conclusion

Paul celebrates the saving work of God and Christ with a variety of metaphors and expressions, presumably because the fullness of salvation cannot be captured by one dimension of God's saving work. If there is a central theme in Paul that summarizes his soteriology, it is that salvation is of the Lord. God foreknew, elected, predestined, and called believers to himself. His grace is so powerful that it conquers sin and inducts believers into the sphere of salvation. Those whom God has chosen will receive the final inheritance promised and will be raised from the dead on the last day. Paul emphasizes that God's saving work is effective in and through Christ. Whether one thinks of justification, reconciliation, redemption, propitiation, salvation, or sanctification, each represents the saving action of God in Christ. Victory over evil powers has come about in and through Christ. Believers praise God in Christ, for Christ has won the victory, reconciled them, and placed them in a right relation to

God. Paul's soteriology also matches another central theme in this book, in that it fits with the already–not yet character of Paul's theology. Believers are now justified, reconciled, redeemed, adopted, and sanctified, and yet in one sense the fullness of these gifts has not yet been experienced. A tension exists between the present possession of such gifts and their final realization. Hence, the Pauline theology of salvation illustrates the already-but-not-yet theme described in chapter 1. The final realization of such salvation is assured because the God who has made believers his people will never forsake them and will empower them until the end. And if God in Christ saves, then believers give thanks and praise forever for the salvation that rescued them. They glorify God in Christ, for the gift is never exalted above the giver.

Pastoral Reflection

From Pauline soteriology it is clear that the work of Jesus must never be restricted to his being an example. Believers are certainly called to be like Jesus and to imitate him. But if the message of the NT is limited to the imitation of Christ, it becomes a new moralism, and then the message of salvation proclaimed by Paul is lost. Pauline theology emphasizes that salvation involves the giving of righteousness to the ungodly. The radical nature of human evil and the greatness of salvation are fundamental to the Pauline gospel. It is also imperative to say that Paul's message does not differ significantly from what we found in the Gospels. Jesus came to die, not merely as an example, but as the new-covenant sacrifice to secure forgiveness of sins. Human beings are rotten trees that need life. Focusing on Jesus without centering on the saving message of the cross actually distorts what the historical Jesus came to do.

7

The Christology of Hebrews–Revelation

———◦◉◦———

The Christology of the remainder of the NT is not as detailed as Paul's, but this is due in part to the brevity, by way of comparison, of the various writings. We remember that Christology includes both the identity of Jesus and what he has accomplished. Hebrews, 1 Peter, 1 John, and Revelation contain the most in-depth treatments, while James, 2 Peter, 2–3 John, and Jude are limited in terms of their christological reflection given the purpose and brevity of these letters. In any case, the centrality of Christ shines in the later part of the NT, showing a fundamental harmony with the Gospels, Acts, and the Pauline writings.

Hebrews

The Christology of Hebrews is richly textured and is an essential theme in the letter. The letter commences with one of the most beautiful and exalted christological texts in the NT (Heb. 1:1–4). God has spoken definitively and finally in the last days in his Son (1:2). Here the author emphasizes that Jesus is the son of David, the messianic king. The Son is described as "the heir of all things" (1:2), which is a clear allusion to the inheritance promised to the Davidic king in Ps. 2:8. Indeed, the name "Son" is part of the inheritance granted to Jesus, by which he has become greater than the angels (Heb. 1:4).

Such an idea is confirmed by the citation of Ps. 2:7 in Heb. 1:5. The author applies this psalm to Jesus himself as David's son. He is the Son who will rule "the ends of the earth" (Ps. 2:8). In other words, Jesus is the one who will fulfill the promises made to Abraham, which will lead to blessing for the whole world. The begetting of the Son (Heb. 1:5) refers to Jesus' installation as the messianic king at his resurrection (cf. Heb. 5:5; Acts 13:33). Jesus is greater than the angels, then, because by virtue of his death and resurrection, he has been crowned as the messianic king. The sonship of Jesus, however, does not only begin at the resurrection. Jesus was the messianic king while he was still on earth, even though his status as the anointed one of Yahweh was hidden from the eyes of most human beings. What Hebrews emphasizes, however, is Jesus' exaltation: his reign over angels and the whole universe that began at his resurrection and ascension. He is God's "firstborn" Son, and as the Davidic heir exercises sovereignty over the people of God (1:6).

Psalm 8, quoted in Heb. 2, considers the majesty of God and the wonders of the created world. What role do apparently insignificant human beings have in a world so vast and magnificent? The psalmist answers, as he reflects on the creation account in Gen. 1–2, that God appointed human beings to rule the world for God. Even though they are now lower than angels, the whole world is destined to be subject to human beings. The author of Hebrews (2:6–8) quotes from Ps. 8 and then comments on it. He acknowledges that presently the world is not under the control of human beings. The sway of death over all demonstrates that human beings suffer under the dominion of hostile powers (Heb. 2:14–15). Human beings have failed, beginning with Adam and Eve, in their quest to domesticate the world for God's praise. The world has become a wreck instead of a blessing.

The failure of human beings is not the end of the story. Jesus is the representative human being. He succeeded where the rest of the human race has failed. In that sense, he is the true human being, the only one who has genuinely lived the kind of life that humans were intended to live under God. In the strongest possible terms, Hebrews emphasizes the true humanness of Jesus, both as the son of Adam (humanity) and as the son of David. As a human being, Jesus was temporarily lower than angels (2:9). Even though the world is not yet subjected to him, he is now "crowned with glory and honor" (2:9). Jesus now sits at God's right hand as the exalted man (1:3, 13) since he has fully atoned for sin and his work is completed. The rule always promised to human beings has commenced with Jesus' exaltation.

Just as Jesus is the faithful son, fulfilling the task at which Adam failed and fulfilling the promises made to David, so too Jesus, like Moses, is God's faithful servant (3:2, 5). God's relationship with Moses was unique in that Moses saw God's "form" and God spoke to him directly (Num. 12:6–8). Despite this exalted position, Jesus is greater than Moses, for he is not merely God's faithful servant but also God's faithful Son (Heb. 3:6). Both David and Moses point toward and anticipate the coming of Jesus. Similarly, the rest given by Joshua during the days of conquest cannot be the final rest given by God, for Ps. 95, written long after the days of Joshua, speaks of a rest that God's people may still inherit (Heb. 3:12–4:11).

Hebrews maintains that Jesus is the true human being, the true Adam. As the faithful Son, he is greater than Moses, and he is greater than Joshua because he grants eschatological rest. He fulfills the promises made to David and therefore rules now as the messianic king. Hebrews emphasizes as well, however, that Jesus rules as a *priest*-king. As we commence with this theme, we are reminded that Christology serves soteriology. As a priest-king, Jesus accomplishes salvation and procures full forgiveness of sins for his people.

According to Hebrews, Jesus is not an ordinary high priest. Indeed, he could not function as a high priest according to the OT law because the high priest hails from the tribe of Levi, whereas Jesus comes from the tribe of Judah (7:13–14). Jesus has a priesthood that is more exalted and greater than the Levitical priesthood because he is a Melchizedekian priest (5:6, 10). The author goes to great lengths to demonstrate that the Melchizedekian priesthood is superior to the Levitical one. He maintains that Melchizedek is greater than Levi because Melchizedek blessed Abraham, and the one who blesses is greater than the one who receives the blessing (7:1, 6–7). Furthermore, Abraham acknowledged Melchizedek's superiority by paying him tithes (7:2, 4, 6, 8). In a sense, Hebrews argues, Levi paid tithes to Melchizedek, since Levi was a descendant of Abraham (7:9–10). In other words, it was always God's intention that the Melchizedekian priesthood replace the Levitical one. The Levitical priesthood was never intended to remain in place forever. A prophecy about a Melchizedekian priesthood would never have arisen if perfection could be obtained through the Levitical priesthood (7:11–12).

The prophecy in Ps. 110:4 is foundational for the argument: "You are a priest forever, after the order of Melchizedek" (Heb. 5:6; 7:17; cf. 7:21). It has also been recognized that Ps. 110 is perhaps the most important OT text for the author of Hebrews, since it refers to one who is both priest and king. In Heb. 5:6 (cf. 7:17, 21) the author seizes upon the word "forever" from Ps. 110:4 to contrast the Melchizedekian priesthood with the Levitical one. Jesus qualifies as a Melchizedekian priest by virtue of his resurrection. His life is "indestructible" (Heb. 7:16). He has no "end of life" (7:3). The Levitical priests could not retain their priestly office because they were mortal and died, but Jesus is a permanent priest "because he continues forever" (7:23–24). "He always lives" (7:25; 13:20–21). The superiority of Jesus' priesthood is evident, for Jesus is the only priest who has conquered death, and doubtless a living priesthood has preeminence.

The superiority of Jesus' priesthood is confirmed also because the Melchizedekian priesthood is ratified by an oath, whereas the Levitical priesthood lacks one (7:20–21). The Levitical priesthood was instituted by God, but it never received a divine oath that it would remain forever. For God to take an oath is highly unusual because his word alone is truth. An oath is added with respect to the Melchizedekian priesthood to underline its perpetuity and superiority.

If Jesus' priesthood is superior to the Levitical priesthood, we are not surprised to learn that Jesus' sacrifice is better than Levitical sacrifices, and in particular the sacrifices offered on the Day of Atonement, because his sacrifice accomplishes forgiveness of sins once for all. Indeed, Jesus did not need to offer sacrifice for his own sins, for he is without sin (4:15; 7:26). The high priests bring offerings for their own sins and those of the people (5:3; 7:27), but Jesus, as the sinless one, offers himself up as the one definitive sacrifice forever (7:27; cf. 4:15). The new covenant, inaugurated and mediated through the death of Jesus, surpasses the old one because atonement has been secured under this covenant (8:7–13; 10:15–18; 12:24). Jesus' priestly sacrifice accomplished "eternal redemption" (9:12) and cleanses the conscience from sin (9:14). He did not merely secure access to God's presence in the tabernacle by his death; he has also entered God's presence in heaven in accomplishing forgiveness (9:12, 24). The OT sacrifices, such as on the Day of Atonement, were offered repeatedly or at least yearly, but Jesus obtained final forgiveness of sins with one sacrifice (9:25–28).

The incarnation of Jesus is suggested by 10:5–10, where his intention in coming into the world was to offer himself (the author using the language of Ps. 40:6–8). He was God's "apostle" (Heb. 3:1): the one whom God sent into the world to accomplish the divine will. Psalm 110 again plays a vital role in his argument, for the psalm refers to a king who sits at God's right hand, reigning forever (Ps. 110:1). Jesus fulfills both the kingly and priestly roles. Indeed, Hebrews clarifies how both roles fit together. He reigns now as the exalted king, sitting at God's right hand *because* he has secured forgiveness of sins once for all by his death (1:3, 13; 8:1; 10:12; 12:2). His kingly work and priestly work are inextricably intertwined.

The tabernacle erected by Moses points forward to something greater and more perfect: the very dwelling place of God in heaven (8:2, 5; 9:11–12, 24). The sacrifices offered under the old covenant could not and did not secure forgiveness of sins. Even the yearly sacrifices offered on the Day of Atonement (Lev. 16) did not bring final forgiveness. Indeed, the various compartments of the tabernacle, and the fact that the high priest could enter the holy of holies only on the Day of Atonement, signified that free access to God was not yet granted (Heb. 9:8). It is evident that the furniture and offerings under the old covenant dealt with external matters that anticipated something better (9:9–10). Jesus secured forgiveness not by offering the blood of animals but by offering his own blood in God's very presence (9:11–14).

The author of Hebrews emphasizes the imperfection of the old-covenant priesthood and sacrifices (7:11, 18–19). The law was only a shadow, not the substance, and hence the sacrifices offered could not bring perfection and true cleansing of the conscience (10:1–4). If the sacrifices of animals truly achieved forgiveness, there would be no need to offer them repeatedly. The repetition of such sacrifices verifies that forgiveness was not obtained through the old covenant, for if forgiveness was granted, then the sacrifices could cease. Furthermore, the sacrifices of animals (10:4) can never be comparable to the sacrifice of a willing and human victim (10:5–10). Animals are constrained by others to offer their blood and have no consciousness of the purpose of their death. The death of Jesus, on the other hand, was the death of a human being, and the very purpose for which he entered into the world was to give his life as a voluntary sacrifice for others. No one could possibly think that the sacrifice of animals could be comparable to the propitiatory (2:17) and willing work of Jesus as high priest.

Under the old covenant the high priests stood, repeatedly offering sacrifices for sins, but Jesus sits at God's right hand because his work is finished forever (10:11–18). The priests continued to offer sacrifices day after day, signaling that final forgiveness had not been achieved, but Jesus secured complete and final forgiveness of sins with one sacrifice (10:14). Jesus' sacrifice fulfills what is promised in the new covenant (Jer. 31:34): complete forgiveness of sins.

According to Hebrews, Jesus established for human beings the rule over creation that was shipwrecked with Adam's sin. To accomplish this victory, however, he himself as God's priest-king had to be a human being. Since human beings are flesh and blood, he had to partake of the same (2:14, 17). He experienced the full range of temptations that beset human beings so that he sympathizes with the human condition (2:18; 4:15). Indeed, Jesus had to suffer in order to be perfected (2:10). "He learned obedience through what he suffered" and thereby was made "perfect" (5:8–9; 7:28). The notion that Jesus became perfect implies imperfection, which seems rather strange, given the exalted view of Jesus explicated in Hebrews. Jesus was not imperfect in the sense that he was stained by sin. Hebrews clearly teaches that Jesus was a perfect and sinless sacrifice (4:15; 7:26). A careful examination of Hebrews reveals that his "perfection" is achieved through suffering as a human being. But this perfection, as Michel (1966: 224) says, includes "his proving in temptation, his fulfillment of the priestly requirements and his exaltation as Redeemer of the heavenly world."[1]

If we engage in a thought experiment, it might help us understand the theology of Hebrews. Could Jesus have atoned for our sins as a ten-year-old? Naturally, this is a question never asked specifically in Hebrews! Still, it seems evident that the answer is no. Jesus would have lacked the maturity and experience as a human being to suffer for the sake of his people at such a tender age. To qualify as an atoning sacrifice, he had to experience the full range of temptation and resist allurements to sin (4:15). The depth of pain

1. I owe this reference and translation to Peterson 1982: 71.

in human existence had to be his, so that he knew what it was to offer up "prayers and supplications, with loud cries and tears" (5:7). Furthermore, to qualify as one who could atone for the sins of others, it was necessary for Jesus to obey his Father in every painful circumstance. It is not enough that Jesus never sinned as a child. It was also necessary for him to demonstrate his faithfulness to God as he was tried in the crucible of sufferings. He could not become a perfect sacrifice apart from enduring the cross (12:2). His obedience to God was demonstrated even when sinners responded to him with implacable hostility (12:3).

The deity of Christ is also clearly taught in the first chapter of Hebrews. Jesus is divine, for he is described as the agent and sustainer of creation (1:2–3). Verse 3 focuses on Jesus' nature. He radiates and shines forth the glory of God. Indeed, Jesus is in the very nature of God, representing to human beings precisely what God is like. When we consider the Christology of Hebrews, we see that the author forcefully emphasizes that Jesus is both human and divine. The two themes adjoin one another and complement each other. The author moves from humanity to divinity and from divinity to humanity easily and without calling attention to such transitions. It seems from this that Jesus' sacrifice for sins as the priest-king is effective because he is both human and divine. Both his divinity and his humanity are necessary for Jesus to accomplish God's saving purposes.

Indeed, Jesus' divinity resounds in the remainder of Heb. 1. The author of Hebrews (1:6), drawing from the LXX of Deut. 32:43, enjoins the angels to worship the Son. In the LXX the one who deserves worship is none other than God himself. Hebrews applies this text to the Son, obviously implying that he is divine. Angels are created by God and serve his will (Heb. 1:7), but the Son is God himself (1:8–9). In 1:8–9 the author cites Ps. 45:6–7. In its original context the psalm is a wedding song, celebrating the king's wedding. What is most striking in the NT is that the Son directly receives the attribution "God" in Heb. 1:8.

Psalm 102:25–27 is another text utilized in the author's christological argument in Heb. 1. In the OT context, the psalmist celebrates Yahweh's work of creation in the created order, which wears down over time. In contrast to Yahweh, who is eternal and the same, creation is temporary and will pass away. Hebrews takes a text that refers to Yahweh and applies it to Jesus Christ (1:10–12). Once again it is evident that the Son has the same status as the Father. Surely only God creates and is eternal. Jesus remains the same from generation to generation. We naturally think here of the famous words in Heb. 13:8: "Jesus Christ is the same yesterday and today and forever."

Christology and soteriology are inseparably wedded in Hebrews. They serve the author's homiletic purpose, whereby he warns his readers about the folly of apostasy. They would thereby reject the one who is greater than Moses, Joshua, and the Levitical priesthood. They would turn away from the one who has fulfilled the promises of the new covenant. They would repudiate the one who as a divine priest-king has secured final and definitive forgiveness of sins. Both Jesus' divinity and his humanity point to the effectiveness of his sacrifice and to his superiority over all that came before. Hence, Hebrews summons the readers to put all their confidence in Jesus as the prophet greater than Moses, the king greater than David, the Melchizedekian priest, and the true man and the true God.

James

The Christology of James is not detailed, but neither is it as negligible as some scholars have alleged. The book opens with the statement, "James, a servant of God and of the Lord Jesus Christ" (1:1). James does not provide an exposition of the statement, but the opening is suggestive and points toward a high Christology. James is a "slave" (AT) of both God and Jesus Christ, and this implies that God and Jesus Christ share the same status as God. The equivalency posited by James is highly significant because his letter has a Jewish character and explicitly affirms monotheism (2:19). James does not work out the implications of the shared status of God and Christ, but given the Jewish flavor of the letter, the fact that he considers himself a slave of both demonstrates that Jesus Christ in some sense has the same dignity as God himself.

In both 1:1 and 2:1, James identifies Jesus as the Christ. It is hardly convincing to say that the title "Christ" here is analogous to using a last name, so that the titular significance of the term has evaporated. The Jewish milieu in which the letter was birthed speaks strongly against such a notion. Since James was a Jew, it is quite improbable that he would use the title "Christ" without thinking that Jesus fulfilled the messianic hope from the OT. Jesus, then, is the promised Davidic king, the fulfillment of the promises found in the Davidic covenant.

James also identifies Jesus the Messiah as "Lord" (1:1; 2:1). His stature as Lord is confirmed by the appellation "glorious Lord" (2:1 AT; cf. 2:7). The glory typically associated with God is ascribed here to Jesus Christ (cf. Exod. 16:7, 10; 24:17; Lev. 9:6; see also Ps. 24:8, 10). Such language suggests Jesus' exaltation and his role as the final judge and thus points to his exalted status. Elsewhere in James, the Father is called "Lord" (1:7; 3:9; 4:10, 15; 5:4, 10, 11). Some of these texts are uncertain, so that in some of these instances Jesus may be called "Lord." James almost certainly has Jesus Christ in view as Lord in some verses (5:7, 8, 14, 15). Bauckham (1999: 138) remarks, "The changing reference of 'the Lord' (*ho kyrios*) within the space of a few sentences in 5:7–11 reflects a high Christology in which Jesus shares the divine throne in heaven and is coming to execute the eschatological judgment of God." The phrase "the coming of the Lord" (5:7, 8) refers to the return of Jesus Christ in his role as the end-time judge, and this fits with the notion that he is the glorious Lord, since he will return as the sovereign one.

The lordship of Christ seems to be in view also in 5:14–15. The sick are anointed in the Lord's name and are raised up by the Lord. Anointing people in the Lord's name probably refers to Jesus Christ, so that Jesus as Lord raises up the sick (5:14–15). The parallels in the Synoptic Gospels and Acts also suggest that Jesus Christ is the one who heals and in whose name the sick are anointed (cf. Matt. 7:22; Mark 6:7; Luke 10:17; Acts 3:6–8, 16; 4:9–12). The name that is invoked over believers in James 2:7 is likely that of Jesus Christ. The Lord's name in the OT clearly refers to Yahweh (cf. Deut. 28:10; Isa. 43:7; Jer. 14:9; Amos 9:12), and hence the reference to Jesus here points to his deity. From both these texts we see that the divine authority of Jesus is evident, for healing is sought in his name, and he has sovereign authority to heal the sick. Further, his divine status is suggested by his name being invoked by believers. The centrality of Jesus is also indicated by his being the object of faith (James 2:1). When James speaks on the important topic of faith and works (2:14–26), faith in Christ is in view. To say in a Jewish context that Christ is the object of faith suggests a high, though implicit, Christology.

James lacks the developed Christology of Paul, Hebrews, John, and even the Synoptic Gospels. Still, we must beware of expecting too much from an occasional letter and reading off it the complete worldview of James. Even with the limited references to Jesus Christ, there are indications of a high Christology. Jesus is the Messiah of Israel and the glorious Lord. He apparently shares the same stature as God, as Lord of all, as the one who is coming again to judge the world. Only those who put their faith in him and live out that faith in daily life will be saved on the last day.

1 Peter

The Christology in 1 Peter is shaped by practical and soteriological interests. The title "Christ" in 1 Peter is not superfluous, for the term "Christ" is used in some instances where Peter focuses on the fulfillment of OT prophecy (1:11, 19; 2:21), or when he emphasizes Christ's sufferings and glory (3:18; 4:1, 13, 14; 5:1, 10, 14), which is closely associated with the fulfillment of prophecy as well. The importance of such a fulfillment is confirmed by 1:20, "He was foreknown before the foundation of the world but was made manifest in the last times for the sake of you." God destined what would happen before history began. Does the statement about Christ being foreknown imply preexistence? The verse is brief, and so it is difficult to say, though on balance the foreknowing of "the Christ" probably implies preexistence.

Since Jesus is also the exalted Lord, believers are to "sanctify Christ as Lord" (3:15 NRSV). He functions as the "Shepherd and Overseer" or the "chief Shepherd" of God's people (2:25; 5:4). Christians "believe in" and "love" Jesus Christ as their Lord (1:8), and their "spiritual sacrifices" are "acceptable to God through Jesus Christ" (2:5). As the exalted one, the Lord Jesus will be revealed again in the future (1:7, 13; 5:4). He will reward his people and bring history to its appointed consummation. Peter also applies an OT text to Jesus Christ that refers to Yahweh. The psalmist implores his readers to "taste and see that the LORD is good" (Ps. 34:8). First Peter 2:3 applies this text to Jesus. We see that Peter holds the common NT view that Jesus shares the same status as Yahweh, without compromising monotheism. Nor does the preeminence of Christ diminish the Father, for the work of Christ brings glory to the Father (4:11).

Peter addresses churches suffering for the faith, and hence he also calls attention to Jesus' suffering and subsequent glory (1:11). The suffering that Jesus endured for the sake of his people is often noted in the letter, especially if we include references to Jesus' death (1:2, 11, 18–19, 21; 2:21–24; 3:18; 4:1, 13; 5:1). The sufferings and glories were predicted by the prophets (1:10–12), and therefore Jesus fulfills what was destined for the Christ all along. The OT sacrifices of lambs pointed toward a greater sacrifice to come (1:19). The reference to a lamb here cannot be restricted to the Passover lamb, regular Levitical sacrifices with lambs, or the lamb of Isa. 53:7. First Peter broadly draws on the OT background about lambs to teach that Jesus is God's spotless and precious lamb whose blood ransomed people from a futile life (1:18–19). The reference to an unblemished and spotless lamb suggests that Jesus was without sin, that he was a perfect sacrifice. Peter explicitly declares that Jesus "committed no sin, neither was deceit found in his mouth" (2:22). He is "the righteous" one who suffered and died "for the unrighteous" (3:18).

The sprinkling of blood in the OT (Num. 19:4, 18–19, 21; cf. Exod. 24:6–8) anticipated the sprinkling of Christ's blood, by which forgiveness of sins is obtained (1 Pet. 1:2). Again we see that Jesus fulfilled what the OT typified. The most dramatic and significant example of the fulfillment of OT prophecy is Jesus' role as the Servant of the Lord. Peter leaves no doubt that Isa. 53 points forward to Jesus. Jesus' freedom from sin and lack of deceit (1 Pet. 2:22) fulfills Isa. 53:9. The bearing of the sins of his people (1 Pet. 2:24) reaches back to Isa. 53:4, 12. The healing that comes through his wounds (1 Pet. 2:24) finds its antecedent in Isa. 53:5. The wandering of his people like sheep (1 Pet. 2:25) hearkens back to Isa. 53:6. The sufferings destined for the Christ are foreshadowed in OT sacrifices and in the Servant of the Lord text. Forgiveness of sins is obtained through the spilling of Christ's blood, by his dying as a substitute for his people. His death as "the righteous for the unrighteous" is the means by which sinners are brought into God's presence (1 Pet. 3:18). In 1 Peter, Christ's death is substitutionary. He dies in place of the unrighteous; as the Servant of the Lord, he dies to atone for their sins, so that the punishment that they deserve is placed on him. Jesus' death is also viewed as a ransom (1:18–19). He freed believers from their sins by his blood; hence the price of the ransom is explicitly indicated. In the OT a futile way of life is associated with the idolatry of paganism (e.g., Lev. 17:7; 1 Kings 16:2; 2 Kings 17:15; Ps. 24:4). Through Christ's death, believers have been liberated from service to false gods to serve the true and living God.

Prophecy is fulfilled not only in the sufferings of Christ but also in the glory that belongs to him as the exalted one. First Peter mentions the pattern of suffering and then glory to encourage those distressed in the present that they too will experience glory after suffering (1:6–7; 4:12–14; 5:6, 10–11; cf. 5:1–4). The hope that strengthens believers is rooted in Christ's resurrection (1:3; 3:21), and his resurrection demonstrated to all that God had vindicated him and crowned him as Lord. We have an allusion to Ps. 110:1 in the claim that he now sits at God's right hand and that all angelic powers are subject to him (1 Pet. 3:22). The one whom God raised from the dead has also been given "glory" (1:21), and 3:22 suggests that the glory he now has consists of his rule at God's right hand. Peter also alludes to Jesus' resurrection in the "stone" prophecies. When he identifies Jesus as "a living stone" (2:4), the word "living" points to his resurrection. The claim that Jesus is "the cornerstone" also suggests his resurrection and exaltation (2:6–7; cf. Ps. 118:22; Isa. 28:16).

In summary, 1 Peter highlights the fulfillment of prophecy in his Christology, and the letter follows the NT pattern in closely linking Christology and soteriology. Jesus is the Christ, the Lord, and the Servant of the Lord, and his suffering and death secure redemption and forgiveness for believers. He fulfills OT prophecy as the son of David and was sacrificed as a spotless lamb. The one who suffered is also glorified and reigns in heaven as Lord. He will return in glory in the future. Indeed, Peter even applies an OT text to Jesus that refers to Yahweh, suggesting that the Father and Jesus Christ share the same status. His suffering and glory are significant because they forecast glory for believers after suffering. Jesus' death is precious to Peter because it redeems from a futile life, and hence the high Christology of Peter undergirds the call to trust in Christ for eschatological salvation.

2 Peter

We could examine the Christology of 1 Peter and 2 Peter together because, in contrast to the view of many NT scholars, a good case can be made for Petrine authorship of both letters.[2] Given the brevity of 2 Peter and its circumscribed purpose, we might expect little by way of Christology. Though the letter is

2. For a defense of authenticity, see Schreiner 2003: 21–36, 255–76.

brief, the Christology is remarkably weighty. We note first of all Peter's assumption that Jesus is the Messiah. He often refers to "Jesus Christ" in the letter (1:1, 8, 11, 14, 16; 2:20; 3:18). Peter does not expound on the significance of the title "Christ," but the repeated use of the term indicates that Jesus' messianic status was a given for Peter. Jesus' lordship is also prominent in the letter. One of Peter's favorite expressions is "Lord Jesus Christ" (1:8, 11, 14, 16; 2:20; 3:18; cf. 3:2), though we will see shortly that he adds "Savior" to this title in some texts. Jesus is also described as "the Master who bought" people by his death (2:1). Jesus is the sovereign Lord, the one exalted by God as Messiah and Master. Because Jesus is Lord, Peter is his slave and apostle (1:1). The "eternal kingdom" belongs to Jesus Christ as Lord (1:11). In some texts the title "Lord" is applied to God (2:9, 11; 3:8–10, 15), though in the texts from 2 Pet. 3 one could argue that the reference is to Christ. Since the term "Lord" fluctuates between "God" and "Christ," it reveals the high status of Jesus Christ in the letter.

Even more compelling evidence attests to Jesus' exalted status. As Lord, Jesus Christ will return with power (1:16). The Father bestowed "honor" and "glory" upon him at the transfiguration (1:17). God's pleasure in Jesus hearkens back to the Servant of the Lord in Isaiah (Isa. 42:1). Peter appeals to the transfiguration because it anticipates and functions as a prelude to the future coming of Christ. The transfiguration testifies to Jesus' lordship over the future, and to the glory and honor that will be his forever. The vision of Jesus' "majesty" (*megaleiotēs*) probably points to his deity (1:16). The word *megaleiotēs* does not necessarily denote deity (cf. 1 Esd. 1:4; 4:40; Jer. 40:9 LXX = 33:9 ESV), but the term is used for God in Luke (9:43). Peter likely uses the term to denote Jesus' lordship and deity.

The high Christology of Peter surfaces in his identifying Jesus as "God" in the very first verse of the letter ("the righteousness of our God and Savior Jesus Christ"; 2 Pet. 1:1). Those reading English translations might naturally think that two different persons are intended, so that God and Jesus are distinguished. In the Greek text, however, both "God" and "Savior" are introduced by the same article, "the" (*tou theou hēmōn kai sōtēros Iēsou Christou*). The Granville Sharp rule, which has been vindicated by recent research, demonstrates that when two singular nouns are joined by *kai* and governed by the same article, they refer to the same entity (Wallace 1996: 270–91). The rule applies only to common nouns, not proper nouns. Readers of the English translations could easily be misled at this point, for neither "God" nor "Savior" is a proper noun in Greek. The grammar, then, could hardly be clearer. Jesus is identified as both God and Savior in this verse.

Other evidence supports the equality of Jesus Christ with God. The final verse of the letter, summing up the whole of 2 Peter's instructions, bids readers to "grow in the grace and knowledge of our Lord and Savior Jesus Christ" (3:18). Peter immediately adds, "To him be the glory both now and to the day of eternity." Since Jesus is the immediate antecedent, Peter ascribes all glory to him. Glory, however, belongs only to God, and therefore we see that Jesus is given the same stature and honor as God himself (cf. 1:17).

Peter is not interested in an abstract discussion of Jesus Christ's divinity. His stature as Messiah, Lord, and God are so important because he is the Savior. God's saving righteousness has been given to believers through the "Savior Jesus Christ" (1:1, 11; cf. 3:2). Peter uses language that hails from the OT. Christians have been chosen (as by lot; *lachousin*) to receive the gift of faith, and "righteousness" should be understood in terms of its OT background as well. Hence, righteousness here refers to Christ's saving work on behalf of his people. The verses emphasize the gift character of salvation. Christ has given believers all that they need for life in the age to come so that they are enabled to please God. He has "called" (*kalesantos*; 1:3) believers by his effective grace to a new life. Believers have received promises of participation in the divine nature. Peter does not refer here to the deification of believers, as if they become "little gods." Sharing the divine nature means that they become morally like God. Even in this present evil age, believers have become like God in that they have escaped from the world's corruption (cf. 2:20), but moral perfection in its fullness will be theirs only when Jesus Christ returns. The work of Christ is also described in terms of his "buying" (*agorazō*) believers from sin (2:1). In other words, believers are redeemed and liberated by Christ from the thrall of sin. His death is the means by which new life has been purchased for those who know God and Christ.

The Letter of 2 Peter emphasizes that Jesus is the Messiah, and hence he fulfills the covenantal promises made to David. Peter does not probe into such a fulfillment deeply but assumes it in his writing. He also emphasizes that Jesus is Lord and even God. The lordship and deity of Christ support his future coming in glory, which was a matter of controversy because the false teachers doubted Christ's return. Further, Peter particularly emphasizes that Jesus is the Savior of his people. Such salvation is experienced through knowing God and Jesus Christ. In this way, God's saving promises are being fulfilled (1:4).

Jude

Despite the brevity of Jude, the Christology of the letter is remarkable. In the OT, Moses and others are described as servants of Yahweh. Jude begins by identifying himself as "a slave of Jesus Christ" (1 AT). If Jude is Christ's slave, then Jesus is his Master and Lord. The lordship of Jesus is clearly a central feature of Jude's Christology, for the intruders "deny our only Master and Lord, Jesus Christ" (4). Nothing in Jude indicates a denial of any particular doctrine about the lordship of Christ. Rather, the infiltrators deny Christ's lordship by the way they live: their libertine lifestyles turn the message of grace into a platform for license. The phrase "apostles of our Lord Jesus Christ" (17) suggests that those so authorized transmit their teaching under Christ's direction. Only those who are the beneficiaries of the Lord's mercies will receive eternal life on the last day (21). Indeed, those who persevere to the end do so because Jesus Christ will "keep" them from stumbling (21, 24). The glory and honor that belong to God are his "through Jesus Christ our Lord" (25). God receives glory not despite or apart from Christ but rather through him.

As the exalted Lord, Jesus will come in the future and inflict judgment on the ungodly (14–15). Jude cites 1 En. 9 here. In 1 Enoch the prophecy clearly refers to God. In taking a text on God's judgment and applying it to Christ's judgment, Jude follows the precedent of other NT writers (cf. 1 Thess. 3:13; 2 Thess. 1:7; Rev. 19:13, 15; 22:12). The coming of Christ is patterned after God's theophany on Sinai, where he came with "myriads of holy ones" (Deut. 33:2 NRSV; cf. Zech. 14:5; Matt. 16:27; 1 Thess. 3:13).

Jude relatively often speaks of Jesus as the Christ (1, 4, 17, 21, 25). The title "Christ" in Jude almost certainly is significant, for there are a number of indications that Jude hails from Palestinian Jewish circles. He cites traditions from the Testament of Moses (Jude 9) and 1 Enoch (Jude 14–15). Significant OT tradition suffuses the letter (5–7, 11). Therefore, when Jude identifies Jesus as the Christ, the title retains its significance, indicating that Jesus is the promised son of David.

1–3 John

The Epistles of John are closely related to the Gospel of John. Despite the reservations of some, the similarity of style points to the same author. Christology plays a major role in 1–2 John, for it is evident from the letters that opponents offered an alternate Christology, which was docetic in character, maintaining that the Christ was not truly and fully human.

Since the secessionists in 1 John denied that Jesus was truly human, John fixes attention on the Jesus of history. The first verse of the letter recalls the past, with John remembering what he heard, saw, and touched (1:1). The subject of these reflections is "the word of life": Jesus himself. The verbs in the first verse climax with touching, so that with each verb the historical actuality of Jesus is emphasized even more. We can hear but not see someone, and we can see but not touch someone, so John begins with hearing, proceeds to seeing, and climaxes with touching. John certifies the space-time nature of the events that transpired by reminding his readers that Jesus was no phantom: John heard, saw, and touched him. The coming of Jesus into history, the incarnation declared in John 1:14, is no illusion. As John declares twice in 1 John 1:2, "the life was made manifest." The collocation of "word of life" and "made manifest" suggests that this is simply another way of saying "the Word became flesh" (John 1:14).

The flesh-and-blood advent of Jesus finds expression elsewhere in 1 John. Forgiveness of sin comes from the shedding of Jesus' blood (1:7). He surrendered his life for the sake of his people (3:16). He came at a certain time in history in that "he appeared to take away sins" (3:5), and he "appeared . . . to destroy the works of the devil" (3:8). We saw in the Gospel of John that the Father is often described as "sending" the Son. The same terminology appears in John's First Letter: "God sent his only Son into the world" (4:9; cf. 4:10, 14; 5:20). If we sum up these texts, we see that John focuses on the incarnation and death of God's Son. Further, it seems that the statements on God sending his Son and the coming of the Son of God imply Jesus' preexistence. Jesus, who is the Christ in the flesh, is also the Son of God, who was with the Father from the beginning (1:1–2).

Those who reject the truth that the historical Jesus is the Christ are identified as antichrists (2:22). Nor does such a denial merely affect their relationship with the Christ. When they deny that the human Jesus is the Christ, they also deny the Father. If they reject Jesus as God's true Son, this is tantamount, whether they realize it or not, to denying the Father as well (2:23). Only those who acknowledge that Jesus is God's Son belong to the Father. Refusal to acknowledge Jesus as the Christ is no trivial error, nor is it simply a temporary lapse of judgment; anyone who separates the Christ from the historical Jesus is an antichrist (cf. 4:2–3).

The historical actuality of the incarnation is expressed vividly in 5:6–8. Jesus as the Christ came into the world both "by the water and the blood." Water here indicates not the physical birth of Jesus but rather his baptism. Blood, as in 1:7, refers to Jesus' death. It is insufficient to claim Jesus as the Christ only at his baptism. One must also acknowledge that Jesus is the Christ at his death, when his blood was shed for sinners.

Apparently, the opponents in 2 John threatened the church with faulty Christology. John identifies those who propound this new teaching as "deceivers," warning that "many" itinerants have spread such an error. The nature of their error is clarified precisely: they "do not confess the coming of Jesus Christ in the flesh" (7). They have embraced the coming of the Christ, and they have probably even identified Jesus as the Christ; what they do not tolerate is any notion that Jesus was truly human. But the one who separates the historical Jesus from the Christ is again identified as "the antichrist" (7). Those who think that they are "progressing" (*ho proagōn*) in their theology but do not persevere in the orthodox teaching have separated themselves from God (9 AT). John repeats what we saw in 1 John 2:23: only those who embrace Jesus as the Christ belong to "both the Father and the Son" (2 John 9). John brooks no opposition on this matter, insisting that those who deny that the historical Jesus is the Christ do not belong to God. In summary, John clearly emphasizes that Christians must embrace Jesus as the Christ. That Jesus is the Messiah is fundamental to Johannine theology, for he says: "Everyone who believes that Jesus is the Christ has been born of God" (cf. 1 John 5:1; cf. 3:23).

John does not restrict his teaching to the claim that the human Jesus is the Messiah; he also emphasizes that Jesus is the Son of God—the unique Son of the Father (1 John 1:3, 7; 3:8, 23; 4:9, 15; 2 John 3). As noted previously, only those who confess the Son also belong to the Father (1 John 2:22–24; 2 John 9). John teaches that the Son of God is himself divine (cf. 1 John 5:20). The first verse of 1 John hearkens back to the Word in the first verse of John's Gospel. Given the affinities with the prologue of John's Gospel, "the word of life" echoes what the Gospel says about "the Word." Just as "the Word" is divine in the Gospel, so too here. The phrase "that which was from the beginning" indicates that the Word is eternal, just as in the Gospel. The one whom the Father "sent" (4:9–10, 14) existed with the Father before he was sent as God's eternal Word.

The uniqueness of Jesus Christ is expressed in other terms by John. Jesus is designated as "the righteous" one (2:1, 29; 3:7), the one who is "pure" (3:3), and the one in whom is no sin (3:5). As the righteous one, he qualifies to serve as an "advocate" (*paraklētos*) with the Father, so that his death provides full forgiveness of sins (2:1). His death provides satisfaction or propitiation for the sins of the entire world (2:2; 4:10). He is, therefore, "the Savior of the world" (4:14; cf. John 4:42). He grants understanding so that believers will have eternal life (1 John 5:20). He keeps believers by his power (5:18). The Gospel of John often refers to believing in Jesus' name or praying in his name (see 1:12; 2:23; 3:18; 14:13, 14, 26; 15:16, 21; 16:23, 24, 26; 20:31). Similarly, we see in John's First Letter that "sins are forgiven for his name's sake" (2:12), and so too faith is in Jesus' name (3:23; 5:13).

Revelation

One of the most astonishing, though often neglected, Christologies in the NT is in the book of Revelation. On three occasions in Revelation, Jesus declares, "I am the first and the last" (1:17; 2:8; 22:13), emphasizing especially his sovereignty over death. What stands out, however, is that the same expression is used of Yahweh in the OT (Isa. 41:4; 44:6; 48:12). Nor would John be ignorant of the OT background, since Revelation is stocked with allusions to and echoes of the OT. We see the same phenomenon with the phrases "Alpha and Omega" and "the beginning and the end." God himself announces that he is "the Alpha and the Omega" at the commencement (1:8) and conclusion (21:6) of Revelation. Similarly, he affirms that he is "the beginning and the end" (21:6). In the latter instance, there may be an echo of Isa. 46:10, where God declares "the end from the beginning." Both "Alpha and Omega" and "beginning and end" point to God's sovereignty over history. Since history commences and concludes with him, no part of history spins out of his control. He rules over the entire expanse of history so that his purposes will not be frustrated. Hence, the significance of Jesus saying "I am the Alpha and the Omega, . . . the beginning and the end" is not lost on the reader (Rev. 22:13). The sovereignty over history exercised by God belongs also to Jesus Christ. The functions of deity are carried out by him. Jesus is "the beginning [archē] of God's creation" (3:14). This does not mean that Jesus is part of the created order, for that would blatantly contradict his being the Alpha and the Omega. It means all things have their origin in Christ (cf. "the origin of God's creation," NRSV).

Another set of remarkable texts should be recognized in which God and Jesus Christ receive the same honor and glory. For instance, Rev. 4 is programmatic for the entire book. John has a vision of God reigning on his throne as creator, and the angelic hosts bow down and worship him as Lord of all. The focus shifts in Rev. 5 from God as creator to Jesus Christ as redeemer, the one who is both the Lion who rules and the Lamb who was slain. In 4:11 the angels worship God, confessing that he is worthy to be worshiped as creator. In 5:9–10 the angels ascribe worthiness to the Lamb, acknowledging that he deserves worship as redeemer. On the one hand, God is "worthy" of "glory and honor and power" (4:11); on the other hand, Christ is "worthy" of "power and wealth and wisdom and might and honor and glory and blessing" (5:12). Obviously, Jesus Christ as the Lamb of God deserves the same honor and glory that belongs to God. Indeed, God and Jesus Christ are worshiped together at the conclusion of Rev. 5: "To him who sits on the throne and to the Lamb be blessing and honor and glory and might forever and ever!" (5:13; cf. 5:14).

The worship of the Lamb, Jesus Christ, along with God cannot be ascribed to a dilution of monotheism. Twice John is so overcome by the glory of the angelic messenger that he bows down to worship the angel (19:10; 22:8–9). In both instances the angel admonishes John that only God should be worshiped, and he forbids John from worshiping an angel. By way of contrast, we notice the oft-repeated collocation of God and Christ in Revelation, so that they receive equal esteem. When judgment is inflicted on the disobedient, people cry out in terror, asking mountains and rocks to fall on them to conceal them "from the face of him who is seated on the throne, and from the wrath of the Lamb" (6:16).

By way of contrast, the redeemed from every cultural and ethnic background stand before God and praise him. They do not merely stand, however, in God's presence; they stand "before the throne and before the Lamb" (7:9). Indeed, they praise God for the salvation that they have received, and yet they place the Lamb on the same plane with God: "Salvation belongs to our God who sits on the throne, and to the Lamb!" (7:10). The kingdom belongs to the "Lord and . . . his Christ" (11:15). Similarly, we read that "the salvation and the power and the kingdom of our God and the authority of his Christ have come" (12:10). Elsewhere those who have been redeemed are described as "firstfruits for God and the Lamb" (14:4). They have both the name of the Lamb and the Father's name on their foreheads (14:1). Those who conquer the second death and reign forever are not merely priests of God; they also serve as "priests of God and Christ" (20:6).

The temple in the new heavens and new earth is no longer a building. The earthly temple always pointed to something greater, or we should say, "someone" greater, so that the "temple is the Lord God the Almighty and the Lamb" (21:22). Nor does the heavenly city need created light, whether of the sun, moon, or stars, "for the glory of God gives it light" (21:23). Characteristically, John does not leave out Jesus Christ, for he immediately adds "and its lamp is the Lamb" (21:23). Finally, God's throne, symbolizing his sovereignty and rule, is erected in the new Jerusalem. And yet 22:3 clarifies that the throne does not belong to God alone: it is "the throne of God and of the Lamb" (22:3; cf. 22:1). The Lamb reigns equally with the Father. This astonishing and frequent collocation of God and Christ indicates that Jesus was considered to be divine in John's theology, that both God and the Lamb are to be worshiped and adored.

John uses other titles to feature the glory of Jesus. He is "the Son of God" (Rev. 2:18). In contrast to its regular appearance in the Gospel of John, the title is used just once in Revelation. When we consider the high Christology of the remainder of Revelation, we have good grounds for concluding that "Son of God" bears the same meaning as in the Gospel. Jesus is the unique Son of the Father, having a special relationship with God. When Jesus masses his armies and prepares to come to judge the world, he is identified as the "Word of God" (19:13), who carries out the divine judgment (cf. John 1:1, 14; Wis. 18:15–16).

Revelation also features Jesus as the Son of Man. As we noted when studying the Gospels, references to Jesus as the Son of Man are scarce outside the Gospels. An allusion to the "son of man" of Dan. 7:13 crops up early in Revelation (1:7). In Dan. 7 the son of man comes with the clouds and appears before God himself, "the Ancient of Days" (7:13). Jesus is explicitly recognized as the Son of Man in John's vision in Rev. 1:13–16.[3] In the vision John sees not the historical Jesus but rather the exalted Christ. The robe that reaches to Christ's feet signifies his priestly authority (1:13). Remarkably, his hair is like white wool and is "white as snow" (1:14 NRSV). The description is astonishing because in Dan. 7 Yahweh's clothing is "white as snow" and his hair is "like pure wool" (7:9). John has not erred in his memory of the biblical account. He modifies the OT account to teach that the Son of Man deserves the same honor and glory as the Ancient of Days. He is to be venerated and

3. Jesus is also likely identified as the Son of Man in Rev. 14:14–16.

worshiped in the same way that God is. Like God, his eyes flame with fire, searching all things so that nothing is hidden from his gaze (Rev. 1:14; 2:18, 23; 19:12). Those who secretly practice evil cannot avoid his penetrating gaze; they will face judgment.

Revelation is addressed to churches in Asia Minor suffering from discrimination and persecution. In response, John highlights Jesus' sovereignty over all. As the Lamb, Jesus is "King of kings" (17:14; 19:16). The same verses affirm that he is "Lord of lords." Paul applies both titles to God in the Pastoral Epistles (1 Tim. 6:15), and in the OT Yahweh is hailed as "Lord of lords" (Deut. 10:17; Ps. 136:3), and in Second Temple literature as "King of kings" (2 Macc. 13:4; 3 Macc. 5:35). Jesus rules over the kings of the earth (Rev. 1:5); it may appear that the political leaders of this world exercise control, but they serve under the authority of Jesus himself. Further, 1:5–6 gives a doxology to Jesus, but doxologies belong to God alone. Jesus is crowned with diadems symbolizing his rule over all, and the fact that no one knows his name demonstrates that no one exercises control over him (19:12). In Hebrew culture, naming signifies authority over what is named, just as Adam exercises his authority in naming the animals in the garden (Gen. 2:19).

In a striking image, Jesus as God's Lamb is also the shepherd of God's people (Rev. 7:17). We have an echo of John's Gospel, where Jesus describes himself as the good shepherd (John 10:11, 14). Jesus' role as the shepherd points to his deity, for in the OT the Lord shepherds his people (Pss. 23:1; 28:9; 80:1; Isa. 40:11; Ezek. 34:12, 15; Mic. 7:14) and leads them to watering places (Ps. 23:2). In some texts the shepherd is a messianic figure (Ezek. 34:23; 37:24; Mic. 5:4). John sees Jesus as fulfilling both the divine and messianic role as the shepherd.

Revelation clearly portrays Jesus as divine, but John also teaches that Jesus is the Messiah (Rev. 1:1–2, 5; 11:15; 12:10; 20:4, 6). The kingdom belongs not merely to God but also to "his Christ" (11:15). As the Christ, Jesus has authority over all (12:10). Those who conquer will reign with him for one thousand years (20:4–6). He has made believers to be priests and a kingdom (1:6; cf. 20:6). The covenant pledge that David's dynasty would persist forever is fulfilled in Jesus, for he holds "the key of David" (3:7). Jesus is "the Lion of the tribe of Judah, the Root of David" (5:5). At the conclusion of the book Jesus declares, "I am the root and the descendant of David, the bright morning star" (22:16). Jesus as Lion of Judah echoes Gen. 49:9, and possibly even Num. 23:24; 24:9. The lion symbolizes the strength, dignity, and royalty of Jesus. The term "root" (*rhiza*) hearkens back to Isa. 11, where a root from Jesse is promised (11:1, 10). He will be endowed with the Spirit, judge righteously, destroy the wicked, and inaugurate peace and righteousness.

Even though Revelation emphasizes the sovereignty and glory of Christ, his death is the fulcrum of all history. He demonstrated his love to believers by freeing them from their sins by his death on the cross (1:5). Despite the threat from the Roman Empire, the fundamental need of believers is freedom from the guilt of sin. Revelation 5 is perhaps the most important chapter in the entire book, for no one is worthy to open the scroll bound with seven seals—no one, that is, except for one. John is informed that "the Lion of the tribe of Judah, the Root of David" can open the sealed book (5:5). And yet when John actually looks to see the conqueror, he sees not a mighty lion but a slain Lamb (5:6). The key to all history and to the outworking of God's promises is the death of the Lamb. Victory over evil comes not through a military triumph, but rather through the suffering of the Lamb. By his blood he "ransomed people" from every ethnic and linguistic background (5:9). Clean white robes signify access into God's presence, and robes are whitened only "in the blood of the Lamb" (7:14).

Those whose names are written in the book of life are enrolled because the Lamb has been slain on their behalf (13:8; 21:27). The 144,000 are sealed (7:1–8) only because they belong to the Lamb. His death is the source of their life. They sing a new song of salvation and have the name of the Father and the Lamb on their foreheads because they have been redeemed by the Lamb (14:1–5). Similarly, believers conquer evil through Christ's blood and their willingness to face death (12:11). The healing of the nations comes from the tree of life (22:2). However, only those who wash their robes have access to that tree (22:14), and we noted in 7:14 that robes are washed and whitened only in the Lamb's blood. On the basis of Christ's death, then, all are invited to take freely of the water of life (22:17). Even though the death of Christ is noted in only a few texts in Revelation, the placement of such is fundamental for the entire book.

The Christology of Revelation is astonishingly explicit and high. Indeed, the Christology is analogous to that in the Gospel of John. Jesus as the Lamb is on the same plane as God and is worshiped as a divine being. He is the Messiah of Israel and the Son of God. He is the glorious Son of Man and the ruler of the kings of the earth. He is King of kings and Lord of lords. Just as God is praised, so too Jesus is praised. Just as God is the Alpha and Omega and the first and the last, so too Jesus is the Alpha and Omega and the first and the last. And it is this Jesus whose death frees believers from their sins and who makes their robes white by his blood. Revelation coheres with a main theme of this book: an exalted Christ secures salvation.

Conclusion

What is most striking about the Christology of the latter part of the NT is that it accords with the major emphases of the Gospels, the Pauline literature, and Acts. In the Gospels we have seen that Jesus is presented as the new and better Moses, the final prophet, the Messiah, Son of Man, Son of God, Lord, and divine. Acts particularly emphasizes that Jesus is the Messiah and Lord, who is risen from the dead. Paul also focuses on Jesus' lordship, emphasizing his divine prerogatives. The lordship of Jesus and his deity are also featured in the later writings of the NT.

Pastoral Reflection

The interest in the identity of Jesus is not speculative. The NT writers did not reflect on the person of Jesus in order to communicate a new metaphysical truth. The identity of Jesus burst through all previous categories and exceeded expectations. But his identity was important to NT authors because of the salvation he had accomplished. Soteriology and Christology are inextricably intertwined. A deficient Christology leads to a deficient soteriology. Or conversely, a reductionistic soteriology does not fit with the NT's high Christology. I am not saying that the NT Christology is only functional. There is ontology here. But the ontology is always connected to soteriology and is never celebrated for its own sake. Athanasius expressed this insight clearly in his famous book *On the Incarnation*. He realized that Jesus as the Christ could not save us from our sins unless he was fully human and fully divine. A mere human being could never redeem us from our sins. Only one who is divine could secure forgiveness so that our consciences would be cleansed of the evil we have done.

8

The Holy Spirit

God's promises of salvation are realized through the work of the Father, the Son, and the Spirit. Thus far we have explored the work of the Father and the Son, and hence it is fitting at this juncture to turn to the work of the Holy Spirit. In the NT the Spirit is the sign that the new age has arrived, that the new creation has become a reality.[1] In other words, as noted in chapter 1, the Holy Spirit represents the intrusion of the already into the present evil age. God's work of salvation is not yet completed, but the Spirit assures believers that the work God has begun will be completed.

In this chapter we shall see that Jesus, the one anointed with the Spirit, is the exalted Lord and pours out the Spirit on his people. The Spirit in Luke-Acts is especially the Spirit of prophecy and power, but his presence also indicates that one belongs to the people of God. Also, as Paul particularly emphasizes, the Spirit indicates that one belongs to God, and the Spirit empowers believers to live a new life. Similar themes are found elsewhere in the NT, signifying a fundamental unity in perception regarding the work of the Spirit.

In my larger work, the contributions of Matthew and Mark on the Spirit are consulted, but since most of what is taught about the Spirit in Matthew

---

1. For the OT background on the Spirit, see Schreiner 2008: 432–35; Hamilton 2006: 25–55.

and Mark is also found in Luke, I will focus on the latter here, for Luke gives us quite a full-orbed theology of the Spirit.

Before examining the Spirit in Luke-Acts, the baptismal formula in Matt. 28:19 will be discussed. Matthew requires baptism not in the *names* of the Father, Son, and Spirit but rather in the *one name*. The one name, however, includes diversity: the threefold Father, Son, and Spirit. Baptism is administered in the divine name, indicating that the Father, the Son, and the Spirit are all divine. Matthew does not give way here to tritheism, for the one name indicates that there is only one God. And yet the Godhead is marked by diversity: the Father, the Son, and the Spirit.

The Spirit and Jesus

Luke could be described as a theologian of the Holy Spirit because he frequently refers to the Spirit in his two-volume work. Jesus' role as the bearer of the Spirit begins in Luke with the virginal conception. The OT contains accounts of elderly and barren parents giving birth to children (Gen. 21:1–7; 1 Sam. 1:1–28). No precedent exists, however, for a virgin having a child. Mary conceived a child not through sexual relations but, miraculously, when the Holy Spirit overshadowed her (Luke 1:35; cf. Matt. 1:18–25). Like Matthew, Luke portrays Jesus as one who experienced the Spirit's work from his conception. He is the unique bearer of the Spirit as the one conceived by the Spirit.

Jesus was anointed by the Spirit at his baptism (Luke 3:22). Luke shares with the other Synoptics the leading of Jesus into the wilderness by the Spirit (4:1). Distinctively, Luke remarks that Jesus returned from his time of testing in the wilderness "in the power of the Spirit" (4:14). His time of preparation and testing was now finished. He had succeeded in the wilderness where Israel had failed. In contrast to Adam and Israel, Jesus was God's obedient Son. He commenced his public ministry full of the Spirit's power, equipped by the Spirit to carry out the will of God. Luke indicates thereby that the whole of Jesus' ministry was conducted in the power of the Spirit. Such a view fits with the summary of Jesus' ministry given by Peter to Cornelius and his friends (Acts 10:37–41).

The centrality of the Spirit is impressed upon the reader by the first event recorded in Jesus' ministry in Luke (4:16–30). The story recorded here contains many of the themes in both Luke and Acts, and so the account is programmatic and fundamental for Luke's two-volume work. The text begins with the words "The Spirit of the Lord is upon me, because he has anointed me to bring good news to the poor" (4:18). Jesus was sent to free the imprisoned, to grant sight to the blind, to free the oppressed, and to herald the grace of God (4:18–19). Jesus described the whole of his ministry here, so that every dimension of his work depended upon the anointing power of the Spirit.

The Spirit and Prophecy

Another broad category for the Spirit in Luke-Acts is what I designate here as "the prophetic Spirit." The Spirit comes upon people so that they communicate the word of God, both in spoken prophetic utterances and in the written scriptural word. In Luke the prophetic word relates to the fulfillment of salvation history. God's redemptive plan is being worked out, and it is advanced by the prophetic words that come from the Spirit. Often in Luke-Acts the Spirit leads his people, especially in terms of mission: the spread of the gospel to the ends of the earth.

When the Spirit comes, people speak forth God's word. When Mary visited Elizabeth, the latter was suddenly filled with the Spirit and spoke loudly an oracle from God (Luke 1:40–45). Earlier, Gabriel announced that John would "be filled with the Holy Spirit, even from his mother's womb" (1:15). Such a filling testifies that John was a prophet of the Lord—indeed, the greatest prophet until the coming of the Christ (7:26–28). Similarly, Zechariah was filled with the Spirit and prophesied, praising God that he was about to fulfill his covenantal promises by causing a son of David to sit on the throne (1:67–79). The words of Simeon should be interpreted similarly (2:25–35). Luke informs the reader that the "Holy Spirit was upon him" (2:25), and that "he came in the Spirit into the temple" (2:27). The prophetic Spirit was upon Simeon so that he was enabled to speak forth the word of God. The Spirit had "revealed to him" previously that his life would not end before he saw the Christ (2:26).

If we take stock of the foregoing texts, we observe a close connection between the "filling" (*pimplēmi*) of the Spirit and prophecy. John the Baptist was a prophet of the Lord and filled with the Spirit from his mother's womb (1:15). Both Elizabeth and Zechariah were filled with the Spirit and prophesied (1:41, 67). The same pattern continues in Acts. When the 120 believers on the day of Pentecost were filled with the Spirit, they spoke in tongues (2:4).

Later in the narrative the apostles were seized by the Sanhedrin and questioned about their activities. Peter defended their actions and was filled with the Spirit. Peter's spontaneous defense before the religious leaders represented a fulfillment of Jesus' promise that the Spirit would teach his disciples how to respond when they were persecuted (4:8–12; Luke 12:11–12). After Peter's defense the religious leaders threateningly warned the disciples not to continue spreading the message about Jesus. The disciples gathered together and prayed. After prayer "they were all filled with the Holy Spirit and continued to speak the word of God with boldness" (Acts 4:31). Again, the filling of the Spirit leads to the proclamation of God's word, to testifying about what God has done in Christ. At Paul's conversion, Ananias laid his hands on Saul (Paul), and the latter was filled with the Spirit (9:17). In the story line of Acts, Paul's being filled with the Spirit led to the dissemination of the gospel to the ends of the earth. On the first missionary journey, Elymas opposed the preaching of Paul and Barnabas. Paul, filled with the Spirit, struck Elymas blind and spoke the word of the Lord against him (13:9–11). The filling of the Spirit immediately leads to an oracle of the Lord. In every instance, the filling of the Spirit is related to bearing witness and speaking out the prophetic word.

The prophetic Spirit led the church as it spread the good news about Jesus Christ throughout the world. Luke often calls attention to the direction the Spirit gave his messengers as the gospel progressed from Jerusalem to the ends of the earth. The Spirit summoned Philip to go and address the Ethiopian eunuch while the latter was riding in his chariot and returning to Ethiopia (8:29). Luke considers the story of Cornelius to be one of the most significant accounts in the spread of the gospel, for Luke tells the story twice, taking up valuable space to communicate this account (10:1–48; 11:1–18). When the men from Cornelius appeared at the house of Simon the Tanner, the Spirit instructed Peter to go with the men and to visit Cornelius and those gathered with him (10:19–20; 11:12). The first missionary journey of Paul and Barnabas commenced when the Holy Spirit summoned Paul and Barnabas to leave Antioch and to travel about, proclaiming the gospel to Gentiles (13:2).

The prophetic Spirit also led the church to consolidate the mission to which it was called. In one of Luke's summary statements, he observes that the church in the regions of Judea, Galilee, and Samaria was "walking . . . in the comfort of the Holy Spirit" (9:31). Such living in the consolation of the Spirit is linked with the expansion of the church in the areas noted. The gospel was taking hold in these regions, fulfilling Jesus' words in 1:8 that the Spirit would empower their mission. When the church met in Jerusalem to consider whether circumcision would be required of Gentiles, Peter reminded them of what happened to Cornelius and his friends. God gave them the Spirit without the distinctive badge of covenant identity (15:8). Hence, the decision not to impose circumcision on Gentiles reflected the leading of the Spirit himself (15:28).

Gift of the Spirit

Jesus was the bearer of the Spirit, but he is also the one who dispenses the Spirit. The conclusion of Luke implies that the gift of the Spirit is vitally connected with Jesus' suffering, death, and resurrection (24:46–49). The message of repentance in Jesus' name is to be proclaimed to all nations, but the disciples must not leave Jerusalem until Jesus sends "the promise of my Father upon you." Only then will they be "clothed with power from on high" (24:49) and receive the strength needed to bear witness throughout the world. Acts resumes where the Gospel of Luke left off; Jesus admonished his disciples not to leave Jerusalem until they receive "the promise of the Father," which is identified as the baptism of the Holy Spirit (1:4–5). The receiving of the Spirit, as at the conclusion of Luke, is necessary for proclaiming the gospel to the ends of the earth (1:8). Before the Spirit is poured out, however, Jesus must ascend into heaven (1:9–11). The Spirit can be given only when Jesus is exalted as Lord and Christ (2:36), sitting at the right hand of the Father on the throne of David (2:30, 34–35). Jesus, as the one exalted to God's right hand, received the Spirit from the Father and in turn poured out this same Spirit on his disciples (2:33). The Spirit was given only after Jesus was exalted, so that Jesus would be prized as Lord and Christ by all nations. Luke does not focus on a diffuse and general testimony to the truth about God through the Spirit. Rather, the Spirit's being given after Jesus' exaltation and ministry always points people to Jesus as the crucified, risen, and exalted Lord. Forgiveness of sins and the gift of the Spirit come only in the name of Jesus (Luke 24:47; Acts 2:38), for there is salvation in no other name (Acts 4:12).

Jesus' gift of the Spirit is described with different verbs in Acts. We have noted already that those who spoke in tongues in 2:4 are said to have been "filled" (*pimplēmi*) with the Spirit. Various other verbs are used to denote the dispensing of the Spirit, including "receive" (*lambanō*, 1:8; 2:33, 38; 8:15, 17; 10:47; 19:2), "pour out" (*ekcheō* or *ekchynnō*, 2:17–18, 33; 10:45–46), "give" (*didōmi*, Luke 11:13; Acts 11:17), "come, come upon" (*erchomai/eperchomai*, Luke 1:35; Acts 1:8; 19:6), "fall upon" (*epipiptō*, 10:44; 11:15), and "baptize" (*baptizō*, Luke 3:16; Acts 1:4–5; 11:16).

If we examine the verbs related to the dispensing of the Spirit, we see that they are mainly used with reference to four main events: the giving of the Spirit to the disciples at Pentecost (Luke 3:16; Acts 1:5, 8; 2:17–18, 33; 11:15–16), to the Samaritans (Acts 8:15–19), to Cornelius and his friends (10:44–45, 47; 11:15–17; 15:8), and to the Ephesian twelve (19:6–7). Another way of summarizing the evidence in Acts is to note which verbs are used with these four events:

1. "receive" (*lambanō*): Pentecost (1:8; 2:33); Samaria (8:15, 17, 19); Cornelius (10:47); the Ephesian twelve (19:2).
2. "pour out" (*ekcheō* or *ekchynnō*): Pentecost (2:17–18, 33); Cornelius (10:45).
3. "give" (*didōmi*): Pentecost (11:17; 15:8);[2] Samaria (8:18); Cornelius (11:17; 15:8).
4. "come upon" (*erchomai/eperchomai*): Pentecost (1:8); the Ephesian twelve (19:6).
5. "fall upon" (*epipiptō*): Pentecost (11:15); Cornelius (10:44; 11:15).
6. "baptize" (*baptizō*): Pentecost (1:5; 11:16); Cornelius (11:16).

2. Since Peter says that God gave them the same gift he gave those on Pentecost, he teaches that the Spirit was given at Pentecost as well.

The verbs overlap in meaning, and so the omission of a verb with one of the events is not necessarily significant. We see the greatest variety of verbs with reference to Pentecost and the Cornelius event, but this is explained by the greater length of the narrative in these two events. The account of the Ephesian twelve has the fewest verbs, but this is reasonable because it is the shortest narrative among the four.

What is the significance of these four events for Luke's theology of the Holy Spirit? Some have argued that Luke's theology of the Spirit is tied to the charismatic gift of the Spirit that empowers for ministry. In the discussion of the prophetic Spirit, we saw that such a conception of the Spirit certainly plays a major role in Luke-Acts. Even in the four accounts that we have just examined, the notion that the Spirit equips for ministry is present. When the Spirit came at Pentecost, the disciples received power to bear witness to the ends of the earth (Acts 1:8; cf. Luke 24:49). Furthermore, the Pentecost account includes one verb omitted in the foregoing analysis. When Jesus baptized the disciples with the Spirit, they were "filled" with the Spirit and spoke in tongues (Acts 2:4). Their "filling" and tongues-speaking were for the purpose of ministry, since a crowd gathered and Peter proclaimed the gospel. We noticed above that in virtually every case, the use of the verb "fill" (*pimplēmi*) is for the purpose of speaking forth God's word.

In these four accounts, Luke does not suggest a rigid separation between the Spirit's empowering and regenerating ministry. The Pentecost narrative and the use of the verb "fill" indicate that empowerment for ministry cannot be washed out of the story. Still, it seems that the main theme in these four events, particularly in the last three accounts, is that those described are inducted into the people of God. The coming of the Spirit in Acts 8; 10; and 19 was not primarily to denote empowering for charismatic ministry but rather to signify that those who received the Spirit belonged to the people of God. The emblem of their membership was their reception of the Spirit. A piece of evidence that supports the case being made here is that the verb "fill" is used only with the Pentecost account and does not appear in the stories about Samaria, Cornelius, and the Ephesian twelve. In the Pentecost story we have an overlap between the themes of empowerment for ministry and induction into the people of God. The remaining three accounts emphasize that various groups of people truly belong to the church of Jesus Christ.

The Pentecost account, then, is not only about receiving charismatic power; it also represents the inception of the Spirit-endowed people of God. Baptism represents initiation language, so that Jesus baptizing with the Spirit (Acts 1:5) indicates the commencement of the new age of the Spirit (2:17–18, 33; cf. Joel 2:28). God gave the Spirit to the believers at Pentecost for the first time (Acts 11:17; 15:8), so that Peter saw continuity between the giving of the Spirit at Pentecost and the gift of the Spirit to Cornelius and his friends. Both groups were baptized into the new age of the Spirit.

Cornelius and his friends received the message by which they were saved from sin and judgment (11:14). Their reception of the Spirit did not involve ministry to others, though doubtless that followed. What Luke highlights here, however, is their inclusion into the people of God. Circumcised Jews avoided eating with Gentiles because they were not part of God's people and did not observe purity laws (11:2–3). Peter's vision about eating unclean animals, then, relates directly to the main point in the account (10:9–16). With the coming of the Spirit and the new age, the food laws of the OT were no longer required for God's people. God had now declared these foods clean (10:15). What is decisive for entrance into the people of God is the presence of the Spirit. Luke is emphatic about the coming of the Spirit on Cornelius and his friends. The Spirit "fell on" them without any summons to repentance and faith (10:44; 11:15) by Peter. It was evident that the Spirit was "poured out" on these Gentiles (10:45; 11:17; 15:8), and hence Peter concluded that the initiation rite of water baptism should be given to them. The function of speaking in tongues at Pentecost was to bear witness to God's great works (2:11) and to provide a bridgehead for the proclamation of the gospel. It also functioned as a reversal of the confusion of languages at Babel (Gen. 11:1–9), anticipating the consummation, when all will understand one another. In the case of Cornelius and his friends, tongues-speaking did not furnish an opportunity for witness and ministry; rather, it confirmed to Peter and the other Jews present that these Gentiles had truly received the Spirit.

The account of the Ephesian twelve (Acts 19:1–7) bears some similarities with the Cornelius account. These twelve disciples were still living, so to speak, under the old covenant. They had not yet received the Holy Spirit (19:2), the mark of living in the new age of redemption. They were living in the transitional period of redemptive history because they had only received John's baptism. Acts 19:4 suggests that they had not yet believed in the one to whom the Baptist directed people, Jesus Christ. The Pentecostal Spirit had not yet been poured out on them. Upon hearing the good news about Jesus Christ, they put their faith in him and were baptized. Their baptism signified their induction into the people of God. The baptism with water was accompanied by the coming of the Holy Spirit at the laying on of Paul's hands. They spoke in tongues and prophesied to verify that they had received the Pentecostal Spirit. The narrative emphasizes that the outpoured Spirit comes only to those who put their faith in Jesus as the exalted Lord.

The fourth incident is quite unusual. The Samaritans believed in the Lord Jesus, received water baptism, and yet they failed to receive the Spirit (8:9–13). This phenomenon may be interpreted in various ways, but here I will relay the view that seems most probable.[3]

---

3. For the various options, see Schreiner 2008: 456–58.

The account could be interpreted as an exceptional incident that is recounted precisely because it is unique. Luke's comment in 8:16 indicates that what occurred in Samaria was anomalous. Here the verb "receive" (*lambanō*) is used three times with reference to the Holy Spirit (8:15, 17, 19), and the verb "fall upon" (*epipiptō*) once (8:16). Since Luke uses the verb "receive" here, there are no grounds for thinking that the Samaritans already had the Spirit when they first believed, and that they merely lacked the power of the Spirit. The gift of the Spirit is normally received at conversion, as Peter clarified in his sermon on Pentecost (2:38). But the text clearly teaches that the Samaritans received the Spirit only when the apostles laid hands on them, and that the Spirit was not in them at all before the laying on of apostolic hands. We see no other example of an interval between believing and receiving the Spirit in Acts. In every other instance the Spirit is received when people repent and believe (2:38; 10:44–48; 11:15–18; 15:7–11; 19:4–7). Indeed, nowhere else in the NT is the gift of the Spirit separated from believing in Christ by some interval.

The key to the narrative is the requirement that Peter and John come and lay hands on the Samaritans before they can receive the Spirit (8:14–17). Philip, one of the seven (6:5) and a person different from the apostle Philip (cf. 8:1), could not dispense the Spirit because he was not one of the apostles. Why must the Samaritans receive the Spirit as it is mediated through the apostolic laying on of hands? The laying on of hands is not required in every instance, for the Spirit fell on Cornelius and his friends without the imposition of hands (10:44–48). The most satisfying answer is that the apostles were needed to mediate the Spirit so that the Samaritan church would not branch off from the Jerusalem church. The church was one church, and God did not give the Samaritans the Spirit apart from the apostles, so that they would not form their own "denomination." The Samaritans had a long history in which they were separate from the Jews, worshiping on Mount Gerizim instead of in Jerusalem, for example, and prizing the Pentateuch instead of the entirety of the OT. John Hyrcanus destroyed their temple on Mount Gerizim during his reign (134–104 BC). The tension between the Jews and the Samaritans is evident also in the NT (Luke 9:51–56; 10:33; 17:16; John 4:9; 8:48; cf. Acts 1:8; 9:31).

I conclude, then, that the primary purpose for the granting of the Spirit— to believers at Pentecost, to the Samaritans, to Cornelius and his friends, and to the Ephesian twelve—is to testify that those who receive the Spirit are members of the people of God. The pouring out of the Spirit signifies that the new age has commenced, and the giving of the Spirit fits with the missionary character of Luke-Acts. Membership in the people of God is not confined to the Jews; it includes Samaritans and Gentiles. In the dispensation of the Spirit, Luke sees the widening mission of the church and the spread of the gospel of Jesus Christ, for in every case the gift of the Spirit is tied to the message of Jesus Christ as the crucified and risen Lord. I am not arguing that a ministry dimension is completely lacking in these four events, for the disciples at Pentecost also bore witness to the gospel of Christ. Still, it seems that the primary purpose was to certify that those who received the Spirit belonged to God's people.

Trinitarian Traces

When we consider Luke-Acts, we see some significant indications that the being of God is complex and must be understood in terms of threeness and oneness. Luke has no texts regarding the Trinity that are as explicit as the baptismal formula in Matt. 28:19. But at Jesus' baptism, the Father speaks and the Spirit descends as a dove, and hence this reference is implicitly trinitarian. The personal and/or divine character of the Spirit is hinted at by other bits of evidence as well. Ananias lied to the Spirit (Acts 5:3), and this is equated with lying to God (5:4). Ananias and Sapphira were indicted for testing the Spirit (5:9), and elsewhere Peter warned against testing God (15:10). We compare this to Stephen's charge that Israel had consistently resisted the Spirit (7:51). The blasphemy against the Spirit also implies that the Spirit is personal (Luke 12:10). The personality of the Spirit is communicated by the letter composed by the Jerusalem Council, which claims that the decision "seemed good to the Holy Spirit and to us" (Acts 15:28). Similarly, "the Holy Spirit has made you overseers" (20:28 AT; cf. 1:8; 13:47). Only a person can appoint someone to an office. Moreover, in this same verse (20:28) we see a reference to "the church of God" and apparently God's own blood, which refers to the blood of Jesus. Hence, Fitzmyer (1998: 680) rightly says about this text, "In any case, one should not miss the triadic nuance of this verse: the explicit mention of 'God,' 'the Spirit,' and the 'blood,' which implies the Son. It is a trinitarian dimension that Luke associates with the Christian community and its governance."

Another text, Acts 1:4–5, witnesses to the Father, Son, and Spirit, though in an indirect way. The promise of the Spirit is from the Father, and presumably the one who baptizes with the Spirit is the Son (Luke 3:16). Similarly, Jesus is exalted to God's right hand and as a consequence pours out the Spirit (Acts 2:33). The "trinitarian" references in Luke-Acts are not prominent, nor are they emphasized. Still, the trinitarian character of what Luke writes is undeniable.

The Spirit in the Gospel of John

John's theology of the Spirit overlaps in some respects with what we see in Luke-Acts, but as we would expect, there are also distinctive themes and emphases in the Johannine teaching on the Spirit. The baptism of Jesus by John is omitted in the Gospel, but John bore witness to Jesus' anointing with the

Spirit (1:32–34). The Spirit's descent as a dove signifies that Jesus has been anointed for his messianic ministry, and perhaps the dove also signals the arrival of the new creation in Jesus' ministry (in Gen. 1:2 the Spirit "hovers" like a bird; cf. also John 3:22–30).

The Spirit in the Gospel of John is the Spirit of life, the Spirit that grants eternal life, the life of the age to come. The Spirit that gives life cannot be separated from the person and ministry of Jesus. After all, Jesus is the one who will baptize his followers with the Spirit (1:33). He will introduce them to the age to come by giving the Spirit. The language of baptism introduces the "water" motif in John's Gospel. John rather frequently associates water with the work of the Spirit. We see antecedents for such a conception in the OT, where "water" and "streams" seem to designate the Spirit (Isa. 44:3; Ezek. 36:25–27; cf. Isa. 12:3; 32:2; 35:7; 41:17–18; 43:20; 44:3; 49:10; 55:1).

The water motif and the giving of life by the Spirit are central in Jesus' conversation with Nicodemus in John 3. Nicodemus misunderstood Jesus, thinking that the call to be born again required reentering a mother's womb. Jesus clarified that one must be "born of water and the Spirit" to enter the kingdom (3:5). A few have seen a reference to physical birth (breaking of water) and spiritual birth (the work of the Spirit) here. It is doubtful, however, that Jesus would bother to state the obvious fact that one must be born physically before one can be born spiritually. Clearly, only those who exist can receive new life from the Spirit! Furthermore, both "water and Spirit" follow a single preposition (*ex*), suggesting that water and Spirit refer not to two different notions but to the same spiritual reality. Most commentators have concluded that John refers to Christian baptism. This interpretation makes much better sense because in the NT, Christian baptism is often associated with new life. If we are persuaded that the dialogue with Nicodemus is historical, then the likelihood of a reference to Christian baptism diminishes because Nicodemus could not have grasped something that did not even exist yet, and Jesus insisted that Nicodemus, being a teacher, should grasp what Jesus was saying (3:10). Others see a reference to John's baptism, and yet it seems unlikely that the necessity of John's baptism would be emphasized in John's Gospel, especially when we consider the Johannine theme that John is merely a witness and not the true light. If anything, the role of the Baptist is subordinated to Jesus in John's Gospel, and so it is quite unlikely that his baptism would be considered necessary to be part of the people of God.

Since Jesus expected Nicodemus to comprehend his insistence on the new birth, the OT furnishes the most likely background to his words. The importance of new birth by the water and the Spirit finds its antecedent in Ezek. 36:25–27. Both water and the Spirit are prominent in Ezekiel. The water signifies cleansing and purification of sins. Only the Spirit of God, as Jesus explained in John 3:7, can grant new life. The work of God's Spirit is a sovereign work, for it is compared to wind that blows mysteriously and apart from human control (3:8).

The relationship between water and the Spirit is illustrated in 7:37–39 as well. One of the great attractions of the Feast of Tabernacles was the water-pouring rite that occurred daily (see *m. Sukkah* 4.1, 9–10; 5.2–4).[4] Jesus stood up on the last day of the feast and claimed that the ritual they practiced, if understood rightly, pointed to him. Those who thirsted should come to him and drink. John 7:39 explains that these rivers of living water refer to the Spirit himself. John clarifies that this life-giving Spirit was not yet available. He would be given only when Jesus was "glorified." Jesus must be exalted on high before the Spirit will be dispensed to his people.

The link between the water and the Spirit adduced in the foregoing texts suggests that the water refers to the Spirit in 4:13–14, where Jesus addressed the Samaritan woman. The Spirit quenches human thirst forever and will spring up to life eternal, bringing to believers the life of the age to come. This is another way of saying that the Spirit grants life, since human beings depend on water for survival.

The Spirit's role in granting life is also expressed in 6:63. Many in the crowd and even some of Jesus' own disciples departed from him after he taught that he is the bread from heaven and that people must eat his flesh and drink his blood to have life. Jesus commented on the scandal that he created (6:61–62), indicating that their offense pierced to the very heart of the matter. Their taking umbrage over him would only be exacerbated, not quelled, if they saw him ascending to the Father, for he would go to the Father via the cross. Hence, the flesh cannot beget life; only the Spirit can do so (6:63). The flesh cannot see that life comes only through Jesus' flesh and blood. Only the Spirit opens eyes so that people perceive the source of life. Jesus' words "are spirit and life" (6:63) because life comes only from the flesh and blood of Jesus—his death on behalf of the world (6:51).

John 20:22 is a difficult text. Jesus commissioned his disciples for mission, sending them just as the Father had sent him (20:21). He then breathes on them and says, "Receive the Holy Spirit" (20:22). Three main interpretations have been suggested. (1) The disciples received the Spirit when Jesus breathed on them, and so John describes the moment of their regeneration. The day of Pentecost in Acts 2, then, represents the occasion when the disciples were clothed with power. Against this, a neat distinction between regeneration and empowering cannot be sustained in John, and so trying to distinguish between the two events in such a way here is unpersuasive. (2) John 20:22 is the Johannine Pentecost. John does not describe Pentecost elsewhere, and so he inserts it here. If we do canonical biblical theology, this solution is unsatisfying. Pentecost plainly comes fifty days after Jesus' resurrection, but

---

4. See also Barrett 1978: 326–27, 335; Köstenberger 2004: 239–40.

John locates this event on the day of resurrection. Furthermore, the events in John 21 suggest that the disciples were not yet clothed with power, and thus the alleged infusion of the Spirit does not seem to grant much confidence or boldness. (3) The best solution seems to be that the event is symbolic of the future reception of the Spirit. If we accept Acts as historically reliable, then John knew about Pentecost because he experienced it. Furthermore, if we date John in the last decade of the first century, it is likely that the churches that he addressed knew about Pentecost as well. Taking the account as symbolic also makes sense in the Johannine context because when Jesus breathed on them, he was not yet exalted, and so the Spirit cannot be given (cf. John 7:39). The action itself also suggests that symbolism is at work. Jesus breathed on them, signifying that he would grant them the Spirit after he had departed.

Only John identifies the Holy Spirit as a "Paraclete" (*paraklētos*). Scholars have intensely discussed the significance of this designation. Some have focused on the legal background of the term, contending that "advocate" summarizes well the meaning of the term. Others have suggested "helper" or "counselor." Attempts to define the word in terms of its background have come to an impasse, and no consensus has been reached in trying to find one term that embraces every usage. The way forward is to investigate the texts in which "Paraclete" is used. One of the primary themes in John 13–17 is Jesus' future absence from his disciples. He informed them that he was leaving and going to the Father. They were filled with sorrow, and so he explained why his absence was for their benefit. Jesus requested that the Father send them "another Paraclete" (*allos paraklētos*) to be with them forever (14:16 AT). Jesus, in other words, is a Paraclete whose personal presence had strengthened the disciples and "kept" them (17:12). That Jesus is a Paraclete is confirmed by 1 John 2:1, in that he functions as an advocate for disciples on the basis of his death. Burge (1987: 140) rightly detects parallels between the ministry of Jesus and the Paraclete: (1) Jesus reveals the Father (John 14:9), and the Paraclete manifests Jesus (14:15–17); (2) Jesus is dependent on the Father for all things (5:19–20; 8:28), and the Spirit is dependent on Jesus (16:13); (3) Jesus glorifies the Father (17:4), while the Spirit glorifies Jesus (16:14). The Spirit is also a Paraclete whose presence will strengthen the disciples in an even greater way. He is with the disciples even now, but he will reside in them in the future (14:17). Thereby they will be enabled to persevere in suffering and to bear witness to Jesus, for the Spirit given to them is the "Spirit of truth" (14:17; 15:26; 16:13). Thompson (2001: 183) rightly adds that the Spirit also performs many of the same functions as the Father: testifying (5:37; 8:18; 1 John 5:9; cf. John 15:26–27); glorifying Jesus (John 5:44; 8:54; 12:23, 28; 13:31–32; 17:1, 5; cf. 16:14); being with the disciples (14:23; 17:11, 15, 26; cf. 14:17); and teaching (6:45; 1 John 2:26–27; cf. John 14:26; 16:13).

The Spirit will "teach" the disciples "all things" (John 14:26), so that the apostles will faithfully pass on the truth about Jesus to their followers. They will be preserved from error by the teaching ministry of the Spirit. Not only will the Spirit teach the apostles, but also he will "bring to your remembrance all that I have said to you" (14:26). The Spirit does not provide an independent access to truth to the disciples. He does not summon them to learn mysteries that are gleaned through some special channel of private revelation. He witnesses to the words of Jesus and reminds them of his words and teaching. They will recall everything that is necessary and crucial from Jesus' teaching, but not in their own capacity.

What is said about the Paraclete here fits with 15:26–27 as well. Jesus had just warned his disciples that while he is absent, hatred will rise against them, and that such hatred is rooted in a detestation of Jesus himself (15:18–25). Jesus promised them that he himself will send the Paraclete "from the Father" (15:26). And yet the Paraclete is also the Father's gift, for he is "the Spirit of truth, who proceeds from the Father" (15:26). This "Spirit of truth" does not convey truth to human beings apart from Jesus, as if he operates as an independent truth revealer to the world. He teaches the truth in that he witnesses to Jesus (15:26). He calls attention to Jesus as the Son of God, the Christ, the one who died so that humans might live. The witness of the disciples, then, must be rooted in the testimony about Jesus borne by the Spirit (15:27).

The meaning of 16:8–11 is notoriously difficult. We should begin by focusing on what is clear in the text. The Spirit's witness before the world is again tied inextricably to Jesus' person and work. The Spirit does not convince the world of truth apart from Jesus the Christ; he convinces the world regarding the truth in Jesus. The Spirit functions as the prosecuting attorney, persuading the world that it is guilty in terms of its stance toward Jesus. It seems, then, that the witness of the disciples will be made effective by virtue of the Spirit's witness through them (cf. 15:26–27).

We consider now the specifics of 16:9–11. The Spirit will convince the world about sin, righteousness, and judgment. The sin of the world centers on the failure to believe in Jesus. The failure to believe in Jesus led to his execution, for no one can take a neutral stand regarding Jesus. One either believes him or hates him (15:18–25). One either embraces him as the Christ or puts him to death as a messianic pretender and a threat to the well-being of the nation (11:48–50).

What is most difficult is determining what is meant by the Spirit's convicting the world about righteousness. Does he convict the world of its lack of righteousness, or about the righteousness of Jesus? If the conclusions suggested above about failing to believe in Jesus are correct, then perhaps both of these matters are included. The world radically misconstrues what righteousness is in that it condemned Jesus to death as an evil impostor and blasphemer. It does not realize that Jesus went "to the Father" by way of the cross for the sin of the world, not because of his own sins. The world has no conception of righteousness because it does not see who Jesus is. At the same time, the

Spirit, who has come now that Jesus is raised and exalted, convinces the world
of its lack of righteousness. Since the world condemned Jesus to death, and
failure to believe in Jesus is the fundamental sin, the crucifixion of Jesus testifies to the unrighteousness of the world. The world does not see Jesus as he
truly is—the Christ, the Son of God, who has come to give life. The Spirit will
convince them that Jesus is the righteous one of God, and as a consequence
the world is unrighteous.

Finally, the Spirit will convince the world about judgment because "the
ruler of this world is judged" (16:11). Obviously, the "ruler of this world" is
Satan (cf. 12:31; 14:30). The world looks at Jesus' execution and concludes
that he cannot be the Messiah and the Son of God. His suffering of "judgment" must have indicated that he displeased God as a messianic pretender.
No one, the world reasons, could be the Christ and end up on a cross. The
Spirit convinces people that the legal decision made by the Roman authorities was misguided and that the Jewish authorities did not interpret his death
accurately. The cross signifies not Jesus' defeat but rather his victory over
Satan. Jesus expelled the ruler of the world by being lifted up high on the
cross (12:31–32). The interpretation proposed here supports the suggestion
that righteousness in John 16:10 has a twofold meaning, referring both to
the righteousness of Jesus and the lack of righteousness of the people. For
here the misconceptions of judgment are also twofold. First, the Spirit will
convince the world of its error about Jesus being judged and rejected by God
on the cross. Second, those convicted will see that the cross accomplishes the
judgment of Satan and Christ's triumph over him. What appears to human
beings to be the defeat of Jesus and his rejection by God is actually the means
by which he defeats the enemy of the human race, Satan, and pronounces a
definitive judgment against him. The witness of the Spirit, referred to here,
does not take place in a vacuum; it occurs through the witness of the disciples,
so that the Paraclete, as Jesus' advocate, convicts the world of its guilt and
Jesus' righteousness as the disciples bear witness to the gospel.

The Spirit's ministry is not limited to "the world" (16:8–11); it is also intended for believers (16:12–14). The teaching ministry of the Spirit is again
highlighted in these verses. The disciples could not grasp all that Jesus would
like to say before the cross and resurrection had taken place. They could not
grasp the fullness of redemptive history until Jesus had died and was risen
and the Spirit was given. Even then, they needed the Spirit to comprehend the
truth. Jesus promised them that the Spirit of truth would come as a teacher
who "will guide" the disciples "into all the truth" (16:13). In other words,
the Spirit would enable Jesus' disciples to comprehend the things that the
historical Jesus desired to speak to them. He would guide them into the truth
about Jesus because Jesus is the truth (14:6). The Spirit would not draw attention to himself or exalt himself, as if he speaks on his own authority. He is
the one sent by the Father and the Son. He is sent by the Father in the name

of the Son to bear witness to the Son. Hence, he will speak "whatever he hears" (16:13) from the Father and the Son. He will bear witness to both the Father and the Son because the Father and the Son share all things in common (16:15). The Spirit's work in the world is not autonomous but rather is dependent upon Jesus. Indeed, one can discern the work of the Spirit only after Jesus is glorified.

The "Paraclete" texts in John indicate that a number of different definitions are fitting for the term. The Spirit is a counselor, helper, advocate, and teacher. Jesus also clarifies that the Spirit will be given only after his departure. The Spirit will come only after Jesus' glorification, after he has been lifted up on the cross and has returned to the Father. The "Paraclete" texts also emphasize that the Spirit works in concert with and in support of Jesus. He does not operate independently; he is Jesus' alter ego. Hence, no true work of the Spirit exists apart from his witness to the Son—his ministry, death, and resurrection. The Spirit is sent by the Father and the Son to glorify Jesus: to convict people of their sin relative to Jesus, and to teach and remind the disciples of the truths that they need in Jesus' absence.

The trinitarian impulses in John burst into the open in Jesus' final discourse to his disciples (chaps. 13–17), where he promised them that the Paraclete will come to them when he departs. Jesus is a Paraclete, and the Spirit is "another Paraclete" (14:16) sent by the Father, who will abide with believers forever. He is known by believers and will dwell in them (14:17). Since he is "another Paraclete," the implication is that he is known as Jesus was known by the disciples. Just as Jesus is in the disciples (14:20), so too the Spirit resides in them.

We see a similar pattern in 14:26. The Father will send the Paraclete to the disciples. The Spirit is not merely a force or impulse, for he will teach the disciples and assist them so that they remember what Jesus taught them. Nor is the Paraclete fully identical with the Father or the Son. He will be sent by the Father, and he will come in Jesus' name. The Spirit, then, is identified with the Father and the Son and yet is distinct from them (cf. 15:26). He teaches and helps disciples remember.

The separation of the Father, Son, and Spirit from one another seems clear from 16:5–11. Jesus is going to the Father via the cross and his resurrection. The Spirit and the Son cannot be identified with each other absolutely, for Jesus explicitly said that he was departing, and when he leaves, he will send the Paraclete. The personal character of the Spirit is also clear, for he will convince the world about sin, righteousness, and judgment. Indeed, Jesus proceeded to say that the Spirit will direct the disciples into all truth and will speak not on his own authority but on the basis of what he hears (16:13). Guiding and speaking, however, are personal activities, indicating that the Spirit shares a personal relation with Jesus and with the disciples. Furthermore, the Spirit will announce the coming things, and such declarations are also the province of persons (16:13–14).

John's Gospel does not articulate the formal doctrine of the Trinity, nor are the relations between the Father, Son, and Spirit explicated in detail. For instance, the Spirit is nowhere called "God." On the other hand, in a number of texts the Spirit is placed together with the Father and Son and clearly works in harmony with them. He cannot be identified absolutely with them, for the Father and Son send the Spirit, and Jesus teaches that he will send the Spirit after he has departed to be with the Father. Nor can the Spirit be identified as a force or an impulse. He witnesses, teaches, speaks, convicts, and declares. He is seen and known by disciples. The church considered the Johannine witness in later formulating the doctrine of the Trinity, noting his personal and divine qualities.

The Spirit in 1 John

The theology of the Spirit in 1 John does not replicate the teaching of John's Gospel, and yet the thought moves in the same orbit. The primacy of assurance fits with the character of 1 John as a whole, for John wrote to assure the readers that they truly had eternal life (5:13; cf. 2:12–14), in contrast to those who had left the church (2:19). John weaves several themes together in addressing the issue of assurance. Those who truly belong to God keep his commands, love fellow believers, and believe that Jesus is the Christ (3:23–24). Believers also know that Jesus abides in them because he has given them the Spirit (3:24). John communicates a similar truth in 4:13 in the midst of his exposition of God's love. Believers have assurance that they abide in Christ and he abides in them because of the Spirit within them.

John is not suggesting that the Spirit's assurance belongs to those who refuse to love others, to those who do not keep God's commands or who deny that Jesus is the Christ. The Spirit is not an independent witness, as if people could claim to belong to God solely on the basis of the Spirit's witness. The strands of love, obedience, and orthodox Christology must be woven together with the Spirit's witness for an accurate grasp of John's theology of assurance. And yet the Spirit's witness cannot be collapsed into love, obedience, and Christology, so that it plays no distinguishing role. John likely refers to an internal work of the Spirit by which he communicates to the heart that one is truly a child of God. In that sense, the Spirit's work is mysterious and inaccessible to others, for the Spirit gives the believer internal confirmation of belonging to God. It is a supernatural and ineffable work that transcends ordinary human discourse or experience.

The Spirit in 1 John also functions as a witness. False prophets with deviant spirits exist, and they must be discerned and rejected (4:1–6). The witness of the Spirit "confesses that Jesus Christ has come in the flesh" (4:2). The spirit that rejects Jesus as the Christ is not God's Spirit but rather is "the spirit of the antichrist" (4:3). The Spirit testifies to the truth and ratifies such an apostolic confession (4:6).

As in John's Gospel, the Spirit does not witness independently to the truth. He witnesses to Jesus, affirming that the historical Jesus is the Christ. The Spirit does not witness to truth subjectively, in the sense that one can claim a private revelation of the Spirit that contradicts the public affirmation that Jesus is the Christ. The anointing that all true believers have received is likely an anointing with the word and the Spirit (2:20, 27). The Spirit witnesses to the truth that Jesus is the Christ, so that the Spirit invariably centers on Jesus himself.

The same theme is confirmed in 5:6–12. John directs his readers to Jesus' baptism and death—his coming by water and blood—emphasizing again that Jesus is the Christ come in the flesh. He adds that the Spirit witnesses to such a reality as the Spirit of truth (5:6). Indeed, the Spirit, water, and blood form an alliance as a threefold witness to the truth of Jesus' person. The Spirit's work, then, affirms historical truths, not private judgments about spiritual realities. The Spirit's witness is inseparably tied to the work of Jesus Christ in redemptive history.

The First Johannine Letter does not explicitly speak of the Trinity. Such a teaching was inserted into some manuscripts at 5:7 by scribes, probably in the midst of later trinitarian controversies. The insertion obviously is later and by no means can be accepted as part of the original text. What we observe in 1 John is actually rather similar to the teaching of John's Gospel. If the anointing refers to the Spirit (2:20, 27), the Spirit works in harmony with the Father and the Son, testifying that Jesus is the Christ come in the flesh (2:22–23). We see that the Father, Son, and Spirit work in concert, as in the Gospel. The Spirit testifies that the Father has sent Jesus in the flesh (4:1–6), confirming that he is the Savior of the world (4:14). The witness of the Spirit to Jesus at his baptism and death (5:6–8) is nothing less than the witness of God himself (5:9). Those who reject the Spirit's witness about Jesus reject God's assessment of Jesus (5:10–11).

The Spirit in Paul's Letters

The Holy Spirit in the Pauline writings is an eschatological gift, fulfilling God's promise of the coming of the new covenant. The end-time gift of the Spirit has been granted to believers by Jesus Christ. Jesus gave the life-giving Spirit to his followers (1 Cor. 15:45), presumably at his exaltation. This same Spirit guarantees the resurrection of believers (15:42–44). As people are converted, the Spirit is given to them as the "firstfruits" (Rom. 8:23). In the OT, the firstfruits function as the anticipation and pledge of the remainder of the harvest. Similarly, the gift of the Spirit guarantees that God will complete the work of redemption and raise believers from the dead. The same Spirit that raised Jesus will raise believers from the dead, for he dwells in them (8:11). The Spirit given to believers is both a seal and a down payment of future redemption (2 Cor. 1:22; Eph. 1:13–14).

The blessing pledged to Abraham (Gen. 12:3) is nothing less than the promise of the Spirit (Isa. 44:3), and this blessing now belongs to believers (Gal. 3:14), indicating that the last days have begun. God has sent the Spirit of his Son into the hearts of believers (4:6). The gift of the Spirit is the mark of the new age and is fundamental for being a Christian (cf. Rom. 8:15; 1 Cor. 6:19; Gal. 3:2, 5; Titus 3:5). The indwelling of the Spirit is the nonnegotiable indication that one is truly a believer (Rom. 8:9). Those who do not have God's Spirit still live in the realm of the flesh: they are unconverted and under the dominion of the present evil age. Since having the Spirit is the sine qua non for believers, they can be simply described as "spiritual" (1 Cor. 3:1; Gal. 6:1). There is no notion here of some believers who are a cut above others, who constitute a spiritual elite (cf. 1 Cor. 2:12, 14). The Spirit himself witnesses with the spirits of Christians, assuring them that they are truly believers (Rom. 8:16). From conversion, believers know that they belong to God because God's love has been poured out into their hearts through the Holy Spirit (5:5; cf. 15:30).

The Spirit in Pauline theology is a Spirit of power. He transforms God's people. We see this clearly in Paul's letter-Spirit contrast, which appears on three different occasions (Rom. 2:29; 7:6; 2 Cor. 3:6). The letter-Spirit polarity should be construed not hermeneutically but in terms of redemptive history. Transformation of human beings did not occur in the old era under the Mosaic law, but such transformation has been effected by the Spirit's power in the new age (Rom. 2:29; 7:6).[5] The transforming work of the Spirit is particularly emphasized in Rom. 8 and Gal. 5. In both contexts Paul contrasts the power of the Spirit with the ineffectiveness of the law (cf. Eph. 3:16). The Spirit sets believers free "from the law of sin and of death" (Rom. 8:2). Since believers have been set free through the Spirit, Paul exhorts them to "put to death the deeds of the body . . . by the Spirit" (8:13; cf. Gal. 5:16, 25; 6:8). Those who are "led by the Spirit of God are sons of God" and daughters of God (Rom. 8:14; cf. Gal. 5:18). The evidence that people have the Spirit is that they are led by the Spirit and manifest the fruit of the Spirit (Gal. 5:22–23). Only those who are filled with the Spirit please God (Eph. 5:18).

The Holy Spirit plays a vital role in ministry. The proclamation of the gospel is not based on human wisdom but is a "demonstration of the Spirit and of power" (1 Cor. 2:4). Indeed, Paul's ministry is characterized by "the Holy Spirit" (2 Cor. 6:6). The proclamation of the gospel from Jerusalem to

---

5. What Paul writes is a generalization. He is not denying that there was a faithful remnant under the old covenant. What is striking to Paul, however, is that the old covenant and the law were not agents of transformation.

Illyricum is the result of the Spirit's power (Rom. 15:19), and so the signs and wonders in the Pauline mission derive from the Spirit. The gospel that Paul proclaimed in Thessalonica was effective not because of Paul's words but because the Holy Spirit was powerfully present (1 Thess. 1:5).

The Spirit grants spiritual gifts to believers for the edification of the church. Even though there are a multitude of gifts, there is one Spirit that stands behind the gifts (1 Cor. 12:4). In the strongest possible terms, Paul emphasizes that the Spirit is the one who gives wisdom, knowledge, faith, or healing (12:8–10). Gifts are not the manifestation of human skill and ability and talent; they are "the manifestation of the Spirit" for the strengthening of the church (12:7). Hence, the gifts exercised can be ascribed only to the work of the Holy Spirit, to his sovereign will (12:11).

The entire discussion of spiritual gifts commences with the claim that no one speaking by the Spirit can invoke a curse upon Jesus; conversely, the one speaking by the Spirit confesses Jesus' lordship (12:3). The discussion of the gifts of the Spirit that follows, then, is subsumed under the banner of the lordship of Christ. The fundamental criterion for determining the work of the Spirit is whether Christ is confessed and embraced as Lord. Interestingly, a trinitarian formula follows in 12:4–6 in a discussion on spiritual gifts. There is "the same Spirit" (12:4), "the same Lord" (12:5), and "the same God" (12:6).

Washing, sanctification, and justification are ascribed to the Spirit (6:11), but they became a reality "in the name of the Lord Jesus Christ." At the same time, the subject of the verbs is God himself. He is the one who washes, sanctifies, and justifies. The close affinity between the Spirit and Christ is apparent in Rom. 8:9–11. The Spirit indwells believers, but the Spirit is identified as "the Spirit of Christ" (8:9) and "the Spirit of him who raised Jesus from the dead" (8:11). Paul switches from the Spirit to Christ, stating that "Christ is in you" (8:10). It is unlikely that Paul collapses the Spirit and Christ together as if they are coterminous in every respect, given the distinctions between the two that permeate his writing. We see a similar alternation in Ephesians. Paul prays that believers will receive strength from the Spirit within (3:16), but the next verse refers to Christ dwelling in the heart (3:17), and this is closely related to experiencing Christ's love (3:19). Believers who have the indwelling Spirit and Christ are filled with God's fullness. In this instance we have a text that is remarkably trinitarian. The Spirit, Christ, and the Father are all said to indwell believers.

And yet the Father is distinct from the Son and the Spirit. The Father elects and predestines people (Eph. 1:4–5) and reveals the purpose of his will (1:9). Jesus redeems believers with his blood and is the agent through whom the Father works (1:7). The Spirit is the seal of God's promise, the guarantee of final redemption (1:13–14). The three are not collapsed together; they are distinguished from one another. Paul continues, however, to affirm that there is only one God (4:6). And yet in the very context in which he reaffirms monotheism, we also find a trinitarian formula with references to the "one Spirit" (4:4), "one Lord" (4:5), and "one God and Father of all" (4:6). Obviously, Paul does not work out the theological ramifications of the formula. In any case, the Spirit seems to be put on the same level with the Father and the Son. We see a similar phenomenon in 2 Cor. 13:14: "The grace of the Lord Jesus Christ and the love of God and the fellowship of the Holy Spirit be with you all." Jesus Christ, the Father, and the Spirit are associated together here in a remarkable way. In other texts, grace flows from the Father, and love is given through the Spirit (Rom. 5:5). Apparently the Father, Son, and Spirit all share divine functions, but the theological implications of the statement are not pursued in detail. Barrett (1973: 345) rightly observes that full "trinitarian orthodoxy" is not worked out here, but we have "a starting-point for such speculative thinking and for its creedal formulation. Christ, God, and the Spirit, appearing in balanced clauses in one sentence, must stand on one divine level." As Barrett further remarks (ibid.), what Paul writes here makes "trinitarian theology, given the setting of Christianity in the following four centuries, inevitable, yet does so unconsciously."

The Pauline theology of the Spirit has many dimensions. The gift of the Spirit represents the inauguration of the age to come, and hence when human beings have the Spirit, there is no doubt that they belong to God. Paul also emphasizes that the Christian life is lived in the power of the Spirit. Here Gal. 3:3 could be taken as the banner verse. The Christian life is not merely begun by the Spirit; it is also continued in the Spirit. The Spirit grants power so that believers are freed to do God's will. The new obedience is not perfect, but it is observable and substantial. The fruit of ministry is also the work of the Spirit. The Spirit empowers those who preach the gospel, so that the work is effective. We also noted a number of trinitarian formulas in the Pauline writings. The relation between the Father, Son, and Spirit remains undeveloped in these texts, and yet there is the clear implication that the three share divine functions.

The Spirit in Hebrews

Hebrews does not refer often to the Holy Spirit. What stands out is the role of the Spirit in the history of salvation, in the fulfillment of the OT that has now dawned in Jesus Christ. One of the most fascinating references to the Spirit occurs with reference to Jesus' atoning sacrifice. Jesus "through the eternal Spirit offered himself without blemish to God" (9:14). Some commentators argue that the author points to Christ's own spirit, while others see a reference to the Holy Spirit. Interestingly, the Spirit is described as "eternal," suggesting the divine character of the Spirit and thus a reference to the Holy Spirit. Of particular importance is the salvation-historical context of the statement.

The sacrifice of Christ secured "eternal redemption" because it was offered "through the eternal Spirit" (9:12, 14). The fleshly sacrifices of animals point toward something greater: the sacrifice of Christ offered through the Spirit.

The Spirit's role in the fulfillment of God's promises is also evident in 6:4. The author chronicles the blessings belonging to the people of God, and perhaps the chief one is that they share (*metochous*) in the Holy Spirit. Despite the reservations of some commentators, the sharing in the Spirit signifies genuine conversion, for the same root is used of partaking of (*metechōn*) milk (5:13). The partaking of milk does not designate an incomplete or partial digestion of milk. Similarly, sharing in the Spirit is *the* mark of new life, the prime indication that believers are Christians. The Spirit is the gift of the new age, and this is confirmed by 6:5, which says that Christians enjoy "the powers of the age to come." The various blessings of believers in 6:4–5 overlap and mutually interpret one another. The Holy Spirit, then, represents one of the blessings of the age to come, indicating that the new age has arrived.

Hebrews 2:4 occupies the same world of discourse. The message proclaimed to the Hebrews is superior to the Mosaic law mediated by angels (2:1–4). The salvation accomplished by Jesus is superior, attested by the fact that he has sat down at God's right hand (1:3, 13), since the final cleansing for sins has been accomplished. God has verified that he has spoken definitively and finally in his Son and his great work on the cross (1:1), in that he has granted apportionments of the Spirit to believers, as well as signs and wonders and miracles (2:4). The gifts of the Spirit, then, signify that the fulfillment of salvation history has arrived. Being made partakers of the Spirit (6:4) and receiving the gifts of the Spirit (2:4) are both tied to the work of Christ.

Hebrews does not reflect on or develop a doctrine of the Trinity. Perhaps the most interesting reference to God, the Son, and the Spirit in Hebrews is found in 9:14 (though whether the Holy Spirit is in view is debated). Here we have a reference to Christ's blood, the work of the Spirit in Christ's life, and the offering made to God. A more indirect reference occurs in 10:29, for God is not explicitly mentioned. Still, he is the one who inflicts punishment on those who spurn God's Son and insult the "Spirit of grace." Here it is remarkable that both the Son and the Spirit are depicted as the objects of insult, and in remarkably personal and provocative terms. Clearly, the author of Hebrews does not develop a doctrine of the Trinity, but some of the clues in the letter are tantalizing and suggestive.

The Spirit in 1 Peter

Categorizing the references to the Spirit in 1 Peter is quite difficult. Most noticeable, perhaps, is the Spirit's relationship to the work of Christ. The first reference to the Spirit is 1:2, where Peter addresses the recipients of the letter and notes "the sanctification of the Spirit." Peter speaks here of the sanctification that Christians receive at conversion. Supporting this is the context of the greeting, for the election and the obedience of the readers signify that they are members of God's people: they truly belong to the church of Jesus Christ.

In 1:10–12 Peter celebrates the special privilege that believers in Jesus Christ enjoy. Unlike the prophets, they live on the other side of the cross. Hence, they understand the significance of the prophecies uttered under the old covenant, and they live in the era in which God's eschatological salvation has penetrated this present evil age. Peter remarks that the prophecies uttered and recorded by the prophets were under the aegis of "the Spirit of Christ." Those who proclaimed the good news of the gospel to the Petrine Christians did so "by the Holy Spirit sent from heaven" (1:12). Both the OT prophets and those who herald the good news of Christ on this side of the cross speak by means of the Holy Spirit. What Peter says here is remarkably similar to what we noted in the Johannine literature. The Spirit witnesses to Jesus Christ. Those who claim a witness of the Spirit but exclude or ignore Jesus Christ deviate from the Petrine view of the ministry of the Spirit, for both the OT prophets and those who proclaim the message of the gospel always call attention to the person and work of Jesus Christ. The reference to the Spirit as the one "sent from heaven" in a context that features the sufferings and glories of Christ suggests that the Spirit is given because of Jesus' exaltation. The Spirit is the gift granted after Jesus' triumph over all his enemies and his being seated at God's right hand (3:22; cf. 3:18).

In 4:14 Peter comforts suffering believers, reminding them that they participate in Christ's sufferings, and that their sufferings, as in the case of Christ, are a prelude to glory (4:13). The association between the sufferings of Christ and the sufferings of believers hearkens back to the Jesus tradition (e.g., Matt. 5:10–12). When believers suffer, however, God's Spirit rests on them (1 Pet. 4:14). The OT background is illuminating here, for we have an allusion to Isa. 11:2, where the Davidic Messiah is endowed with the Spirit of the Lord. Peter implies that the Spirit that rested on Jesus also rests upon the disciples. As the Spirit-anointed Messiah, Jesus pours out the same Spirit on his disciples, and their endowment with the Spirit is particularly evident when they suffer.

If we reflect on the Spirit in 1 Peter, what stands out is the Spirit's role with reference to Jesus Christ. The new age in redemptive history has dawned, and the Spirit witnesses to Jesus Christ. The age of fulfillment has commenced with Christ's resurrection, which was the result of the Spirit's work (3:18). The same Spirit that raised Christ will also raise believers on the last day (4:6). Believers are cleansed from their sins by the blood of Christ, and the Spirit sets them apart at conversion (1:2). The Spirit spoke through the prophets and declares his word through those proclaiming the gospel, and in both cases the Spirit testifies to Jesus Christ as the crucified and risen Lord (1:10–12). The Spirit has been given to believers—sent from heaven—now that Jesus Christ is exalted. Jesus, as the Spirit-anointed Messiah, sends the same Spirit upon believers that rested upon him (4:14). Now that the new age of redemptive history has dawned, believers are God's new temple animated by the Spirit, and they offer "spiritual sacrifices" (2:5), which means that their sacrifices are offered through the Holy Spirit. Peter knows of no work of the Spirit apart from Jesus Christ, and the Spirit's work becomes prominent after Christ's death and resurrection precisely because he came to bear witness to Jesus.

Further, we have a trinitarian formula in 1:1–2. God foreknows believers, so that they are "elect exiles." The Spirit sanctifies them, and Jesus sprinkles them with his blood. The formula suggests the divine function of Father, Spirit, and Son. The threefold reference gains special prominence because it opens the letter, signifying from the outset that the saving work is accomplished by the Father, the Spirit, and Jesus Christ.

The Spirit in James, Jude, and 2 Peter

James, Jude, and 2 Peter are included together here because these letters say little about the Spirit. Again we must recall that such a state of affairs does not indicate a lack of interest in the Spirit or a rejection of what other NT writers say about the Spirit. All the writings under consideration here are occasional and remarkably brief. James may not mention the Holy Spirit at all. The only direct reference may be in James 4:5, which happens to be one of the most disputed verses in the entire letter. If the reference is to the Holy Spirit, the Spirit's dwelling in believers is noted.

It may be that James uses wisdom where other writers speak of the Spirit. For instance, James exhorts his readers who are bereft of wisdom to ask God. He gives generously and gladly to those who request such a gift (1:5). The admonition is similar to what we find in Luke 11:13, where Jesus assures his disciples that God gives "good gifts" to his children; indeed, God will "give the Holy Spirit to those who ask him!" Wisdom in James 3:13–18 manifests itself by its fruit. What is striking here is that the evidence of true wisdom is comparable to the fruit of the Spirit (Gal. 5:22–23). The overlap between wisdom and the Spirit is suggestive, not definite. In any case, James does not specifically point his readers to the Holy Spirit, but the reference to wisdom is not remarkably far from such a conception.

In Jude we find two references to the Spirit. The first instance reminds us of James 3:15 and is perhaps one indication (among a number of others) that both Jude and James hail from Palestinian Christian circles. The interlopers in Jude have disturbed the church with their libertinism. Jude upbraids them for causing "divisions" and for being "worldly" (AT; *psychikoi*) and "devoid of the Spirit" (19). Being "worldly" and "devoid of the Spirit" are two different ways of describing the same reality (cf. 1 Cor. 2:14; Rom. 8:9). These intruders did not share the fundamental mark of authentic Christian faith, for they lacked the Holy Spirit. They lived entirely and wholly on a natural plane.

In Jude 20–21 readers are exhorted to keep themselves in God's love. One way to do this is to pray in the Holy Spirit. Jude refers to the prayer animated by the Spirit, and such prayer should be woven into the fabric of the everyday Christian lives of believers.

Interestingly enough, we also see a trinitarian formula here. Believers are to keep themselves in the love of God (20–21), and this plainly refers to the Father. They are to pray in the Holy Spirit and await the mercy of the Lord Jesus Christ. In these two verses, then, Jude refers to the Father, the Spirit, and the Son. The reference to the Trinity is primitive, and certainly no ontological reflection is included. Yet we can hardly deny that the threefold reference is suggestive, and it seems to place the Spirit on the same level as the Father and Jesus Christ.

Only one reference to the Holy Spirit occurs in 2 Peter. The text, 1:21, is well-known, for Peter speaks of the Holy Spirit carrying along the writers of Scripture. Human beings spoke the word, and yet ultimately the inscripturated word is the result of the Spirit's work. Human beings clearly chose to write the words deposited in Scripture, and yet Peter insists that the human will was not ultimate, for the biblical word is finally attributed to the will of God and the work of his Spirit in moving people to write the word of God. Perhaps there is even a trinitarian dimension to 1:19–21. We are reminded that prophets spoke from God as they were inspired by the Holy Spirit, but the subject of the Spirit's inspiration is the "morning star" of 1:19, which is Jesus Christ.

The Spirit in Revelation

The Spirit in Revelation is the Spirit that speaks and prophesies and witnesses to Jesus Christ. The message that John proclaims is inspired by the Spirit. On four different occasions, John emphasizes that he was "in the Spirit" (1:10; 4:2; 17:3; 21:10). This expression occurs at decisive places in the book: at the inception of the book and John's vision of heaven, and also in the contrast between the two cities, Babylon and the new Jerusalem.

The Spirit also speaks in the seven letters sent to the churches of Asia Minor. Each letter is intended for a specific church—Ephesus, Smyrna, Pergamum, and so forth. Nevertheless, the individual letters also apply to all the churches. Each letter closes with the exhortation, "Let anyone who has an ear hear what the Spirit is saying to the churches" (2:7, 11, 17, 29; 3:6, 13, 22 NRSV). The content of each of the seven letters represents the words of the Spirit addressed to the churches. Remarkably enough, each of the letters also claims to come from the Son of Man, for the introduction of each letter has "the words of [Jesus Christ]" (2:1, 8, 12, 18; 3:1, 7, 14). The words of the risen Christ, the Son of God, therefore, are also the words of the Holy Spirit (cf. 14:13; 22:17).

A striking text on the Holy Spirit occurs in the grace benediction in 1:4–5. Tucked in between the Father and the Son is a reference to "the seven spirits who are before his throne." Grace and peace never come from an angel or an apostle; they always come from God or Jesus Christ. Hence, the seven spirits here cannot be angelic. The referent is almost certainly to the Holy Spirit. The number "seven" is used to denote the fullness and perfection of the Spirit, since it is typical for apocalyptic literature to use numbers symbolically. The significance of the number "seven" is apparent from the beginning of the Scripture in the creation of the world (Gen. 1:1–2:3). We have seen that Revelation emphasizes the prophetic role of the Spirit, the speaking forth of God's word. In this verse, however, we have a trinitarian formula, for grace and peace come from the Father, the Spirit, and the Son. Apparently, the Spirit shares divine prerogatives with the Father and the Son.

Jesus is also said to have the seven spirits of God (Rev. 3:1). It is likely that the first usage of seven spirits, in 1:4, functions as the interpretive lens by which the seven spirits should be understood. If so, then the point is likely that Jesus is the one endowed by the Spirit. Perhaps there is an allusion here to Isa. 11:2, where seven different qualities are related to the Spirit, and the one upon whom the Spirit rests is none other than the descendant of Jesse— the messianic king.

God sits on his throne in Rev. 4, and his glory is stunningly beautiful. Before God's throne are "seven torches of fire, which are the seven spirits of God" (4:5). The seven "torches" (*lampades*) allude to the golden lampstand with seven lamps in Zechariah (4:2). The lampstand in Zechariah is filled by the two olive trees, Joshua and Zerubbabel. The power for Joshua and Zerubbabel to build the temple, however, comes from the Spirit. Hence, God declares, "Not by might, nor by power, but by my Spirit says the LORD of hosts" (4:6). Perhaps there is also an allusion to Isa. 4:4, which speaks of "a spirit of judgment" and "a spirit of burning" by which Israel is cleansed. The seven spirits burning before God's throne may refer to God's power and holiness, which make approaching God's throne a fearful thing. If this analysis is correct, then the Spirit is associated with God himself in his power and holiness.

The last reference to the seven spirits of God occurs in Rev. 5, where the Lamb is worshiped. The Lamb has seven horns and seven eyes, and John remarks that these "are the seven spirits of God sent out into all the earth" (5:6). The seven horns and seven eyes indicate that the Lamb is all-powerful and all-knowing. Nothing can conquer him, nor does anything escape his searching gaze (cf. 1:14; 2:18; 19:12). The sending out of the seven spirits suggests a commonplace in NT theology. The Spirit is sent out to human beings as a consequence of Jesus' death and his victory over evil. The crucified and exalted Jesus gives his people the gift of the Holy Spirit.

In Revelation, John stresses that the Spirit is the Spirit of prophecy. John speaks to his contemporaries by the Spirit. The Spirit speaks to the churches of Asia Minor in the letters to the seven churches and invites all to come to Jesus for life (22:17). The Spirit authoritatively pronounces that those who die in the Lord are blessed and now enjoy rest from their labors (14:13). The Spirit of God is closely related to Jesus Christ. The messages from the Spirit to the churches, as we noted above, also are the words of the Son of Man. Jesus is the one endowed with the Spirit (3:1), and the Spirit is given to believers as a result of his death (5:6). That the Spirit comes when Jesus is glorified is a central theme in the Gospel of John (see 7:39; 16:7–15; cf. 14:16–17, 25–26; 15:26; 20:22). The Spirit is placed on the same plane as the Father and the Son, for grace and peace come from him (Rev. 1:4–5). He is the holy and powerful Spirit that resides with God (4:5). He grants resurrection life to believers (11:11), vindicating those who suffered for Jesus. John has no interest in ontological speculation about the Holy Spirit, but clearly the Spirit is personal, for he speaks and issues invitations. Further, he performs divine functions such as granting life and giving grace and peace. The trinitarian character of Revelation is striking: as we have noted previously, grace benedictions come only from God. We have a trinitarian wish for grace and peace from the Father, the Spirit, and Jesus Christ in 1:4–5.

Conclusion

The gift of the Spirit is prophesied in the OT and given in the NT, and so the Spirit is the signature and mark of the commencement of the new age. The Spirit testifies that the new creation and new exodus have arrived, that the day of fulfillment has come. Such fulfillment certainly centers on Jesus Christ. The Gospel writers emphasize that Jesus was uniquely anointed with the Spirit, beginning with his baptism, so that his entire ministry was carried out in the Spirit's strength. Jesus is not only the bearer of the Spirit but also the one who gives the Spirit to his people. In Acts the gift of the Spirit signifies that one belongs to the people of God. Such theology is not limited to Acts, for Paul insists that the Galatians have no need of circumcision to belong to the people of God because the powerful work of the Spirit is evident among them and in them (3:1–5).

The Spirit is also the Spirit of prophecy. Often in the NT those who speak for God are said to be animated by the Spirit, and in many of these texts the focus is on the fulfillment of God's saving promises. The blessing that God has promised to the whole world has arrived with the gift of the Spirit. But the giving of the Holy Spirit is tied to the ministry, death, resurrection, and exaltation of Jesus Christ. The NT writers do not conceive of a ministry of the Spirit apart from the work of Jesus Christ as the crucified and risen one. The spread of the word to all nations in Acts and the Pauline Letters is empowered by the Spirit, so that the Spirit is the means by which the mission goes forth, but the gift of the Spirit is conveyed through the preached word of the gospel. There is no diffuse and general work of the Spirit apart from Jesus Christ. The revelation and teaching ministry of the Spirit emphasized in John's Gospel is anchored in the work of the historical Jesus. The Spirit has come to glorify Christ and to instruct believers further regarding his death and resurrection.

Pastoral Reflection

The Spirit grants power for ministry but also strengthens believers so that they live in a way that pleases God. This too signals the arrival of the new age, for the law was unable to transform human beings, but the Spirit energizes human beings to obey God in contrast to the inability and weakness of the law. The Spirit's work in granting life is linked to the assurance granted to believers by the same Spirit: those who have experienced God's love are assured by the witness of the Spirit in their hearts. Finally, although no formal doctrine of the Trinity is worked out or explicated in the NT, there are numerous indications of a trinitarian framework in the NT documents. Quite a few trinitarian formulas are found in the NT, and in a number of texts the Father, Son, and Spirit work together in accomplishing salvation for believers. It is difficult to believe that the Father and the Son are personal in these instances while the Spirit is subpersonal or conceived of as a force. All through Christian history, believers have gathered to worship in the name of the triune God: Father, Son, and Spirit. This worship is directed to the God who saves through the work of the Son and the Spirit. If the saving promises of God bring glory to God through Christ, then the Holy Spirit also plays a central role in this whole process, particularly in calling attention to Jesus Christ.

9

The Problem of Sin

We have seen thus far that the promises of salvation were fulfilled with the coming of Jesus Christ and the work of the Holy Spirit. The new age and new creation and new covenant have indeed dawned. But why is the saving work of the Father, Son, and Spirit needed? The saving work of God presupposes that human beings need to be rescued from sin. At this juncture, therefore, we will back up to investigate the plight from which human beings need to be rescued.

The Synoptic Gospels

The Synoptic Gospels presuppose that the people of God, Israel, need a saving work of God. The proclamation of John the Baptist in the wilderness (Matt. 3:3) and the call for baptism in the Jordan suggest that Israel was, so to speak, on the wrong side of the Jordan. They needed to confess their sins (3:6) in order to receive forgiveness, so that God's covenant promises to Israel would be realized. They were not protected from God's wrath simply because Abraham was their father (3:9). A genealogical connection to the progenitor of the Jewish people does not ensure that one will be a recipient of God's salvation.

159

Human beings are vividly described as rotten trees (7:17–19; 12:33; Luke 6:43–44). The evil that besets human beings is not limited to evil actions that need reformation and correction. The "tree" itself has a deep-seated pollution, requiring a new good tree in place of the rotten one. Jesus announced that human beings are not "righteous" but are "sinners." He uses the metaphor of sickness to depict what ails people (Matt. 9:12–13). Unfortunately, many, especially the religious leaders, refused to admit that they were afflicted by a disease, insisting that they were righteous and in no need of a physician. Human pride refuses to acknowledge spiritual poverty and the radical need for renewal.

By nature, the hearts of all people are dull and insensitive to the things of God; nor are people genuinely interested in hearing and seeing what God has to say to them (13:15). Mark emphasizes that the same malady afflicted the disciples. They suffered from hard hearts that resisted the revelation of God in Jesus (Mark 6:52; 8:17, 21). They failed to grasp the significance of Jesus' teaching, and their failure cannot be attributed merely to intellectual incapacity. At bottom they were also idolaters, and so they quarreled about which of them was the greatest and would receive the highest rewards in the kingdom (9:33–37; 10:35–45; Luke 9:46–48; 22:24–27).

Those who sin despise God. They are dead and separated from life and are lost (Luke 15:24, 32). The lostness of human beings is captured by the aphorism "The Son of Man came to seek and to save the lost" (19:10). The older son in the parable of the two sons continued to insist on his goodness, claiming to have obeyed his father perfectly (15:29). He despised the younger son and castigated him for his immorality, all the while failing to see his own evil.

The sinfulness of human beings is most evident in the rejection of Jesus. Those who fail to acknowledge Jesus will be denied by him (Matt. 10:32–33). Those who are scandalized by Jesus stand in opposition to God himself (11:6). In the story line of the Gospels, the sin of Israel culminated in the betrayal and crucifixion of Jesus the Messiah. When he appeared in Israel's midst, God's chosen one was not embraced but murdered.

In the Synoptic Gospels, sin is described colorfully. All people are stained by sin and selfish wills, even the religious leaders. The "tree" is rotten and needs to be made good. A stubborn and evil heart displays itself in a life of evil, one where God is not prized and where people are corrupted by pride. Hence, all are called upon to repent, and this repentance reveals itself in hearing and heeding the kingdom message proclaimed by Jesus.

The Gospel of John and the Johannine Letters

The sin of human beings is portrayed by John with striking images. For instance, those who sin live in the realm of darkness. Walking in the darkness is not accidental, nor is it some cruel trick of fate. People "love" the darkness because they love practicing evil (John 3:19–20). They flee from the light because the light exposes their evil motives and deeds (3:20). Those who hate dwell in darkness, revealing that they belong to the old age, in which darkness reigns, instead of the new era, in which the light is dawning (1 John 2:8–11).

John also uses a spatial metaphor to delineate those who live in the realm of darkness. They are "from below," while Jesus is "from above" (8:23). Another way of saying this is that they are restricted to this world, which is dominated by evil. John typically uses the term *kosmos* to refer to the world of human beings that oppose God and his will. Even though Jesus "was in the world" and made the world, human beings did not know him or embrace him as the Son of God (1:10). The world neither knows nor loves the Father (17:25). Jesus came to the world, and God demonstrated his love for the world by sending Jesus so that the world would be saved (3:16–17), thus also revealing that the world's natural state is one of condemnation and judgment. The world hates Jesus because he reproves its evil and exposes it (7:7; 8:26). It rejoices mightily over Jesus' death (16:20). Satan is the world's ruler (12:31; 14:30; 16:11), and hence all unbelievers live under his dominion (1 John 5:19), and they pay heed to the world's wisdom (1 John 4:5; 2 John 7). The world cannot and will not receive the Spirit, who witnesses to the truth (John 14:17). The world believes the lies of the antichrist instead of receiving the witness to the truth (1 John 4:1, 3, 5). Those who love the world do not belong to God (2:15–17). Because the world is devoted to evil, it will not receive a revelation of Jesus' identity (John 14:19, 22) unless the Spirit convicts the world of its sin (16:8).

There is not an absolute dualism between Jesus' flock and the world, as if the former know nothing of evil. The disciples know evil all too well, but they have been liberated by the work of the Lamb of God, who atoned for their sins (1:29).

Jesus unflinchingly taught that those who refused to believe in him would die in their sins (8:21, 24). Those who did not believe in Jesus have the devil as their father (8:44); they were children neither of God nor of Abraham (8:39–40, 42, 47). They desired to kill Jesus, even if they denied that such was their intention (8:37, 40; cf. 8:59; 10:31). Because they were enslaved to wickedness and refused to trust in Jesus, they lived under God's wrath (3:18, 36). Those who practice wickedness will be raised for judgment on the last day (5:29). John defines sin as lawlessness (1 John 3:4), which means a refusal to do the will of God and to keep his commandments. Lawlessness, then, cannot be restricted to failure to observe God's commands. Lawlessness signifies rebellion against God and a stubborn refusal to submit to him.

Another way of describing the power of sin is to say that those who are born into this world are spiritually blind. If human beings would humble themselves and admit that they are blind, then they would truly see (John 9:39–41). But pride and stubbornness invade the human heart so that people fail to admit that they walk in darkness. If they were willing to carry out God's will, they would realize that Jesus' teaching was from God (7:17). They refuse to come to Jesus for life (5:40) or receive him in the Father's name (5:43). Such rejection of Jesus stems from a lust for human approval and the glory and honor that comes from peers (5:44; 9:22; 12:42–43).

John starkly portrays human sin. The world is opposed to the things of God. Even the Jewish people, who were God's chosen ones, rejected Jesus the Messiah. Human beings live under the rule of Satan; they reside in the darkness rather than in the light; they are from below instead of from above; they love lies instead of clinging to the truth; they hate the light because the darkness seems beautiful to them. The supreme manifestation of sin is the refusal to believe in Jesus. Human beings prefer praise and glory from other humans over the love of God. Sin, then, is lawlessness, for it represents the refusal to believe in Jesus as the Christ; it is a fierce rebellion that refuses to submit to Jesus as Lord.

Acts

Acts does not reflect deeply on human sin, though this is hardly surprising, given the genre of the literature. We should also remember that what Luke says about sin should be added to what is found in Acts. In Peter's sermon on Pentecost, he exhorted his hearers to save themselves "from this crooked generation" (2:40). The wording hearkens back to Deut. 32:5 and Moses's song about Israel, where Israel is faulted for having a heart far from God. Stephen also reached back to Israel's history and found the same sins present in his day as in former generations. The people were "stiff-necked" and "uncircumcised in heart and ears" (Acts 7:51). Israel's apostasy at the incident of the golden calf revealed that the people were "stiff-necked" (7:39–41; cf. Exod. 33:3, 5; 34:9; Deut. 9:6, 13). Israel's uncircumcised heart indicates that the people are unregenerate (Lev. 26:41; cf. Deut. 10:16; Jer. 4:4; 9:25–26). Stephen argued that idolatry was characteristic of Israel's history (Acts 7:42–43). The Jews of his day had fallen prey to the same sin; they claimed to treasure God's law but failed to observe it (6:11, 13–14; 7:39, 53).

The inability to keep God's law is also featured in Peter's comments at the Jerusalem Council (15:10–11). Peter did not merely indict other people for sin; he admitted that Israel itself had been unable to keep the law. Acts 13:38–39 should be interpreted along similar lines. Instead of freeing people from sin, the Mosaic law exposes the sins that people have committed, showing that all fall short of God's favor.

The evil that pervades human life came to a climax in the crucifixion of the Lord and Messiah, Jesus of Nazareth. Stephen declared that Israel regularly persecuted and killed the prophets (7:52), and now his generation had betrayed and murdered the "Righteous One" (7:52). The apostles boldly preached to the Jews that they had sinned egregiously in crucifying the Messiah (2:23; 3:13, 17; 4:10–11; 5:30; 13:28). The Jews' persecution of the messengers of the gospel also signaled their rejection of God's salvation.

Luke in Acts argues that sin characterized Israel's history. Indeed, Israel always failed to observe the law, showing that a selfish will dominated their lives. Sin reached its apex in the crucifixion of Jesus Christ, the agent of God's salvation. Hence, all are called upon to repent and to put their trust in Jesus Christ in order to escape the coming judgment.

The Pauline Literature

The fundamental sin is the failure to praise and thank God, to glorify him as God (Rom. 1:21). Indeed, all the "sins" humans commit are a consequence of their rejection of God as God (1:24, 26, 28). Since God is not worshiped as God, he hands human beings over to sins by which their lives and society are degraded. The inclination to idolatry is manifested in human boasting. For instance, the division in Corinth over the wisdom of the ministers (1 Cor. 1:10–4:21) troubled Paul because the root problem was pride. The same concern animates Paul in addressing the "knowers" in 8:1–11:1. They despised the weak, who thought they were defiled in eating idol food. Indeed, the arrogance of the knowers led them onto the precipice: Paul warned them that they were flirting with idolatry (10:1–22). Such is scarcely surprising, for pride exalts self as God instead of worshiping and honoring the one true God. The Corinthians were also prone to boast in the gifts that they exercised, particularly those who had the flashy and spontaneous gift of speaking in other tongues (12:1–14:40).

God judges those who fail to keep his law. Jews, who were taught the law from their earliest years, tended to view the possession of the law as an indication of their favored status. But they were condemned because they failed to do what the law demands; they practiced "the very same things" that they condemned in Gentiles (Rom. 2:1; cf. 2:3). Mere possession of the law does not stave off judgment; obedience is necessary as well (2:12–29).

All people without exception have sinned. Paul does not open a crack in the door by suggesting that some have responded positively to the revelation of God evident through the created world. The wrath of God is visited upon all people (1:18), and all are without excuse (1:20; 3:4). Jews are not superior to Gentiles, for "all" are "under sin" (3:9). The OT catena in 3:10–18 drives home the conclusion. Not even one person is righteous. "All have sinned and fall short of the glory of God" (3:23).

No one can be righteous before God or receive the Spirit by "works of the law," for all fail to do what is required by the law (3:20, 28; Gal. 2:16; 3:2, 5, 10). The term "works of the law" has been the subject of considerable debate, especially with the onset of the "new perspective" on Paul. Various interpretations of "works of the law" have been proposed. Some have argued that the term refers to legalism. Those supporting the new perspective claim that the works of the law focus on the identity markers of the law, those parts of the law that separate Jews from Gentiles, such as circumcision, purity laws, and Sabbath. Both of these views should be rejected. Even though legalism existed in Judaism in Paul's day, the phrase "works of the law" should not be defined as legalism. The phrase refers to the commands of the law. Nor is it clear that works of the law concentrate on the badges of the law, such as circumcision and dietary restrictions. In Galatians, works of the law became an issue because of circumcision and food laws, but Paul widened the discussion to include the law as a whole (Gal. 2:16, 19, 21; 3:10). Comparable phrases in Jewish literature most likely refer to the entirety of the law (4QFlor 1.7; 1QS 5.21; 6.18; 4QMMT; cf. 2 Bar. 4.9; 57.2). The argument of Rom. 1:18–3:20 also supports the notion that "works of the law" refers to all the deeds required by the law. Paul did not criticize the Jews for trying to impose boundary markers on Gentiles. He found them guilty before God because they failed to keep God's commands (cf. 2:21–22). Paul slides easily and without comment from "works of the law" (3:20, 28) to "works" in general (4:2, 4, 6). The phrase "works of the law" is inapposite in reference to Abraham because he did not live under the law. In 9:11–12 Paul defines "works" as doing something good or bad. Since Paul moves straightforwardly from "works of the law" to "works" and defines "works" as the performance of something good or bad, "works of the law" refers to the actions required by the law.

The same conclusion should be drawn in regard to Gal. 3:10: "For all who rely on works of the law are under a curse; for it is written, 'Cursed be everyone who does not abide by all things written in the Book of the Law, and do them.'" The most natural way of interpreting this verse is to supply the proposition that no one keeps everything the law requires (cf. Eph. 2:9; Titus 3:5). Paul argues that works and works of the law do not and cannot save, for all have sinned. All fall short of God's standard. Even Abraham was ungodly (Rom. 4:5).

Is there any polemic against legalism relative to the law? Since the Reformation, scholars have been nearly unanimous in seeing such a polemic. The issue exploded into prominence with the publication of E. P. Sanders's *Paul and Palestinian Judaism* in 1977. Sanders forcefully argues that Judaism was not legalistic. Judaism, says Sanders, espoused not meritorious righteousness but covenantal nomism. Jews did not teach that one must weigh merits to obtain salvation; rather, all Jews were inducted into the covenant by election, by the grace of God. They must maintain their place in the covenant by keeping the law, but their entrance into the covenant was due to God's covenantal mercy, not their law keeping. The observance of the law was a response to God's grace, not an attempt to gain his grace. Sanders's work had an immediate impact and is a salutary correction of those who caricatured Judaism and failed to see anything but legalism in it. Still, it seems that Sanders overemphasized his own insight. Significant challenges to Sanders's paradigm have demonstrated that his view does not account for all the evidence in a satisfactory way. Elliott (2000) maintains that Judaism during the Second Temple period typically fore-casted the salvation not of all of Israel but only of those who kept the Torah. Avemarie (1996; 1999) has demonstrated that the two themes of election and works stand in an uneasy tension in Tannaitic literature, so that one cannot merely say that works are always subordinate to election. Gathercole (2003) has come to similar conclusions in his study of Jewish literature during the Second Temple period, showing that works played a significant role in gaining salvation (see also Das 2001: 12–69). A study of nomism in Jewish literature indicates as well that the Judaism of Paul's day was diverse, and there were streams in Jewish thinking that do not accord with Sanders's conclusions.[1]

When we examine the Pauline writings, it seems that there are indications that he engaged in a polemic against legalism. Legalism is defined here as the view that one's works are the basis of a right relation with God, so that one can boast in what one has accomplished. For example, the critique of boast-ing in the law suggests that some thought their obedience qualified them for reward (Rom. 3:27; 4:2–5, 13–16). Paul's polemic against works as the basis of salvation must be directed against those who believed that works qualified them to receive the inheritance. Otherwise, Paul's remarks are merely theo-retical and address a problem that he did not face in his ministry. It is much more probable that Paul addresses a real problem that people faced. Some apparently believed that their works were the basis of their right relationship with God, and Paul counters that claim.

Nor is the polemic against works reserved for only a few texts. Works of the law are contrasted with faith in Jesus Christ in Gal. 2:16. Indeed, in this single verse Paul places works of the law and faith in Christ against each other three times. Doing and believing are contrasted also in 3:10–12. Those who think that they can be justified by works of law are cursed because all fail to do what God requires. On the contrary, as Hab. 2:4 affirms, righteousness with God is obtained not by doing but by faith. Indeed, righteousness by doing the law and by trusting in God are specifically contrasted with one another in Gal. 3:12. The law demands works to obtain eschatological life, but faith operates on a different principle: looking to Christ for the removal of the curse (3:13–14). Hence, if the inheritance were received on the basis of keeping the law, then God's promise and faith are ruled out as the basis of God's gift (3:18). Since

---

1. See especially the essays on variegated nomism in Carson, O'Brien, and Seifrid 2001.

the inheritance is given by virtue of God's promise, it surely will be realized, and it is received by those who trust God instead of by those who work for God (cf. also Rom. 9:30–10:13; Phil. 3:2–9).

The new perspective on Paul rightly sees that Paul is concerned about the exclusion of the Gentiles from the promise (Rom. 4:9–12). Salvation is open to all without distinction, both Jews and Gentiles, by faith in Christ Jesus (1:16; 2:6–11; 3:9, 22–23, 29–30; 4:9–12, 16; Gal. 3:7–9, 14; Eph. 2:11–22). But Paul also engages in a polemic against works as the basis of salvation, for those who trust in their own works trust themselves and their own goodness rather than the grace of God.

Human beings do not merely commit sins. They also are in bondage to sin, so that sin rules over them. Paul remarks that "sin reigned in death" (Rom. 5:21). Death here refers to both spiritual death—separation from God—and physical death. Sin as a power rules over those who live in the realm of death. Before people become believers, they are slaves to sin (6:6, 16–18, 20, 22) and cannot escape its grasp on their own. Those who live under the Sinai covenant are enslaved to sin (Gal. 4:24–25). The subjugation of humans under sin is expressed in the "under" sayings in Paul. Unbelievers are "under a curse" (3:10), "under sin" (3:22), "under law" (Rom. 6:14–15; Gal. 3:23), "under a pedagogue" (Gal. 3:25 AT), "sold under sin" (Rom. 7:14), and "under the elements of the world" (Gal. 4:3 AT). For Paul, to be "under law" is equivalent to being under the old age of redemptive history, so that being under law and being under sin are equivalent realities (5:18). The law functioned as a pedagogue or babysitter (3:23, 25), supervising people until the time of the promise, until the coming of Christ. Those who live under the law are in bondage to sin (Rom. 7:14–25) and cannot carry out the requirements of God's law. They inevitably set their minds on the things of the flesh (8:5). Since they still live in the realm of the flesh, they cannot observe God's law, nor do they have any ability to please God (8:7–8). Their hostility to God cannot be removed merely through willpower.

The claim that "the power of sin is the law" (1 Cor. 15:56) functions as an epigrammatic summary of Rom. 7:7–25. The law itself is holy and good (7:12), but sin has wrapped its tentacles so tightly around human beings that it brings the law under the orbit of its influence. The law has not led to the restraint of sin; it has formed an unholy alliance with sin, so that sin has increased all the more (5:20; 7:13). All of this testifies to the impotence of human beings in Adam.

The impotence of human beings with regard to spiritual reality is communicated in a variety of ways by Paul. The natural person—that is, the person without the Spirit—does not welcome the truths of the Spirit and indeed has no capacity for such understanding (1 Cor. 2:14). The unregenerate push the truth of the gospel away from themselves, for they find their pleasure in doing evil rather than in embracing the truth (2 Thess. 2:10–12). Unbeknownst to them, Satan is their god, and he has spun a veil over the minds of unbelievers so that they fail to see the beauty of Christ (2 Cor. 4:3–4; cf. 3:14). They have been snared by the devil, and he holds them as prisoners, so they invariably do his will (2 Tim. 2:26) even as they trumpet their own freedom. The state of unbelievers is spiritual death, and the consequence of that death is sin (Eph. 2:1, 5; cf. Rom. 5:12).

Unbelievers live under the thrall of the world, the devil, and the flesh (Eph. 2:1–3). We could say that the captivity is sociological, spiritual, and psychological. It is sociological in that unbelievers follow the dictates and fashions of the world. It is spiritual in that the devil works in their hearts to bring about disobedience. It is psychological in that the unregenerate follow the desires of the flesh. Unbelievers, whenever possible, follow the desires of their hearts, and yet this so-called freedom to indulge in desires is nothing other than slavery.

All are born into the world as "children of wrath" (2:3), destined for destruction. Those who do not belong to Jesus will face the coming wrath (1 Thess. 1:10; 5:9). They live in spiritual darkness (Eph. 5:8; Col. 1:13; 1 Thess. 5:4–5), oblivious to the truth that shines in Christ (Eph. 4:17). Their thinking about reality is twisted (4:17), so that they have become fools instead of wise (Rom. 1:21–23). Their intellectual dullness is due to their being cut off from the life of God, and the consequence is lives given over to evil (Eph. 4:18–19). They serve idols rather than believing in and obeying the true and living God (1 Thess. 1:9), so that they are enslaved to false gods (Gal. 4:8). Paul does not envision anyone inhabiting a neutral place. One is aligned with righteousness or lawlessness, light or darkness, Christ or Satan, God's temple or idols (2 Cor. 6:14–16). Gentiles who do not trust in Christ are separated from Israel and have no portion in God's covenant promises. Since they do not know Christ, they are without hope and separated from God (Eph. 2:12).

The alienation of human beings from God is often expressed by Paul with the term "flesh" (sarx). The word "flesh" is used in a variety of ways by Paul. It denotes human beings (e.g., Rom. 3:20; Gal. 2:16), life in the body (e.g., 1 Cor. 15:39; Gal. 2:20; Phil. 1:22, 24), or descent, kinship, and earthly relationships (Rom. 1:3; 9:5; Eph. 6:5). But Paul uses the term distinctively and often to refer to what people are in Adam. Those who are spiritually dead are "in the flesh." "Flesh" should be understood in redemptive-historical categories instead of ontologically. Unbelievers are in the flesh because they are in Adam (Rom. 5:12–19; 7:5; 8:5–8; Col. 2:13; cf. Eph. 2:11), and hence they belong to "the present evil age" (Gal. 1:4) instead of the one to come.

All people enter the world as sinners because they are sons and daughters of Adam. The two central characters in human history are Adam and Christ. Sin entered the world through Adam, and as a consequence of sin, death reigned over all (Rom. 5:12). The consequences of Adam's sin are relayed with five statements in 5:15–19: (1) death entered the world through his one trespass; (2) his one sin brought condemnation; (3) his one sin inaugurated the reign of death; (4) his one trespass resulted in condemnation for all people; (5) his disobedience led to the many becoming sinners. The consequences of Adam's sin are death, sin, and condemnation. Paul does not specifically explain how Adam's sin led to these consequences for all. It seems most likely that he views Adam as the covenantal head for humanity, just as Christ is the covenantal head for the new humanity. In any case, human beings do not enter the world suspended neutrally between good and evil. As sons and daughters of Adam, they are spring-loaded to do evil (cf. 1 Cor. 15:21–22).

Paul's theology of sin is multifaceted and profound. The root sin is the failure to thank and glorify God for his goodness—the worship of the creature rather than the Creator. The sinfulness of human beings manifests itself in coveting and in boasting: in coveting because whatever human beings desire most is their god, and in boasting because human beings take incredible pride in what they have accomplished. Sin can also be measured objectively and is universal. In other words, all human beings everywhere fail to do what God requires. They violate his written law or the law inscribed upon their hearts. The "works of the law" cannot bring salvation, for no one carries out what the law demands. Instead of curbing sin, the law reveals sin. Indeed, the remarkable subtlety of sin comes to the forefront in that sinners who fail to keep God's law become proud of their so-called morality and obedience and think it to be sufficient to merit salvation. The problem with human beings is not superficial, for the human race is enslaved to sin, and both sin and death rule over all. Human beings, after all, are born into the world as sons and daughters of Adam: by virtue of their union with Adam, they are under the reign of sin and death and are condemned before God.

Hebrews

When we examine the General or Catholic Epistles and Revelation, we do not find an in-depth discussion on human sin, nor do any of the writers contemplate intensely the state of human beings before salvation. It is obvious from Hebrews that sin consists in unbelief and disobedience (e.g., 3:12, 18; 4:2–3, 6, 11). The apostasy that the author warns the readers against is described in the following ways: hardening of the heart (3:8), testing God (3:9), going astray (3:10), dullness of hearing (5:11; 6:12), falling away (6:6), deliberate sin (10:26), spurning God's Son, profaning the blood of the covenant, and outraging the Spirit of grace (10:29), and refusing and rejecting what God says (12:25).

The author speaks of the "dead works" of unbelievers (6:1; 9:14). This expression refers to the evil deeds of unbelievers that lead to death. The author of Hebrews, drawing on the OT, believes that human beings suffer from guilt because of sin and need to be forgiven. The author also teaches that Jesus frees believers from slavery to and fear of death (2:14–15). Death, then, appears to be a consequence of sin, and Jesus' high priestly ministry serves as the propitiation for sins that bring death (2:14–18).

James

James is replete with exhortations against sin, but the author does not reflect specifically on why believers need the saving work of God. James 1:13–15 opens an interesting window on sin. No one can blame God for sin, as if God actually seduces people so that they sin. Sin finds its origin in human desires that lure and entice people to wrongdoing. Human beings have various desires, and if they capitulate to evil desires, they sin, and sin in turn leads to death. Further, sin is the portion of all people, without exception, for "we all stumble in many ways" (3:2). The "we all" in this context includes believers, even those who teach and lead the church. Even a single sin marks one out as a transgressor (2:10). Here James sounds remarkably similar to Paul. No one can claim to be righteous for refraining from adultery while at the same time violating another commandment. Any infraction identifies one as a lawbreaker. James also describes sin as spiritual adultery (4:4), drawing on the OT, where Israel's forsaking of God is nothing less than spiritual harlotry. Sin, in other words, is treachery in that people long for the favor and approbation of the world rather than friendship with God. Sin is not merely the doing of evil; it is fundamentally personal, involving the rejection of God's lordship over one's life.

1 Peter

The unbelief of unconverted Gentiles is designated as "ignorance" (1:14). Such ignorance is not restricted to the intellectual realm; it also manifests itself in evil behavior that finds its roots in desires contrary to God's will. Their lives were characterized by "futile ways inherited from your forefathers" (1:18). Peter likely has in view the idolatry that was typical among Gentiles, passed on from generation to generation. Their idolatry was futile and vain in that it separated people from the true and living God. The Gentile past of the readers is also communicated in 4:2–4. Those who do not know God live for human passions and desires. Unbelievers are those who refuse to obey the call of the gospel (2:8; 4:17; cf. 3:20). They are lost and thus need to be won to faith in Christ (3:1). They need forgiveness of sins through the death of Jesus Christ (2:24). Another way of putting it is that all people are born into the world sick, and thus they need the healing work that comes from the forgiveness of their sins. Before people hear the gospel, they are straying from God and wandering from the truth (2:25; cf. Isa. 53:6). They are unrighteous and separated from

God, and the only way they can be brought to God is through the death of Jesus Christ (1 Pet. 3:18).

2 Peter and Jude

Jude wrote to counteract intruders who have entered the church (or churches), encouraging and warning believers to resist their influence. Even though the letter is brief, sin plays a large role because condemnation of the interlopers takes center stage. Jude emphasizes throughout that sin leads to final judgment. He uses the term "ungodly" (*asebeia* word group) to depict the sin of the false teachers who have had such an adverse influence (4, 15, 18). The term indicates a refusal to submit to God's lordship, and it manifests itself in Jude in a libertine lifestyle, particularly in terms of sexual sin (4, 6–8). Unbelievers are worldly people (19) who think that they belong to the people of God. The term "worldly people" (*psychikoi*) recalls 1 Cor. 2:14, where Paul says that natural persons do not and cannot welcome the teaching of the Spirit because they lack the Spirit. So too, here in Jude the intruders are separated from God and live within the realm of this world because they are bereft of the Spirit.

In many respects, 2 Peter is similar to Jude because it too is written in response to false teachers, though in this case the false teachers seem to have come from within the community (2:1). Peter, like Jude, emphasizes the wickedness of the false teachers and their certain judgment (see esp. 2 Pet. 2). Perhaps they interpreted the Pauline gospel so that it became a platform for libertinism (3:15–16; cf. 2:2, 7, 10, 12–14, 18–19). Human beings have sinned before God, and so they need to be cleansed of sin to receive forgiveness (1:9). The natural state of human beings is expressed in the phrase "the corruption that is in the world because of sinful desire" (1:4). Believers have escaped the "corruption" (1:4) or "defilements" (2:20) of the world in coming to know Jesus Christ. Such corruption or defilement is rooted in a desire for what is evil. Human beings naturally incline toward and choose to carry out actions that are wicked. The use of the word "escape" (*apopheugō*; 1:4; 2:20) implies that formerly believers were held captive by corruption and sin. This is confirmed by 2:19, where unbelievers are said to be "slaves of corruption." They trumpet their freedom with great fanfare, but apart from Jesus Christ they cannot escape the clutches of sin. Sin is also intensely personal in that it manifests itself in the denial of Jesus Christ as Master and Lord (2:1). Such a denial applies especially to those who claim to be believers and who participate in the Christian community.

Revelation

Revelation often proclaims God's judgment against those who sin and fail to repent (e.g., 2:5, 16, 21; 3:3; 9:20–21; 16:8–9). Human beings will face God's

wrath unless they turn from their evil ways. The author obviously is not san-
guine about human goodness, nor is he blind to the corruption that is endemic
to human society and governmental structures. Human beings are sinners, and
they need to be freed from their sin to enter the heavenly city (1:5; 14:4). Sin
is portrayed as a filth that defiles and destroys human beings (22:11). Those
who are unclean and who practice evil will not be allowed to enter (21:27)
unless they wash their robes. God will judge people on the last day according to their works (20:11–15; 22:12, 15). Those who indulge in falsehood and
idolatry and plunge into sin will be condemned (22:15).

According to Revelation, the fundamental evil of human beings is idolatry.
Human beings do not want to admit that they are poor, blind, and naked (3:17),
and the context here indicates that even believers are tempted to indulge in illu-
sions about their own goodness or lack thereof. Unbelievers cling to their idols
and evil deeds even when judgment strikes (9:20–21), even cursing God when
judgment comes and stubbornly refusing to repent (16:9). They blaspheme
and revile God because they hate him (13:6). They give their allegiance instead
to the beast: the Roman emperor and empire with all its glory and promise
of financial prosperity. Hence, they worship the beast instead of the one true
and living God (13:8, 12, 15). They curse God because his judgments intervene
and prevent the carrying out of their own schemes (16:11). They demonstrate
their hostility to God by making war with the Lamb (17:14; 19:11–21). Hence,
they slay believers, who belong to the Lamb (16:6; 17:6; 19:2). They long for
the riches of Rome and are grieved when Rome is judged (18:7, 9, 11–15, 19).
They neither give glory to God (16:11) nor worship him (14:7).

Conclusion

When we consider the entirety of the NT, we see that sin is described in a variety of ways, communicating thereby the complexity and fullness of what is
involved. Sin often is defined as the failure to keep what God has commanded,
particularly in the Mosaic law. This is a particular focus of Paul, though we see
the same theme in Acts and James. Both Paul and James maintain that only
complete and perfect obedience constitutes true obedience. Any infraction
marks one out as a lawbreaker. John sums up the message of the NT when he
says that "sin is lawlessness" (1 John 3:4). Those who sin stand guilty before
God and are deserving of his judgment. Indeed, God's wrath is poured out
on those who are disobedient and guilty before him.

The heart of sin is the failure to worship, praise, and thank God (Rom.
1:21). It involves the worship of the creature rather than the Creator. John
describes the same reality as loving the honor and praise of human beings
more than the honor and praise of God (John 5:44). The root sin is idolatry,
and idolatry manifests itself in human boasting and pride. Legalism is another

species of this same sin, for religious persons think that they are pleasing to God because of their virtue (even though they are not nearly as virtuous as they think). Hence, religion becomes the vehicle for self-congratulation and self-absorption rather than the worship of God. Depending on one's own works is folly, for it looks to the capability of human beings.

All human beings enter the world as sinners and condemned because they are sons and daughters of Adam (Rom. 5:12–19). Sin blinds human beings to their own wickedness and tricks people into thinking that they are righteous. Sin is not merely a matter of peccadilloes or mistakes. Human beings are fiercely rebellious and stubborn, which is captured in the metaphor of being stiff-necked. The sin of human beings is manifested supremely in the crucifixion of Jesus of Nazareth. All enter into the world spiritually dead toward God and heading toward physical death and judgment. By nature, humans are children of wrath and are rotten trees. From birth, they are under the dominion of the old age of the flesh instead of the new age of the Spirit. They are a brood of vipers instead of children of God.

Pastoral Reflection

The power and depth of sin function as the backdrop to God's saving promises, for such promises represent astonishing good news, given the devastation that sin inflicts on human beings. With the coming of Jesus Christ, the era of salvation and deliverance has dawned; with the death and resurrection of Jesus, the tyranny of sin and death has ended. As believers we continue to struggle with sin, so there is no room for triumphalism in our lives. A recognition of our sin keeps us humble, and hence our hearts resonate with Martin Luther when he said on his deathbed, "We are beggars. This is true." But believers in Christ face death with confidence, for they are assured of a future resurrection and complete victory over sin because of their union with Christ.

10

Faith and Obedience

———

In the previous chapter, we saw that human beings as sons and daughters of Adam refuse to esteem God as God and to give him thanks and praise. They long for autonomy rather than theonomy. In this chapter, we consider what human beings need to do to be delivered from this age of sin and death. The response expected of human beings can be summarized under the terms "faith" and "obedience." We shall see that these terms summarize well the various NT writings.

The Synoptic Gospels

In order to be saved, believers must recognize their desperate need for God and his righteousness. Those who are aware of their poverty in spirit receive the blessing of the kingdom (Matt. 5:3). Those who thirst for righteousness will be satisfied with the righteousness that comes from God himself (5:6). Faith recognizes that human beings are spiritually sick and need a physician for healing: human beings lack righteousness, and such righteousness will come only from God himself (9:12–13; Mark 2:17; Luke 5:31–32). Faith seeks God as its prime good, and such seeking of God is not a onetime event but rather a lifetime pattern of asking, seeking, and knocking (Matt. 7:7–8; Luke 11:9–10).

Faith is illustrated in the account of the centurion. He was convinced of the power of Jesus' word to effect a new reality. The centurion's faith exceeded what Jesus had found in Israel (Matt. 8:10; Luke 7:9). Nor can this faith be limited merely to physical healing, for Jesus, according to Matthew, proceeds to say that Gentiles will enjoy the kingdom banquet, while many of those from Israel will be excluded (Matt. 8:11–12). Hence, the faith that brought healing was also evidence of saving faith in Jesus. The woman suffering from a hemorrhage for twelve years was convinced that touching the hem of Jesus' robe would bring healing. Jesus affirmed that her "faith has saved" her (9:22 AT). Again, this faith is not restricted to physical healing, though certainly it is the case that faith brought healing. The Synoptics use the term "saved" because physical healing here functions as an emblem for spiritual healing. Hence, in both Mark (5:34) and Luke (7:50), Jesus immediately adds the words "Go in peace," signifying a new relation to God.

The link between physical healing and eschatological salvation should not be pressed in every case. The story of the healing of the paralytic, however, illustrates that such a theme is present here as well (Matt. 9:2–8). Jesus healed when he saw the faith of those who took so much trouble to bring the paralytic to Jesus. The healing, however, becomes an emblem for the forgiveness of sins, and it seems that such forgiveness is given in response to faith.

The healing of the blind should be interpreted along the same lines. In Matthew's Gospel, Jesus healed the blind men on account of their faith, for they believed that Jesus could perform the miracle (9:28–30). In the story about Bartimaeus, Jesus was acclaimed as David's son, and he declares, "Your faith has saved you" (Mark 10:52 AT; Luke 18:42), pointing to a deeper reality than the recovery of physical sight. Each account emphasizes that the healing was not merely physical. The blind man followed Jesus to Jerusalem. He was a disciple who was willing to follow Jesus as he went to the cross. The same theme is evident in the account of the ten lepers who were healed by Jesus (Luke 17:11–19). Only the Samaritan returned and voiced thanks and praise to God, displaying his worship of Jesus. His physical healing, the praise in his heart, and his worship of Jesus point to a greater reality. Thus Jesus declared, "Your faith has saved you" (17:19 AT).

The fundamental requirement given to Jesus' followers is faith. This is summarized in his words to Jairus: "Do not fear, only believe" (Mark 5:36). What astonished Jesus in Nazareth was that those in his own hometown lacked faith (Matt. 13:53–58). Jesus reproached the Jews because they were unbelieving (17:17). The demon was expelled from the Syrophoenician woman's daughter because of the woman's persistent faith in Jesus (15:22–29). Luke emphasizes the faith of the sinful woman who intruded upon the feast at Simon's house (7:36–50). She manifested her love for Jesus by washing his feet, drying his feet with her hair, and anointing them with ointment. Her love for Jesus flowed from the recognition that her sins had been forgiven. On the basis of 7:47, some have argued that she was forgiven *because* of her love. But the parable of the two debtors suggests otherwise, since it is the one who was forgiven a great debt who loved much, indicating that love is the consequence of forgiveness. The story concludes with Jesus saying, "Your faith has saved you; go in peace" (7:50). The woman was not saved on the basis of her love; she was saved because she trusted in Jesus for the forgiveness of her sins, and as a result of that forgiveness, she overflowed in love for Jesus.

The story of the Pharisee and tax collector should be interpreted similarly, even though the word "faith" does not appear in the account (18:9–14). The Pharisee clearly thinks that he is "justified" (18:14) before God because of his devotion to righteousness, for he refrains from theft and sexual sin and lives justly. Moreover, he goes beyond the call of duty by fasting and paying tithes on items that are not even required by the law. The tax collector, on the other hand, puts his trust in God for forgiveness, imploring God for mercy. This account is remarkable because it clearly shows Jesus speaking against the notion that human beings can gain God's forgiveness on the basis of their works. It also suggests that some in Judaism believed that righteousness could be secured through works. Otherwise, the parable would be addressing a problem with which no one struggled! Further, the Pauline teaching on justification is anticipated in this text, for Luke clearly implies that the tax collector is right with God because of his faith in God.

In the Synoptic Gospels, faith can never be separated from a new way of life, a new obedience in the lives of Jesus' followers. This is illustrated in Mark 1:15: "Repent and believe in the gospel." Genuine belief does not exist without repentance (cf. Matt. 4:17), and indeed all repentance flows from faith. The relationship between faith and repentance is illustrated well in Jesus' insistence that people turn and become like children (Matt. 18:3–4; cf. 19:14). Each of the Synoptic Gospels often stresses the new kind of life that is necessary to enter the kingdom. Such statements, however, do not contradict the truth that faith saves rather than works. The changed life of disciples is a fruit of faith and the result of faith. Those who follow Jesus in discipleship do so because they trust in him. The obedience of believers should never be construed as if it were independent of faith. On the other hand, it is unthinkable that the new relationship to Jesus would be anything less than transforming.

Matthew's emphasis on obedience illustrates the point being made. Those who do God's will are part of the family of God (12:46–50). In the parable of the soils, only those who bear fruit truly belong to God (13:18–23). The rich ruler would be saved only if he gave up all his possessions and followed Jesus in discipleship (19:21). Those who refuse to take up their cross and follow Jesus but instead try to preserve their own lives will be ruined (16:24–26). Only those who follow Jesus in radical discipleship will be saved on the last day. They must be willing to sacrifice comfortable homes and cut family ties for the sake of following Jesus (8:18–22). Those who love family members more than Jesus are unworthy of him, for those who become Jesus' disciples must be prepared to die for his sake (10:37–39).

Only good trees that produce good fruit will be spared on the day of judgment, for people will be judged by every word uttered (12:33–37). Those who obstinately refuse to forgive others will not be forgiven by God on the day of judgment (6:14–15; 18:21–35). Anything that causes people to stumble or fall away must be removed from their lives. Jesus uses hyperbolic language of cutting off a foot or hand or gouging out an eye (5:29–30; 18:8–9) to portray the radical steps that must be taken to avoid apostasy. Both anger (5:21–26) and lust (5:27–28) must be conquered by believers, and they cannot be allowed to take root in the hearts of Jesus' disciples. Jesus' true disciples are not those who profess to do the Father's will (i.e., the Pharisees), but rather those who actually carry out the Father's will by repenting. Faithful slaves do what the master commands and will be duly rewarded, but unfaithful slaves will be excluded from the kingdom and will weep and gnash their teeth (24:45–51; cf. 25:1–13).

In the parable of the talents, those who did the master's bidding were rewarded, but the one who out of laziness did nothing and hid his talent was thrown into the outer darkness, where there is "weeping and gnashing of the teeth" (25:14–30). Jesus' judgment of the sheep and the goats is in accordance with what they have done, whether they have shown mercy and love to believers: "one of the least of these" (25:45). Again, the issue is not merely a matter of rewards disconnected from eternal life, for the unrighteous "will go away into eternal punishment, but the righteous into eternal life" (25:46).

Jesus' radical call to his disciples is evident throughout Matthew. On the final day people must enter the narrow gate to be saved (7:13–14). The narrow gate for Matthew clearly refers to obedience: the changed life demanded of Jesus' disciples. The false prophets will not receive a reward, for they are not good trees (7:15–20). Instead of producing good fruit, their lives are wicked and fail to conform to God's will. Simply calling on Jesus as Lord does not qualify one for the kingdom (7:21–23). People may even do miracles, exorcise demons, and utter prophecies yet still be excluded from the kingdom because of their failure to do God's will. Only those who build securely on the foundation will survive the storm of the final judgment (7:24–27). Building on the foundation, in this context in Matthew, clearly means to hear and do Jesus' words.

Some conclude that Matthew's emphasis on obedience contradicts the Pauline gospel, where righteousness is obtained by faith rather than through works. Matthew certainly emphasizes the new life of obedience that is required to enter the kingdom of heaven. Still, we should not exaggerate the polarity between Matthew and Paul. Matthew recognizes that human beings are poor in spirit (5:3); only those who recognize their poverty of spirit will receive the power of the kingdom. In other words, people need the power of the kingdom to live in the new way demanded by Jesus. The new life that is needed is possible only with God and cannot be conjured up through human effort (19:26). The call to obedience is nothing less than radical commitment to Jesus, so that disciples are willing to follow him and to prize him above everything. The call to follow Jesus and to obedience should not be interpreted as if perfection were necessary to obtain the final reward. God demands perfection (5:48), but forgiveness is the last word for those who repent. The prayer that Jesus taught his disciples recognizes the need to ask for forgiveness of sins (6:12), presumably every day. The ultimate basis for the forgiveness of sins is the death of Jesus, which inaugurates the new covenant (26:28). Obedience is required to enter the kingdom, even to the end of one's life: "But the one who endures to the end will be saved" (10:22; 24:13). Those who acknowledge Jesus will be acknowledged before God, but those who deny him will be rejected (10:32–33). The obedience demanded in Matthew reveals whether one treasures Jesus above all else. Further, such obedience is the fruit of faith. It is not the case that obedience is conceived of as the basis for entrance into the kingdom; Jesus' death is the only basis for the forgiveness of sins, but those who trust Jesus demonstrate such faith by a new way of life.

The Johannine Literature

The Gospel of John uses the verb "believe" (*pisteuō*) ninety-eight times, indicating the centrality of the theme. Perhaps the use of the verb places the emphasis on believing as an action, excluding any notion of a passive faith. The importance of believing is indicated by the purpose of the Gospel as stated in 20:31. Such a concluding statement hardly surprises, for John often emphasizes that those who believe in Jesus receive eternal life (3:15–16, 18, 36; 6:40, 47), and that those who put their trust in Jesus will never die (11:25–26). Conversely, those who fail to believe in him will face death because of their sins (8:24).

John's use of "believe" indicates that human beings receive eternal life by believing. Eternal life is not obtained by working for God; human beings cannot "atone" for their evil. Jesus Christ has come into the world as the Lamb of God to remove sin (1:29). The "work" that God requires, then, is contrary to human expectations. "This is the work of God, that you believe in him who he has sent" (6:29).

In John, belief is not a vague entity, as if an amorphous faith qualifies one for eternal life. Saving faith is radically Christ centered. One must believe in Jesus' name (1:12) and trust that God's love has been manifested in the giving of Jesus (3:16–18; cf. 16:27, 30; 17:8, 21). Alternatively, John can say that one must believe in the Father (5:23–24), but it is precisely the Father who sent Jesus (5:37–38; 12:44). Those who refuse to confess Jesus as "I am" will perish in sin (8:24 AT; cf. 13:19). A blind man put his faith in Jesus as the "Son of

Man" (9:35). Genuine disciples confess with Martha, "I believe that you are the Christ, the Son of God, who is coming into the world" (11:27). The content of saving faith is captured best by the purpose statement in John's Gospel, which affirms that Jesus did his signs so that people would acknowledge him as the Messiah and the Son of God, and as a result enjoy eternal life (20:31).

The centrality of faith in Jesus is evident also in 1 John. God's command is "that we believe in the name of his Son Jesus Christ" (3:23). Those who have been born of God believe "that Jesus is the Christ" (5:1). Those who believe "that Jesus is the Son of God" overcome the world (5:5; cf. 5:4). If one fails to believe that Jesus is God's Son, then one dismisses God's testimony as a lie (5:10). The purpose statement of John's First Letter is remarkably similar to the purpose statement in the Gospel (cf. 5:13). For John, the faith that saves is faith in Jesus as the Son of God, as the Messiah who has come in the flesh (2:22–23).

The dynamism of faith is expressed through many other terms in John, so that it is clear that faith is living and active. Faith receives, obeys, drinks, hears, comes, beholds, eats, abides, goes, knows, sees, follows, enters, hates, loves, and more.

Several sensory metaphors convey what it means to believe in Jesus—for example, hearing, seeing, drinking, and eating. In some contexts in John, the word "hear" (*akouō*) refers to an "effective" hearing, so that the one who hears lives. Those who are spiritually dead yet "hear the voice of the Son of God . . . will live" (5:25). Not all "hear" Jesus' voice in this way, for this kind of hearing is a believing hearing. Those who have "heard and learned from the Father," therefore, certainly will come to Jesus (6:45; cf. Isa. 54:13). Such hearing in this instance inevitably leads to "coming" and believing in Jesus, whereas those who do not belong to Jesus cannot "hear" (*akouō*) his difficult teaching (John 6:60; 8:43). Jesus declares, "Whoever is of God hears the words of God. The reason why you do not hear them is that you are not of God" (8:47). Jesus' sheep hear his voice because they belong to his flock, and they flee from the voice of strangers (10:3, 5, 8, 27). Jesus came to witness to the truth, and "everyone who is of the truth listens to my voice" (18:37).

Faith can also be described as "seeing" Jesus, as perceiving him for who he really is. The one who "sees" (*theōreō*) Jesus also "sees" the Father, who sent him (John 12:45). Probably the verb "seeing" in 6:40 is synonymous with "believing," so that genuine faith entails seeing who Jesus is. The account of the blind man in John 9 plays off on the idea that those who believe see who Jesus truly is. The blind man saw that Jesus is the Son of Man, but the Pharisees who claimed to have spiritual sight and were unwilling to admit to their blindness were enveloped in darkness (9:35–41).

The vitality of faith is communicated through the sensory actions of drinking and eating. Those who drink the water given by Jesus will slake their thirst forever. Those who believe in Jesus will find that their thirst is satisfied (6:35).

Anyone who is parched should come to Jesus and drink freely (7:37–38). Indeed, people must drink Jesus' blood to obtain life (6:54, 56); that is, people must believe in Jesus as the crucified Lord to gain life. The image of drinking blood would be especially scandalous to Jews, given the OT prohibition against consuming blood. It emphasizes that the death of Jesus must be embraced wholly and without reservation by those who are saved.

The same truth is conveyed by the metaphor of eating. The verbs *esthiō* and *trōgō* are used to signify eating Jesus' flesh (6:50, 53, 54, 56, 57, 58). All the references to eating are found in John 6, where Jesus declares that he is the bread of life. The image of eating is another way to describe the faith that leads to life (6:29, 35, 36, 40, 47, 64, 69). One must eat of Jesus as the bread of heaven in order to escape death (6:50). John particularly emphasizes that people must "eat" Jesus' flesh to live, which is a clear reference to the cross (6:51). Hence, Jesus emphasizes that one must eat his flesh and drink his blood in order to enjoy eternal life (6:53–54, 56–58). Faith is not a mere acceptance of the notion that Jesus died; it is the active ingesting of that truth, so that believing in Jesus' death is one's food and drink. Those who believe feed on Jesus' death as the very source of their life.

The active nature of faith is conveyed by the verb "receive" (*lambanō*). The Jews did not "receive" (*paralambanō*) Jesus, but those who "receive" (*lambanō*) become God's children (1:11–12). The religious leaders did not receive Jesus, even though he came in the name of the Father (5:43). Conversely, those who received Jesus also received the Father (13:20). The disciples' reception of Jesus is evident in that they have received and welcomed his words (17:8).

Coming to faith is also described as coming to know God and Jesus Christ. Knowing is conveyed by the verbs *oida* and, especially, *ginōskō*. The use of both verbs reflects John's love for synonyms. The centrality of knowing is expressed clearly in 17:3: "And this is eternal life, that they may know you the only true God, and Jesus Christ whom you have sent." Believers "know" Jesus as God's holy one (6:69). They "know that this is indeed the Savior of the world" (4:42). Those who are willing to do the Father's bidding will know whether Jesus is truly from God (7:17; cf. 17:8, 25). The world is condemned for not knowing Jesus (1:10) or the Father (7:28; 8:19). Knowing the truth is what liberates human beings, and it is the Son himself who is the truth that sets people free (8:32, 36). Jesus' sheep know him and follow him because they know his voice (10:4–5, 14). Those who know Jesus also know the Father (14:7), but those who persecute believers reveal that they have not known the Son or the Father (8:55; 16:3; cf. 17:25).

Those who believe in Jesus "come" (*erchomai*) to him for life. Unbelief is manifested in the refusal to come to Jesus to receive life (5:40). Those who practice evil shrink from the light and refuse to come to it in order to spare themselves humiliation, whereas those who practice truth "come to the light" so that it is evident that the good work done in them is from God (3:20–21).

The correlation between "coming" and "believing" is evident in 6:35, for those who "come" to Jesus will satisfy their hunger, and those who "believe" in Jesus will slake their thirst. Jesus invites all who thirst to come to him (7:37). Coming to Jesus is essential because Jesus teaches in no uncertain terms that "no one comes to the Father" except through him, for he is "the way, and the truth, and the life" (14:6). Coming to Jesus portrays the action of those who believe, but such coming can be ascribed only to the grace of God because all those whom the Father has granted to the Son certainly will come to Jesus (6:37). Indeed, those who are not drawn by the Father cannot come to Jesus (6:44), whereas those who have been taught by God will come (6:45). It is not as if some desire to come but God prevents them from doing so; rather, unless one is drawn by the Father, one has no inclination to come to Jesus for life. Hence, Jesus says, "No one can come to me unless it is granted him by the Father" (John 6:65). Such coming to Jesus is alternatively described as being "drawn" (*helkō*) by the Father to Jesus (6:44; 12:32).

Genuine faith moves toward Jesus. This is evident also in John 6. Many of Jesus' disciples took offense at his teaching and ceased to follow him (6:66–69). Jesus asked the Twelve if they wished to depart from him as well. Peter replied, "Lord, to whom shall we go? You have the words of eternal life" (6:68). Peter and the other disciples have "gone" (*aperchomai*) to find life. Faith "enters" (*eiserchomai*) into the pastures of salvation and trusts in Jesus as the good shepherd (10:9). Faith "follows" (*akoloutheō*) Jesus just as sheep follow their shepherd (10:4, 27), but Jesus' disciples run from strangers and refuse to follow false shepherds (10:5). Because Jesus is the light of the world, those who "follow" him will escape the darkness and enjoy "the light of life" (8:12). Disciples of Jesus must be willing to give up their entire lives to him and lose their lives in order to gain them for eternal life (12:25). This kind of surrender is what it means to "follow" Jesus (12:26). Jesus summons disciples to "follow" him at both the beginning and the end of John's Gospel (1:43 [cf. 1:37]; 21:19, 22), so that the call to follow Jesus functions as bookends for the material within.

Those who believe in Jesus "abide" (*menō*) in him. "Eating" and "drinking" are vivid ways of saying that one "believes" in Jesus, and those who eat Jesus' flesh and drink his blood "abide" in him (6:56). Those who "remain" (*menō*) in his word are genuine disciples. Genuine faith is clearly persevering faith, a faith in which one continues to trust in Jesus. In John 15, remaining in Jesus is compared to abiding in a vine, so that just as one cannot bear fruit apart from staying connected to a vine, neither can disciples bear fruit unless they remain in Jesus (15:4–6). As in 8:31, remaining in Jesus means that disciples continue in his teaching (15:7). Those who do not continue to abide will be destroyed forever because they will be severed from the vine (15:6). Remaining in Jesus is expressed concretely by obeying his commands (15:10; cf. 15:16).

The converse of believing in the Son is to "disobey" (*apeitheō*) him (3:36). Only those who "hate" their lives will save them on the last day (12:25). Genuine love for Jesus is expressed in keeping his word and obeying his commands (14:15, 21, 23–24). Jesus declares that his disciples have kept his word (17:6). Those who keep Jesus' words will conquer death (8:51). Jesus' supreme command is that disciples love one another (13:34–35; 15:12–17), and this love is to be patterned after Jesus' self-giving love for the disciples, his laying down of his life for his sheep.

According to John, mere belief does not save. Many put their faith in Jesus because of the remarkable signs that he was doing (2:23). However, Jesus did not entrust himself to such people, for he knew what was in their hearts, discerning that they did not truly grasp that his signs pointed to the necessity of faith in him (2:24–25). John observes that many "believed" in Jesus during the Feast of Tabernacles (8:30). As the narrative unfolds, however, it becomes clear that their purported faith in Jesus was not an abiding faith, for by the end of the story (8:59), they desired to kill Jesus! The same kind of inadequate belief is reflected in 12:42–43. Many of the authorities "believed in" Jesus, and yet they refused to acknowledge him openly because they did not want to face the wrath of the Pharisees and be expelled from the synagogues. Such "faith" is not saving faith, since it does not publicly embrace Jesus, and since those who hide their faith "save" their lives instead of "losing" them for Jesus' sake (12:25).

The Johannine Epistles repeat many of the themes noted in John's Gospel, indicating that saving faith is a transforming faith, not a merely passive belief. Those who claim, therefore, to have "fellowship" with God—to be members of his people (1 John 1:3, 6–7)—must live in accord with their profession. Only those who live in the light, in a way that pleases God, truly belong to him. God's children are those who "[walk] in the truth" (2 John 4; 3 John 3–4). Those who claim to "know" Christ but fail to obey his commands reveal that they do not truly know him (1 John 2:3–6). We might think that John advocates perfectionism, but he clarifies that it is those who claim to be without sin altogether who are outside the circle of God's people (1:8, 10). The secessionists from the church apparently were convinced that they were completely free from sin (1:8, 10). The rationale for their position is lost to us because John does not bother to explicate it in his letter, presumably because his readers knew their position all too well. Believers are devoted to goodness rather than to evil; when they sin, they freely acknowledge it (1:9).

The change in the lives of believers is evident because they love brothers and sisters in the community of faith (2:7–11; 3:11–15; 4:7–16). The evidence that new life has commenced, that believers "have passed out of death into life," is love for fellow believers (3:14). Such love expresses itself concretely in meeting the needs for food and shelter that other believers have (3:17–18). Nor can anyone claim genuine love for God without keeping his commands (5:3).

First John regularly refers to those who are born of God and the consequences of this new life. Those who are truly born of God live righteous lives (2:29). John declares: "Those who have been born of God do not sin" (3:9).[2] "We know that those who are born of God do not sin" (5:18). "No one who abides in him sins" (3:6). "Everyone who does what is right is righteous" (3:7). "Everyone who commits sin is a child of the devil" (3:8). "All who do not do what is right are not from God" (3:10). These statements have been interpreted in various ways: (1) John teaches that Christians are perfect, but it is incorrect to say that John teaches that Christians can live perfect lives, for he has already stated that it is those who are convinced that they are without sin who are deceived (1:8, 10). (2) Others have suggested that John refers to an elite group of Christians who have reached a special status in which they no longer sin. However, such a reading would seem to fit with the theology of the secessionists, who claimed to be a cut above the believers in the Johannine churches. Moreover, the text does not restrict godly living to a special group of Christians but rather claims that all believers without exception—all those born of God—do not sin. Hence, a spiritual elite cannot be in view here. (3) Others suggest that only willful and deliberate sins are intended, but there is no evidence in the text that only a special category of sins is in view. (4) An intriguing suggestion is that John refers to the sin unto death (5:16–17). Believers, therefore, are spared from the sin that leads to apostasy. Despite the truth in this viewpoint, we lack evidence that John confines himself only to apostasy. He appears to refer to sin in general.

Another view (5) is that believers do not sin as long as they are abiding in Christ. This solution might work if the verse on abiding were the only one, but it hardly explains the claim that those who are born of God do not sin. The text does not say that those who have new life only desist from sinning when they are abiding; it insists that freedom from sin marks out all those who are regenerated. (6) It has also been suggested that John refers to an ideal that is not always realized, but such a view seems to undermine John's argument, for then the secessionists could be placed in the category of those who do not always attain the ideal. John, however, excludes them from new life because of their disobedience. (7) The best solution, therefore, is that John speaks of the pattern and direction of one's life. The lives of believers are marked out by an orientation toward goodness and obedience. Many scholars have defended this view by noting the present tense of the verbs in 3:4–10, though scholarship has questioned whether such weight can be assigned to the verbal tense. Even if the present tense does not establish this view, placing these verses in the context of 1 John as a whole assists us in understanding John's meaning. John does not speak of perfection but rather of a new direction and way of life. Genuine believers do not lead antinomian lives; they reveal their new life by their new behavior. Nevertheless, John is not suggesting that their behavior

2. The citations in this paragraph are from the NRSV.

will be without any moral blemish at all, for otherwise there would be no need to confess one's sins (1:9).

Those who have left the community reveal that they have loved the world more than God, and that they do not truly belong to him (2:15–17). For John, perseverance is the mark of genuine faith and authenticity. What he says in 1 John 2:19 coheres well with the discourse in John 8:30–59. John does not think that those who have left the church were genuine believers; he argues that their secession demonstrates that they were never authentic (cf. 2 John 8–9).

For John, salvation is obtained by believing. This theme is prominent in both his Gospel and in 1 John. Still, believing is not passive; it is dynamic and transforming. The work that God requires is to believe that Jesus is the one sent by God (John 6:29), and hence eternal life comes from belief alone. Still, believing cannot be separated from coming to Jesus, following him, hearing him, eating and drinking him, keeping his commands, and loving brothers and sisters. The belief that saves is one that perseveres and manifests itself in practical and concrete ways. The belief that saves confesses that Jesus is the Christ and the Son of God. It looks to him for the forgiveness of sins and for eternal life.

Acts

Faith and obedience are two sides of the same coin in Acts, just as they are in the Gospel of Luke. Unbelievers are regularly called upon to repent and turn from their sins (2:38; 3:19; 13:24; 17:30). When Paul summarized the gospel for King Agrippa, he said that human beings "should repent and turn to God, performing deeds in keeping with their repentance" (26:20; cf. 5:31–32; 15:19). In other texts, however, faith is required, and nothing is said about repentance (e.g., 8:12; 13:12, 38–39; 14:27; 15:7, 9; 16:31; 17:12, 34; 18:8).

The emphasis in some texts on believing and in others on repentance may seem puzzling, even contradictory. The apparent difficulty is resolved when we realize that faith and repentance are ultimately inseparable for Luke. The close relationship between these two is apparent from a number of texts. For instance, we noted that Paul summoned the Athenians to repent (17:30), but later those who responded are identified as those who believed (17:34). Another instructive example surfaces in Acts 9. When Peter healed the bedridden Aeneas, Lydda and Sharon "turned to the Lord" (9:35). When he raised Tabitha from the dead, "many believed in the Lord" (9:42). The two miracle stories conclude with similar responses. Luke did not intend for readers to draw a disjunction between turning to the Lord in repentance and believing in him.

We noted above how Peter emphasizes that Cornelius and his friends were saved because they believed (10:43; 15:7, 9). But in 11:18 the Jews in Jerusalem described the conversion of Cornelius and his friends in terms of God granting them repentance. The vital relationship between belief and repentance is evident in 11:21: "A great number who believed turned to the Lord." The same collocation appears in 20:21, where Paul summarized his ministry as one that calls for "repentance toward God" and "faith in our Lord Jesus Christ." Luke does not explain the logical or temporal relationship between faith and repentance, but he does see them as inseparably joined in God's saving work.

The indissoluble relationship between faith and repentance is confirmed by the need for persevering faith. Initial decisions of faith do not guarantee final forgiveness of sins. One must continue in the faith and not apostatize. When Gentiles responded positively to the gospel in Antioch, Barnabas "exhorted them all to remain faithful to the Lord with steadfast purpose" (11:23; cf. 13:43; 14:22). Perhaps the most notable example of such a departure was Simon (8:9–24). Before embracing the gospel, Simon practiced magic and was venerated in Samaria as one who had God's power. When Philip proclaimed the gospel, Simon believed and was baptized. It appears from the narrative that Simon's initial belief was not genuine but rather was a subterfuge, since he was impressed by the miracles Philip did. Luke indicates that genuine faith endures. It produces works "in keeping with repentance" (26:20).

We can summarize Luke in Acts, then, as emphasizing the indissoluble nature of faith and repentance. They are two sides of the same coin. What Luke teaches in Acts fits with what we saw in his Gospel. There we saw the refrain "Your faith has saved you," but Luke also strongly emphasizes that true disciples follow Jesus. Both the Gospel of Luke and Acts underscore that faith and repentance are necessary for salvation.

The Pauline Literature

The human response of faith is fundamental, according to the Pauline gospel. Human beings are "justified by faith" (Rom. 5:1), which means that people stand in the right before God through faith. Faith trusts in the forgiveness of sins achieved through Christ on the cross. Human beings are to put their faith in God, who sent Jesus as the crucified and risen one (4:24–25). Paul emphasizes that human beings are justified by faith (Rom. 1:17; Gal. 3:11), seeing in Hab. 2:4 a grounding for this claim. A right relation with God is obtained "through faith in Jesus Christ for all who believe" (Rom. 3:22; cf. 3:25–26, 28; Gal. 2:16; 3:2, 5; Phil. 3:9).

Many scholars, however, read the foregoing texts in a remarkably different way, claiming that the verses refer to "the faithfulness *of* Christ" rather than "faith *in* Christ." A number of arguments are presented in support of "faithfulness of Christ." (1) In Rom. 3:3 *tēn pistin tou theou* clearly refers to the faithfulness of God. (2) In 4:12 *pisteōs . . . Abraam* means "the faith of Abraham." (3) It is argued that the genitive in such constructions is most naturally understood as subjective. (4) If one takes the genitive as objective, then faith in Christ is superfluous because in the key texts (e.g., 3:22; Gal. 2:16; Phil. 3:9), Paul already mentions the need to trust in Christ. (5) The "faithfulness of Jesus" is another way of referring to Jesus' obedience, which achieved salvation (Rom. 5:19; Phil. 2:8). (6) The coming of "faith" refers to redemptive history (Gal. 3:23, 25), designating the faithfulness of Christ at this time in salvation history. (7) The focus in Paul's theology is the work of God in Christ, not the human response of faith.

Despite the arguments supporting a subjective genitive, there are good reasons to prefer an objective genitive, so that Paul refers to "faith *in* Christ." (1) The genitive object with "faith" is clear in some instances (Mark 11:22; James 2:1). (2) A genitive object with other verbal nouns shows that an objective genitive with the noun "faith" is quite normal grammatically—for example, "knowledge of Christ Jesus" (*tēs gnōseōs Christou Iēsou*; Phil. 3:8 AT). (3) Hence, those who claim that the genitive must be subjective fail to convince. (4) The texts that use the verb "believe" in a verbal construction and the noun "faith" with the genitive are not superfluous but rather emphatic, stressing the importance of faith to be right with God. (5) Paul often contrasts works and human faith. Hence, seeing a polarity between works of law and faith in Christ, both of which are human activities, fits with what Paul does elsewhere. (6) On the other hand, nowhere else does Paul, in speaking of Jesus Christ, use the word "faith" to describe his "obedience." (7) The salvation-historical argument fails to persuade as well. Certainly, Gal. 3:23, 25 refer to the coming of faith at a certain time in redemptive history. But such an observation hardly excludes faith in Christ, for faith in Christ becomes a reality when he arrives and fulfills God's promises. We should not pit redemptive history against anthropology. (8) Nor is the emphasis on faith in Christ somehow Pelagian, as if it somehow detracts from God's work in salvation. A human response of faith does not undercut the truth that God saves, particularly if God grants faith to his own (Eph. 2:8–9).

The only hope for right standing with God, then, is to trust what God has done in Christ rather than depending on one's attainments. Human boasting is ruled out because human beings rest on what Christ has done to save them (Rom. 3:27–28; 4:1–3). Faith calls attention to the power of God, who justifies the ungodly (4:5). A new reality is called into existence by the death and resurrection of Christ, so that a new relation with God is established through faith in Christ (4:17–25).

Faith is fundamental to the Pauline gospel because it is always allied with grace, for faith rests on and believes in what God has accomplished through the crucified and risen Lord. If righteousness can be achieved through adherence to the law, then the death of Christ becomes superfluous (Gal. 2:21). Faith glorifies God because it looks to him for every good gift and blessing, acknowledging that all comes from him. This helps explain why Paul can say that "whatever does not proceed from faith is sin" (Rom. 14:23). Abraham's faith was not merely a passive acknowledgment of God's existence. He believed in a God who raises the dead and calls into existence that which does not yet exist (4:17). As he trusted in God, "he gave glory to God" (4:20). We see that faith gives God glory because it honors him as trustworthy, confessing that his promises will be realized.

Paul does not understand faith to be a momentary feeling that vanishes. Saving faith is a persevering faith. Those who "received" the message of the gospel belong to God (1 Cor. 15:1–2), but they have believed "in vain" if they do not continue to cling to the faith that they embraced. Faith alone saves (cf. 1 Tim. 1:16), but genuine faith produces fruit and leads to a change in one's life. The emphasis on perseverance and fruit in Paul does not contradict his teaching that justification is through faith and not works. Good works are always understood as the fruit of faith, and they function as evidence that faith is genuine. They never stand independently of faith, as if works alone can justify. Those who are a new creation in Christ Jesus do good works that are ordained for them (Eph. 2:10), but these works are the result of the new creation.

Warnings are common in the Pauline Letters, instructing his readers to continue in the faith in order to escape eschatological destruction. Those who have fallen from the faith experience God's "severity," and believers must "continue in [God's] kindness" or they "will be cut off" as well (Rom. 11:22). God's severity here refers to eschatological judgment, for in the context of Rom. 9–11, the fate of unbelieving Jews is considered. Believers who cave in to the desires of the flesh will die—they will not experience eternal life (8:13; cf. Col. 3:5–6)—but those who rely on the Spirit and slay fleshly desires will enjoy life forever.

Similarly, in 1 Cor. 6:9–11 Paul warns his readers that those who practice unrighteousness will not inherit God's kingdom. When Paul declares that "the wages of sin is death" (Rom. 6:23), he addresses believers and warns them about the consequences of sin. The consequence is not merely physical death, for here death is contrasted with "eternal life." Death refers to the final judgment of the wicked. Nor does Paul reserve his warnings only for weak Christians. All believers need to be admonished about the need to continue walking in God's ways. Paul lived in such a way that he might share in the saving blessings of the gospel (1 Cor. 9:23). The image of the race and receiving a reward in 9:24–27 illustrates the need for perseverance to obtain end-time salvation. The Corinthians should not deceive themselves, as if sharing in the sacraments magically protected them from any harm (cf. 10:14–22). The sins of Israel in the wilderness stand as a warning to believers, so that they will avoid the same fate. Those who presume to stand at the last judgment regardless of their behavior need to be awakened from their slumber, for those who disregard warnings are liable to fall.

It is sometimes difficult to discern the line between apostasy and significant sin. Believers who had blatantly sinned during the Lord's Supper were disciplined with sickness (11:17–34). Such judgments of the Lord spared believers from final condemnation (11:32). On the other hand, the factions present in the congregation clarified who was approved or "genuine" (*dokimoi*; 11:19) in the church. It seems, then, that those who fall away were never genuine believers. Their apostasy confirms their inauthenticity.

Those who sow to the flesh will harvest corruption, whereas those who sow to the Spirit will harvest eternal life (Gal. 6:8). The contrast demonstrates that sowing to the flesh will result in eschatological judgment. Such a stern saying may seem surprising in Galatians, the letter of faith, freedom, and life in the Spirit. What it shows, however, is that faith and life in the Spirit lead to a new way of life in which faith produces the fruit of the Spirit.

Paul does not promise that believers will be vindicated on the last day regardless of their actions. Those who deny Jesus will be denied by him on the last day (2 Tim. 2:12). Yet not all sin constitutes a denial of Jesus. Believers may act in a faithless manner and sin without committing apostasy (2:13). God is faithful to believers in such instances and will not reject them as his own. Some, however, claim to know God, but the way they live denies that they truly know him (Titus 1:16). Only those who turn from wickedness will be residents in the Lord's house in the end; those who veer away from the truth never truly belonged to God (2 Tim. 2:18–19).

Paul teaches justification by faith and judgment according to works. Romans 3:28 is rightly interpreted to say that believers are justified by faith alone, and yet faith always produces good works, so that the faith that saves is a persevering faith. Works and faith are inseparable in Paul, for good works are always the fruit of faith. Faith looks outside itself to Jesus Christ as the crucified and risen Lord for salvation. It anchors itself to the God who gives life where there is death, trusting that God will raise believers from the dead on the last day. Hence, the call to good works in Paul's writings does not focus on the inherent power of human beings to do what is good and right and true. Every good thing is the fruit of faith and due to the power of God. Perseverance cannot be equated with perfection; it is nothing less than continuing to trust in God's grace until the final day. In considering Paul's teaching, we see that his emphasis on faith and works is quite compatible with the rest of the NT. Indeed, it appears that Paul and James, though they emphasize different truths, are compatible after all.

Hebrews

The issue of faith and obedience in Hebrews will be probed initially by exploring the warning passages in Hebrews. The Letter to the Hebrews as a whole is a homily (13:22) in which the author exhorts the readers not to depart from the Christian faith by relapsing back into Judaism and the sacrifices offered under the old covenant. Many attempts have been made to identify the situation of the readers more precisely, but unfortunately the details elude us. The author portrays Christ as the Melchizedekian priest in order to urge his readers to remain faithful to the end. The theology of the book, in other words, points to and serves the warnings. The call to faith and obedience is the purpose for which the letter was written.

Identifying the precise parameters of the warnings in Hebrews is difficult. If one includes the exhortation to faith, the warnings may include 2:1–4; 3:7–4:13; 5:11–6:12; 10:19–12:29. McKnight (1992) helpfully argues that the warnings in the letter must be interpreted together or synoptically. One warning should not be isolated from the other in our attempt to understand them, for the admonitions in the letter are intended to produce one single effect or response in the readers.

If we consider all the warnings, we see that various expressions are used to implore the readers to remain faithful to Christ and the gospel. The readers should not "drift away" from the gospel proclaimed to them (2:1). They must not harden their hearts (3:8, 15; 4:7), "be hardened by the deceitfulness of sin" (3:13), or have an "evil, unbelieving heart, leading you to fall away from the living God" (3:12). The wilderness generation failed to enter God's rest because of disobedience (3:18; 4:6, 11), and the author entreats his readers to avoid the same fate. Such disobedience, however, stems from unbelief—the failure to believe in God's promises (3:19). The wilderness generation failed to put their trust in the good news proclaimed to them, and only believers enter into God's rest (4:2–3). The oscillation between faith and obedience in 3:7–4:13 indicates the inseparable relationship between them. The admonitions should be interpreted not as a call to moralism or a rigorous perfectionism but rather as a call to faith.

The readers are warned that those who have once experienced numerous blessings from God cannot repent if they fall away (6:4–6). In Heb. 6 the author is not reflecting on those who have fallen away but rather is admonishing and encouraging his readers not to turn away from the gospel that they have embraced (cf. 6:11–12). We also see further evidence that the warning here relates to apostasy and not merely to lack of fruitfulness in the Christian life. A radical defection seems to be in view, for it is described as "crucifying once again the Son of God . . . and holding him up to contempt" (6:6).

The author also warns the readers against sinning deliberately (10:26). The sin is described as a spurning of God's Son, profaning the blood of Christ that inaugurated the new covenant, and outraging God's gracious Spirit (10:29). By way of contrast, the readers should not forsake their confidence in Christ and lose the reward (10:35). In other words, they are to continue to endure in doing the will of God (10:36) instead of shrinking back (10:38–39). Those who shrink back reveal that they do not believe in God or trust his promises.

The warning in 10:26–39 supports the claim that the sin in view is apostasy. Willful persistence in sin refers to deliberate sin, which is identified in the OT as sin "with a high hand," for which there is no forgiveness (cf. Lev. 4:2, 22, 27; Num. 15:30; Deut. 17:12; Ps. 19:13). For those who sin willfully "there no longer remains a sacrifice for sins" (Heb. 10:26). In other words, if the readers turn away from the cross of Christ for the cleansing of their sins and consciences, no other sacrifice will avail. Reverting to the OT cult will not offer any help, for animal sacrifices cannot take away sins (10:4). If the readers rely on such sacrifices for forgiveness, they deny the efficacy of Christ's atonement and thus cut themselves off from the only means by which sins can be forgiven. The threat of judgment, fire, vengeance, and recompense points to the final judgment inflicted by God upon unbelievers (10:27, 30). Nor can anyone be considered a genuine believer who tramples on Jesus as God's Son, treats Jesus' blood as if it were defiled and unclean, and outrages the Spirit that gives grace (10:29).

Hebrews 10:39 reveals clearly that final destruction or salvation is at stake. Those who "shrink back . . . are destroyed" (*apōleian*), but those who trust God "are saved" (NRSV). The word for "destroyed" (*apōleia*) is used regularly in the NT to denote those who will be ruined and destroyed forever in the final judgment. When we turn to Heb. 11, we realize that the warning texts call upon the readers to trust in the gospel. Warnings are a summons to faith, a call to trust God until the end. Faith looks toward the future and is assured that God will fulfill his promises, particularly the promises of eschatological blessing. Faith can rely on God's future promises only because it is grounded in the work of Christ on the cross, which has secured complete cleansing from sin (7:1–10:18). For the author of Hebrews, failure to trust God for the future demonstrates that one has lost confidence in what Christ has achieved in the past through his cross and resurrection. Those who rest in the cross of Christ will not turn away from the atonement that he provided and revert to the sacrifices offered under the OT cult. Hebrews emphasizes faith in what God has promised, for the gospel calls each person to keep believing in what Christ has achieved through the cross. Genuine faith believes that God "exists and that he rewards those who seek him" (11:6), but for the author of Hebrews, this future reward is not a mere belief in God's existence and his reward. Faith rests on what Christ has done in securing forgiveness of sins and in inaugurating the new covenant.

Hebrews 11 also remarkably supports the inseparable relationship between faith and obedience, and at the same time it verifies that faith precedes obedience, so that all obedience derives from faith and is rooted in faith. The connection between faith and activity is evident in the following statements: "By faith Abel offered" (11:4). "By faith Noah . . . constructed an ark" (11:7).

"By faith Abraham obeyed" (11:8). "By faith he went to live in the land of promise" (11:9). "By faith Abraham . . . offered up Isaac" (11:17). "By faith Isaac invoked future blessings" (11:20). "By faith Jacob . . . blessed each of the sons of Joseph" (11:21). "By faith Joseph . . . made mention of the exodus of the Israelites and gave directions concerning his bones" (11:22). "By faith . . . Moses was hidden for three months" (11:23). "By faith Moses . . . refused to be called a son of Pharaoh's daughter" (11:24). "By faith he left Egypt" (11:27). "By faith he kept the Passover" (11:28). The supreme exemplar of faith is Jesus, "who for the joy that was set before him endured the cross" (12:2).

The dynamism of faith is evident. Faith acts, obeys, and endures. The author of Hebrews does not fall prey to moral rigorism that demands perfection of his readers. He summons them to believe in God's promises secured in the death of Christ, to trust in the cross until the end. Faith is not a mere passive acceptance of the gospel; rather, it reaches into the very soul and transforms one's life. It should be clear, then, that Heb. 11 cannot be detached from the larger epistolary context of Hebrews. Only those who trust God and do not shrink back (10:38–39) will enter the heavenly city.

Scholars have also discussed whether those who receive the warnings are Christians. The debate centers on 6:4–6. Are those who have "been enlightened," "tasted the heavenly gift," "shared in the Holy Spirit," and "tasted the goodness of the word of God and the powers of the age to come" Christians? Some have argued that they are "almost Christians." That is, they have come remarkably close to Christian faith without actually becoming members of the people of God. They have been enlightened in the sense that they know a significant amount about the Christian faith, and yet this knowledge has not led them to salvation. They have tasted and sampled the heavenly gift, but they have not ingested it and made it their own. They have had experiences of the Holy Spirit and spiritual gifts, but the Spirit did not indwell them. They have even experienced the delight of the word of God without ever embracing it truly. Such an interpretation explains how such could fall away (6:6). They fell away because they never were Christians. Similarly, in 10:29 those who are said to be "sanctified" enjoy an outward cleansing (cf. 9:13–14). They were not truly set apart for the things of God. Those warned came close to accepting the Christian faith, but they repudiated it after initial positive experiences.

The proposed interpretation has its attractions, but it fails to convince. The most natural way of reading the description of the addressees is to identify them as believers. In 10:32 the word "enlightened" (*phōtizō*) is repeated from 6:4, and clearly it refers to the time of the readers' conversion. Determining precisely what it means to taste the heavenly gift is difficult. The metaphor of tasting is also used of their experience of God's word. In each case tasting does not mean that the readers merely sampled the heavenly gift and God's word and the powers of the coming age. The verb "taste" (*geuomai*) is used of Jesus' tasting death in 2:9. Surely the author does not mean that Jesus did not experience death fully. Tasting indicates that Jesus underwent death in all its fullness. Similarly, the author addresses readers who have ingested the heavenly gift and have experienced the powers of the age to come and the joy of God's word. Most important, the author says that the readers "shared in the Holy Spirit" (6:4). The word "shared" (*metochos*) does not denote an inferior experience with the Spirit. Just a few verses earlier, a verbal form (*metexchōn*) is used of ingesting milk (5:13). There is no suggestion that the illustration points to only a sipping of milk or a slight ingestion of it. So too, the most natural way to read the verses is to understand the author to be saying that the readers have received the Holy Spirit. The reception of the Holy Spirit is the hallmark of being a Christian. The same argument applies to 10:29, where those addressed are said to be "sanctified" "by the blood of the covenant." It will not do to say that the sanctification here is merely outward or ceremonial, for the blood in view here is the blood of Jesus. The OT sacrifices purify only externally and outwardly, but the blood of Christ cleanses the conscience and is effective, in contrast to the sacrifices offered under the old covenant. The author does not give any indication that he addresses those who are "almost Christians."

The warning passages are controversial in another respect in the history of the church. Do they teach that genuine believers can be irretrievably lost so that they are condemned in the final judgment? In early church history some understood any serious postbaptismal sin (e.g., murder and adultery) as disqualifying one from future entrance into the kingdom. This interpretation fails to see that the sin that leads to irrevocable judgment, according to Hebrews, is apostasy, by which the atonement provided by Christ is abandoned. Still, it is clear that the earliest interpreters believed that apostasy was possible. Most scholarly work on Hebrews agrees, arguing that the author threatens the readers with eschatological judgment if they depart from the gospel. The threat, it is argued, would be idle if such apostasy were impossible; in addition, there must have been examples in the author's mind of those who had committed such apostasy, such as the wilderness generation of Israel (3:7–4:13) or Esau (12:16–17).

A few have maintained that believers are addressed in these verses, but that the punishment threatened relates to loss of rewards and not to eschatological destruction. I have argued above that the threats are of such a nature that the punishment described cannot be limited to loss of rewards. Still others, as we noted previously, argue that those who are warned are "almost Christians." Hence, those who fall away were not genuine believers but only appeared to be Christians. The problem with this view, as is often noted, is that there is no compelling evidence, as we have seen, that the readers are described as "almost Christians." We cannot segregate the warnings in Heb. 6 from the rest of the letter, and elsewhere the readers are addressed as believers.

I suggest a different answer to the controversy. The author of Hebrews writes to warn those in the church not to fall away. His purpose is not to answer the question, "Were those who have fallen away genuine Christians?" He does not look back retrospectively and assess the state of those who have departed from the Christian faith. The intent of the letter is quite different. The author addresses those in the church who were tempted to revert to Judaism in order to avoid discrimination and persecution. He does not cast a glance backward, contemplating the state of those who have lapsed, and ask whether they were ever genuine believers. He is walking forward, urging his readers to adhere to the gospel and continue in the faith until the return of Jesus Christ. The warnings are *prospective*, designed to prevent the readers from drifting away from the gospel that they embraced. We misread Hebrews when we ask, "Can genuine Christians apostatize?" Asking the wrong question frames the discussion in a way that gives a wrong perspective on what the author says. The author does not specifically address the question of whether Christians are capable of committing apostasy; rather, he writes stern warnings so that they will avoid apostasy.

But surely, one could object, the writer was aware of those who had departed from the Christian faith. Under the old covenant he mentions Israel in the wilderness (3:7–4:13) and the defection of Esau (12:16–17). There is no doubt that the writer was familiar with some who had departed from the Christian faith. However, the point here is that he does not address that question specifically. There are some indications that believers have a certain hope that is irrevocable (e.g., 6:13–20; 10:14). The author functions as pastor, warning his readers not to depart from Jesus Christ and the atonement that he has provided. But he also is optimistic that his warnings will succeed (6:9–12), for he knows that God's promises are sure, like an anchor, providing a hope that reaches inside the veil (6:13–20). Hence, he seems to believe that the warnings will actually be a means by which his readers will persevere and be assured of their salvation.

The importance of obedience and perseverance is woven throughout the Letter to the Hebrews, for the readers were tempted to relapse into Jewish practices to avoid persecution. Returning to Judaism is no light matter for the author, for he views it as a repudiation of the cross and a denial of the gospel. Those who fail to endure in the Christian faith and revert to Judaism will face eternal destruction. Some in the history of interpretation have taken Hebrews more rigorously than the author intends. He does not threaten judgment for any significant postbaptismal sin. We should not read him to say that those who murder or commit adultery after conversion are necessarily damned, as serious as those sins are. God's wrath is reserved for those who deny the gospel of Christ, for they no longer rely on the death of Jesus for the forgiveness of their sins. There is no atonement for sin for those who turn aside from the only basis for atonement. The call to perseverance, as the whole of Hebrews clarifies, is a call to faith. Those who endure to the end put their faith in the death of Jesus Christ for the forgiveness of their sins. They profess that their only hope on the day of judgment is the purification accomplished by Christ as the Melchizedekian priest. Only those who continue to trust God in the future by remaining within the Christian church reveal that they have found in Jesus Christ final forgiveness of sins.

James

James clearly emphasizes that good works are necessary to avert final judgment. But the call to endurance (1:2–4) should not be confused with perfection. Moral perfection cannot be obtained in this life, and indeed James notes that "we all stumble in many ways" (3:2). Here "stumble" (*ptaiō*) should be defined as "sin," as the use of the same term in 2:10 confirms. Hence, the moral perfection promised by James must be eschatological. On the other hand, enduring trials in a way that pleases God is not optional for James, for those who do so "will receive the crown of life" (1:12), which refers to eternal life itself.

The necessity of obedience brings us to James's famous discussion of faith and works in 2:14–26. Some scholars affirm that James contradicts the Pauline view of justification by faith apart from works. The arguments supporting a contradiction are quite impressive: (1) James specifically denies that justification is by faith alone (2:24), whereas Paul teaches that believers are justified by faith alone (Rom. 3:28); (2) Paul claims that Abraham was justified by faith, but James asserts that he was justified by works in sacrificing Isaac (Rom. 4:1–8; Gal. 3:6–9; James 2:21); (3) Paul appeals to Gen. 15:6 to support Abraham being justified by faith apart from works (Rom. 4:3; Gal. 3:6), but James (2:23) cites the same verse from Genesis to substantiate justification by works. The arguments that favor a contradiction between Paul and James are certainly striking, but James is more likely responding to a distortion of Pauline teaching, as we shall see below.

Various solutions have been suggested to reconcile the discrepancy between Paul and James. One possibility is that James and Paul mean something different by the word "works" (*erga*). Historically, Roman Catholic interpreters have suggested that Paul excludes ceremonial works as playing a role in justification, whereas James refers here to moral works. The Reformers disagreed with the Roman Catholic interpretation, maintaining that works in Paul could not be limited to ceremonies such as circumcision or the observance of days. Interestingly, the new perspective on Paul typically identifies the works that Paul rules out for justification as those that erect barriers between Jews and Gentiles, so that the focus is on circumcision, food laws, and Sabbath. Obviously, those who endorse the new perspective are coming from a different place than Roman Catholic scholarship of the sixteenth century, and yet the interpretations share a fascinating convergence at this particular point. The new perspective solution fails, as I argued earlier, for it is not evident that Paul restricts "works of the law" or "works" to ceremonial works or those laws that divide Jews from Gentiles. Hence, it is not evident that Paul and James use the term "works" in a different sense.

What is likely, however, is that Paul and James use the term "justify" (*dikaioō*) with a different nuance. Paul uses the word *dikaioō* to refer to a righteousness given to the ungodly. He shockingly insists that it is the ungodly who are declared to be righteous by virtue of the righteousness of Christ. James, on the other hand, uses the verb *dikaioō* to refer to those whom God declares to be righteous by good works. On the other hand, the common view that *dikaioō* in James means "proved to be righteous" or "shown to be righteous" is incorrect, for such a definition does not fit with how the word is typically used. Instead, *dikaioō* means "declare righteous" in James and Paul; but in contrast to Paul, James says that those who obey God are declared to be in the right.

The soteriological context in James is evident, for he asks if a faith without works can "save" (*sōzō*; 2:14). The word "save" almost certainly refers to deliverance from God's wrath on the day when the Lord returns (cf. 5:7–9), which is the same meaning that it often has in Paul. Both "save" and "justify," then, relate to one's standing before God, not the opinion of human beings. James appeals to Genesis to support the need for works (2:21), and there is no suggestion in that chapter that the sacrifice of Isaac was commanded so that other people would commend Abraham.

If James uses *dikaioō* to refer to a declaration of righteousness by virtue of works, whereas Paul uses the term *dikaioō* in an unusual way to refer to the gift of righteousness granted to the ungodly, then do James and Paul contradict one another? Another proposed solution is that James differs from Paul because he uses the term to refer to eschatological justification: the pronouncement to be made on the last day. Such a reading brings us closer to resolving the differences between Paul and James, but it still does not quite succeed. The term "justify" is eschatological in Paul: it refers to the final judgment that has been announced ahead of time. Paul surely emphasizes that believers are *now* justified by faith (Rom. 5:1). The final verdict already belongs to believers who are in Christ Jesus (8:1). Significantly, James frequently uses the word "save" to refer to eschatological deliverance (1:21; 2:14; 4:12; 5:20). Paul often uses the verb "save," as I argued earlier, to refer to end-time deliverance as well. Evidence is lacking, however, that James and Paul use the verb "justify" (*dikaioō*) differently in this sense. We can agree that "justify" is eschatological in that it represents God's verdict pronounced on the judgment day. James, however, emphasizes that this verdict has already been pronounced in history, just as Paul does. The most natural way to read 2:21 is to conclude that Abraham was "justified by works *when* he offered his son Isaac on the altar" (NRSV, stress added). One could argue that the participle should be translated as causal, but even so, the aorist passive "he was justified" (*edikaiōthē*) seems to point to a justification that belonged to Abraham *in history* (cf. 2:25). James appears to use the word "justify" within the same time frame as Paul, referring to the final verdict of God that has already been announced in advance.

I have argued that James and Paul use the term *dikaioō* with a different nuance: James to refer to the declaration of righteousness pronounced by virtue of the works performed, and Paul to the verdict by God that the ungodly who trust in Christ are righteous. Still, it does not follow that James and Paul ultimately contradict one another. We must recognize that they address different situations and circumstances, and those situations must be taken into account in understanding the stances of Paul and James relative to justification. Indeed, we are on the way to resolving the tension between James and Paul in seeing how they both use the term "faith" (*pistis*). When James says that faith alone does not justify, faith here refers to mere intellectual assent. For instance, demons affirm monotheism, but such "faith" is not wholehearted and glad-hearted assent that leads demons to embrace Jesus Christ as Lord and Savior. Instead, the faith of demons is theologically orthodox but leads them to shudder because they fear judgment (2:19). The faith that saves, according to Paul, embraces Jesus Christ as Savior and Lord, placing one's life entirely in his hands. James criticizes a "faith" that notionally concurs with the gospel but does not grip the whole person. In other words, James does not disagree with Paul's contention that faith alone justifies, but he defines carefully the kind of faith that justifies. The faith that truly justifies can never be separated from works. Works will inevitably flow as the fruit of such faith. Faith that merely accepts doctrines intellectually but does not lead to a transformed life is "dead" (2:17, 26) and "useless" (2:20). Such faith does not "profit" (*ophelos*; 2:14, 16 RSV) in the sense that it does not spare one from judgment on the last day. Those who have dead and barren faith will not escape judgment. True faith is demonstrated by works (2:18). James does not deny that faith alone saves, but it is faith that produces (*synergeō*) works and is completed (*teleioō*) by works (2:22). The faith that saves is living, active, and dynamic. It must produce works, just as compassion for the poor inevitably means that one cares practically for their physical needs (2:15–16).

James and Paul do not actually contradict one another on the role of faith and works in justification. James affirms as well that faith is the root and works are the fruit. James addresses a situation different from Paul's, for the latter denies that works can function as the basis of a right relation with God. A right relation with God is obtained by faith alone. Paul responds to those who tried to establish a right relation with God on the basis of works. He argues that God shockingly declares those who lack any righteousness to be in the right if they put their faith in Christ for salvation. James counters those who think that a right relation with God is genuine if there is faith without any subsequent works. James looks at God's pronouncement of righteousness from another angle: not as the fundamental basis of one's relation to God but rather as the result of faith. James responds to antinomianism, whereas Paul reacts to legalism.

James recognizes that all believers sin in numerous ways (3:2), and that even one sin makes a lawbreaker of the one who commits it (2:10–11). Being sinners, humans lack the capacity to do the works required to merit justification. They are saved by the grace of God, for in his goodness and generosity he granted believers new life (1:18). Even faith is a gift of God, for God chose some "to be rich in faith and heirs of the kingdom" (2:5). It seems, then, that Paul and James do not contradict one another. Both affirm the priority of faith in justification, and both also affirm that good works are the fruit of faith but are not the basis of justification. Hence, what James teaches fits with Paul's teaching and with what we have seen elsewhere in the NT.

1 Peter

Peter writes to churches facing suffering, encouraging them to "stand firm" in God's grace (5:12). Many scholars think that this admonition sums up the message of the entire letter. On the one hand, believers are exhorted to stand and remain faithful to the gospel; on the other hand, only God's grace grants them the ability to stand and endure to the end. Ethical admonition permeates the letter.

Conversion is described as "obedience to Jesus Christ" (1:2) or as the purification of "your souls by your obedience to the truth" (1:22). In these contexts Peter does not think of ongoing obedience in the Christian life as in 1:15–16. The context of the opening (1:1–2) indicates that conversion is in view: being chosen by God for salvation, set apart by the Spirit so that they are in the sphere of the holy, and sprinkled by Jesus' blood for the forgiveness of sins. Those who believe in Jesus will escape eschatological humiliation on the last day (2:6–7). Faith is described as coming to Jesus, the living stone (2:4). Peter also uses the metaphor of tasting (2:3), drawing on Ps. 34:8. Those who believe taste the goodness and kindness of the Lord. The image of tasting the Lord's kindness captures the richness of faith, for faith embraces Jesus as Lord, finding him to be satisfying and fulfilling. It "comes" to him and submits to him as Lord.

If the message of 1 Peter can be summed up as "stand firm" in grace (5:12), it seems that the same theme appears in the admonition to "resist" the devil, "firm in your faith" (5:9). Perseverance and endurance are rooted in faith, in placing one's trust in what God has done in Christ on the cross. The ongoing role of faith is clear because God guards his people, ensuring that they will enjoy end-time salvation "through faith" (1:5). Peter also teaches that believers will enjoy a final reward if they obey (2:19–20). Those who long to inherit the eschatological blessing and to enjoy good days must live in a godly fashion (3:10–12). Even though the citation from Ps. 34 in 1 Pet. 3:10–12 relates to life in this world, Peter considers entrance into the land typologically so that it forecasts possession of the heavenly inheritance. Such an inheritance will be given only to those who refrain from evil and seek peace. Those who practice evil will experience God's judgment. What we find in 1 Peter is characteristic of the NT. Saving faith always leads to a changed life, so that there is a new obedience. Such obedience is necessary for an eschatological inheritance, but it is still conceived of as a fruit of faith. Good works are not the basis for receiving salvation, but they are the necessary fruit of faith for life eternal.

2 Peter and Jude

Both 2 Peter and Jude are addressed to churches in which false teachers with antinomian lifestyles and agendas threaten the church. Both writers, therefore, naturally emphasize the need for perseverance and obedience. Though Jude says nothing about faith, the emphasis on God's grace (1–2, 24–25) indicates that enduring to the end cannot ultimately be attributed to the work of believers.

Peter emphasizes the judgment of the false teachers, repeating many of the themes found in Jude (2 Pet. 2). The role of faith in receiving God's saving righteousness is stated in the introduction to the letter (1:1–4). Contrary to the view of some, Peter thus does not fall prey to works-righteousness or moralism. In 1:5–7 he exhorts his readers to pursue godly virtues, for God has given them all they need to live godly lives (1:3–4). The imperative is rooted in the indicative. Indeed, all the virtues listed in 1:5–7 flow from faith.

Second Peter argues that those who live in an ungodly way are "ineffective or unfruitful in the knowledge of our Lord Jesus Christ" (1:8). To be forgetful of the forgiveness of sins is not a trifling matter (1:9), for godly qualities (1:5–7) are necessary "to confirm" one's "call and election" (1:10 NRSV). Those who lack such virtues, therefore, will not enjoy eschatological salvation. On the other hand, those who practice such virtues "will never fall" (1:10), which means that they will never commit apostasy.

Peter threatens, as did Jude, judgment for those who disobey (2:4–10a), but he adds the theme that God is able to preserve those who belong to him, adducing the examples of Noah and Lot. The authenticity of the faith of Noah and Lot was demonstrated by their perseverance in the midst of societies that were utterly corrupt. If God could preserve them in the midst of such evil cultures, then surely he will guard the believers in the Petrine communities.

The false teachers denied "the Master who bought them" (2:1). They had escaped the world through their knowledge of Christ, but subsequently they denied him, presumably by the way they lived (2:20–21). Peter wrote to the church so that they would not follow the same pattern as the false teachers, who professed to believe in Christ but then departed from "the holy commandment"

(2:21). The mark of genuine Christians, according to Peter, is perseverance. Those who defect from the faith demonstrate that they are dogs and pigs: unclean animals that do not truly belong to the holy community (2:22).

The fundamental message of 2 Peter, then, is to warn believers not to be swept away by the libertinism of the false teachers (3:17). Instead, they are to continue growing in grace and in the knowledge of Jesus Christ (3:18). They are to "be diligent to be found by him without spot and blemish, and at peace" (3:14). Believers must be diligent to be blameless before him, so that they will receive their eschatological reward. Such blamelessness involves repudiating the false teachers and staying true to the gospel until the end. Nevertheless, we are reminded from 1:5 that godly living is the result of faith, and hence the call to perseverance should be interpreted as a summons to a life of faith.

Revelation

In some ways the book of Revelation is remarkably similar to Hebrews. John writes to churches in Asia Minor that were facing discrimination and persecution in their newfound faith. The readers were enticed by the culture of their day. If they participated in emperor worship *and* showed devotion to Jesus, life would be much easier (13:1–18). They would stifle questions about their loyalty to the political structure in which they lived, and they would fit in with the cultural ethos of the day, in which people worshiped many gods and found them useful for a variety of purposes. John does not tolerate any compromise with Rome, nor does he countenance emperor worship. Those who worship the beast, which almost certainly is a designation of the Roman emperor, do not have their names inscribed in the book of life (13:8). He threatens those who worship the beast with eternal torment and the fierce wrath of God (14:9–11).

Most commentators agree that Babylon represents the city of Rome (17:18), the commercial center of the Roman Empire. Believers would find Rome alluring because it was a glorious jewel, holding out the promise of economic prosperity. John, however, identifies it as a "whore" (17:1 NRSV), and those who compromise with Rome "have committed fornication" (17:2; 18:3, 9 NRSV). They have gotten in bed with Rome and pandered to its power to secure their own future. They have joined hands with a city that has spilled the blood of God's holy ones (17:6; 18:24; 19:2). For John, "fornication" here is not literal but rather denotes worship of this world.

The situation of the letter explains why John emphasizes perseverance and endurance. Believers must conquer and overcome (*nikaō*) to the end in order to receive eternal life. In each of the letters to the seven churches, he exhorts the readers to conquer (2:7, 11, 17, 26; 3:5, 12, 21): he means that they must heed John's admonitions to obtain the final reward. Such conquering is not optional. "To the one who conquers I will grant to eat of the tree of life, which is in the paradise of God" (2:7). The "tree of life" alludes to the tree of life in Genesis (2:9; 3:22) and refers to eternal life. That conquering is required for obtaining an eschatological inheritance is even clearer in 2:11: "The one who conquers will not be hurt by the second death." The second death is the lake of fire, and those whose names are not recorded in the book of life are cast into the lake of fire (20:14–15; cf. 21:8). Only those who walk with Jesus in white will receive a reward (3:4). Those who conquer will be adorned with white robes, and their names will not be removed from the book of life (3:5).

The necessity for believers to overcome can also be described as repentance (2:5, 16, 21–22; 3:3, 19). If believers fail to repent, Jesus will remove their lamp-stand (2:5). Those who stubbornly persist in sexual sin and do not repent will experience distress and even death (2:21–23; cf. 3:3, 16, 19). The Christian life cannot merely be an initial moment of repentance. Believers must be faithful to death to obtain the crown of life (2:10). If they are to avoid judgment, they must "hold fast" their faith until Jesus comes (2:25; 3:10–11).

John does not concentrate on the faith that produces obedience but rather on the obedience that is required to receive the final reward. If Revelation was written by the same John who wrote the Fourth Gospel, it is clear that elsewhere John places emphasis on believing as the sum and substance of what God demands of human beings. In Revelation, on the other hand, we see the same kaleidoscope from a different perspective. Genuine faith cannot be isolated from the whole of life, as if it were simply a private and subjective experience. The whole of the NT clarifies that faith does work, that it has a transforming effect. Hence, John writes to summon believers to endure even if they are destined for imprisonment or death (13:9–10). Those who endure must keep God's commands and continue in "their faith in Jesus" (14:12). The last phrase, *pistin Iēsou*, should be translated "faith in Jesus" (as in ESV), so that faith in Jesus is inseparable from obedience. Those who belong to the Lamb are "faithful" (17:14). They are willing to give their lives for the sake of their devotion to Jesus (20:4).

Final judgment is according to works. The context of the seven letters, as argued above, exhorts believers to persevere until the end in order to receive salvation. Hence, the judgment and reward according to works relates to eternal life (2:23). Blessing is reserved for those who keep the words of John's prophecy (1:3; 22:7). When Jesus comes and passes judgment from the white throne, he will repay each one in accord with their works (20:11–15; 22:12).

Some might read Revelation as if it excludes the necessity of faith. However, we must remind ourselves of the specific purpose of the book. John writes to exhort believers to persevere and obey in order to receive a final reward. The threat that believers face impels John to emphasize the necessity of faithfulness, and so he focuses on the result of faith rather than on the faith that produces such obedience. John emphasizes that only those who do God's will and keep his commands will receive the final reward. Those who fail to worship God and the Lamb and give their devotion to the beast will face judgment.

Conclusion

The variety of situations addressed in the NT literature and the diverse purposes of the writings mean that various themes are emphasized. In some instances faith is trumpeted as the only means by which the blessing of eternal life is received, whereas in other cases the necessity of obedience and discipleship takes center stage. In this chapter I have argued that there is a fundamental unity of approach throughout the NT. Faith is fundamental and primary for a right relation with God or for receiving eternal life. Human beings cannot obtain an eternal reward on the basis of their works, for human sin intervenes and rules out works as the pathway for blessing. Faith receives from God the salvation accomplished through Jesus Christ. Faith looks away from itself and gives glory to God as the one who delivers human beings from sin and death. Indeed, faith specifically casts its hope upon Jesus Christ as the crucified and risen Lord. Saving faith finds its roots in the cross of Jesus Christ, and so faith looks outwardly to what God has done in Christ instead of gazing inwardly upon the ability of the human subject.

The faith that saves, however, is not an abstraction, and it cannot be separated from repentance and the transformation of one's life. The NT writers never imagined a passive faith that could be sundered from a life of discipleship. Paul himself, the champion of faith, insists that true faith manifests itself in love, that only persevering faith is saving faith. Those who do not practice good works will not inherit God's kingdom. Virtually all the NT writers emphasize that one must persevere to the end in order to be saved on the eschatological day. Only those who overcome will receive the final reward. Those who fall away from the living God will face him as a consuming fire. Believers confirm their calling and election by their good works: as James says, the faith that saves must be accompanied by good works. The priority of faith in the NT rules out legalism, but it also eliminates antinomianism. Those who have truly come to know Jesus Christ keep his commandments and by their love for fellow believers show that they are truly born again. Only those who enter through the narrow gate of obedience will be saved. Purported believers may do signs, wonders, and exorcisms, but if they do not bear good fruit, they demonstrate that Jesus never knew them as his own.

Pastoral Reflection

The new life of believers reveals the object of their trust. It demonstrates whether they are a rotten tree or a healthy one. The NT writers do not call on dead trees to produce fruit; they call for a new tree and a new creation. Such newness is the work, as we have seen, of the Father, the Son, and the Spirit. It has already burst onto the scene with the death and resurrection of Christ, and yet believers await the final act in the drama: the coming of Jesus Christ to complete the saving work that has been inaugurated.

11

The Law and Salvation History

———◦◉◦———

In the preceding chapter, we saw that the life of believers can be described in terms of faith and obedience. Obedience in the NT should never be separated from faith, for all obedience that is pleasing to God flows from faith. In considering the life of believers, we must now investigate the role of the law. Are believers required to obey what is commanded in the OT law? I shall argue here that the NT view of the OT law demonstrates both continuity and discontinuity with the OT.[1] Hence, the answer to the question is complex.

Matthew

Matthew's view of the OT law must be integrated with the narrative framework and theology of the Gospel. The kingdom has been inaugurated in Jesus Christ, and he is the promised Messiah, the Lord, the Son of Man, and the Son of God. What the OT promised, therefore, is fulfilled in him.[2] Some scholars understand Matthew as endorsing a conservative view of the OT law. For instance, only Matthew says that those in distress from the siege of

---

1. This chapter is considerably abbreviated. The discussion of Mark, John, 1–2 John, Revelation, James, 1 Peter, and 2 Peter and Jude is omitted here, and the discussion of the other literature is also pared down. For a fuller exposition, see Schreiner 2008: 617–72.
2. For the fulfillment formulas in Matthew, see Schreiner 2008: 70–79.

Jerusalem should pray that their flight might not occur on the Sabbath (24:20), and only Matthew commends offering sacrifices in the temple (5:24). Believers are even enjoined to do whatever the Pharisees teach (23:2–3), which is quite astonishing in light of the sharp criticisms of the Pharisees that permeate the Gospel. Justice, mercy, and faith are exalted above tithing, but tithing is still commended and does not appear to be abolished (23:23–24).

From the foregoing texts, it might appear that Matthew only argues for continuity in his view of the OT law. Certainly, Matthew focuses on the fulfillment of the law in Christ (5:17–20), but this fulfillment also involves some discontinuity. The new wine must be placed into new wineskins (9:14–17). Jesus did not clearly abolish the Sabbath, and yet he is the sovereign Lord and interpreter of the Sabbath (12:1–14). The wise scribe in the kingdom is like the householder who rightly assembles both new and old and relates the old to the new (13:52). The wise scribe, in other words, does not merely repeat the old but rather explains how the old relates to the new and is fulfilled in the new: now that the new has arrived, the old does not retain precisely the same status.

We could overstate the element of continuity in Jesus' teaching in Matthew. Warning about the dangers of flight during the Sabbath (24:20) should not be understood as necessarily ratifying the ongoing validity of the Sabbath. Jews living in Israel would find travel difficult on the Sabbath in any case. Similarly, Jesus' words about offerings (5:24) and tithing (23:23–24), if taken seriously as words of the historical Jesus, addressed Jews who lived under the OT law. They do not, therefore, necessarily endorse sacrifices and tithing in perpetuity.

The entire law finds its fulfillment in Christ, but the time of fulfillment means that believers are not under the prescriptions of the law in the same way as before. Matthew (15:1–20), like Mark (7:1–23), includes the account about the tradition of the elders and Jesus' saying that only what comes out of a person defiles. Matthew, unlike Mark, does not add the comment that Jesus thereby cleansed all foods (cf. Mark 7:19). Some have concluded from this that Matthew promotes a more conservative view of the law. Such a conclusion is difficult to sustain, for the declaration that foods entering the mouth do not defile clearly sets aside OT prescriptions (15:11, 17–18).

A clear indication of discontinuity in Matthew relates to the temple tax required of every Israelite (Exod. 30:11–16). Jesus sovereignly declared to Peter that the sons are free from paying the tax (Matt. 17:24–27). Matthew does not state why this regulation is no longer in force, but if we consider the narrative outline of his Gospel, we receive a clue. The temple tax was required for the ransom of each Israelite. In Matthew, however, Jesus' death provides the ransom for each one (20:28). Further, Jesus predicts the destruction of the temple, signifying God's judgment on the old order (Matt. 24). In Jesus the new has arrived, and his coming means that the old must be interpreted in light of the coming of the kingdom and salvation in Jesus.

The most extensive discussion on the law in Matthew appears in 5:17–20. Jesus emphasizes that he has come to fulfill rather than abolish the law, so that even the least of the commandments should not be relaxed but rather enforced. This statement could be understood as saying that every single law of the OT must be observed by Christians. We must recall, however, that the word "fulfill" (*plēroō*) is regularly used in fulfillment formulas in Matthew, and that OT prophecies find their goal in Jesus Christ. Furthermore, we have already observed that the entirety of the OT law is not binding for Matthew. Otherwise the temple tax would continue to be an obligation. Hence, Jesus likely means that the OT law continues to be authoritative for believers, but only insofar as it is fulfilled in Jesus Christ. Such a fulfillment means that there are elements of continuity and discontinuity. Moreover, the subsequent verses (5:21–48) reveal that Jesus is the sovereign interpreter of the law. The contrast between "You have heard that it was said" (5:21, 27, 33, 38, 43) and "But I say to you" (5:22, 28, 32, 34, 39, 44) indicates that the law points to Jesus and is fulfilled and interpreted by him.

In this section, Jesus often counters his contemporaries' misinterpretations of the law. The prohibition against murder cannot be restricted merely to avoidance of murder; it also includes unrighteous anger (5:21–26). The Pharisees and scribes limited the prohibition against adultery to the physical act (5:27–32), but Jesus located adultery in the heart, contending that those who desire women in their hearts are guilty of adultery. Similarly, those who divorce their wives and marry others are guilty of adultery unless their spouses are guilty of sexual sin (5:31–32; 19:3–12). It is unclear that here Jesus actually abolished the OT law about divorce in Deut. 24:1–4. The text in Deut. 24, in any case, does not commend divorce but simply restricts it.

We seem to have a clear abrogation of the OT law when Jesus forbade his disciples to take oaths (Matt. 5:33–37). But a closer look suggests that he responded to an abuse of oath-taking practiced in his day. When we consult 23:16–22, we learn that some Jews engaged in evasive language and faulty reasoning in oath-taking, and hence Jesus corrects an abuse.

Jesus appeared to cancel the OT law in overturning the prescription "an eye for an eye and a tooth for a tooth" (5:38). Instead, he enjoined his disciples to nonresistance and to doing positive good to those who mistreat them (5:38–42). It seems, however, that Jesus countered a misinterpretation of the OT law instead of abolishing it. The principle of "an eye for an eye and a tooth for a tooth" reaches back to judicial contexts in the OT (Exod. 21:22–27; Lev. 24:17–22; Deut. 19:15–21). Punishment should be proportional to the crime, and hence, cruelty that inflicts excessive penalties on the one committing the infraction must be avoided. Similarly, lax sentences given out of partiality to the defendant are prohibited as well. What Jesus spoke against here is the practice of applying the judicial principle that the punishment should fit the crime to the *personal* sphere.

Nor did Jesus abolish the OT law when he said that disciples should love their enemies (Matt. 5:43–48). He again reacted to a misinterpretation of the OT that justified hating one's enemies. Love of neighbor extends to all without discrimination (Lev. 19:17–18). If Israelites saw an ox or donkey of an enemy wandering, they were to return it (Exod. 23:4). If they saw the donkey of one who hated them needing help from a burden, they were to render assistance (23:5). It seems, therefore, that Jesus corrected a misapprehension of the OT law.

In summary, the Matthean view of the law is complex. The law points to and is fulfilled in Jesus. The law finds its climax in the arrival of the kingdom and the coming of Jesus as the Messiah, the Lord, the Son of Man, and the Son of God. He is the sovereign interpreter and Lord of the Mosaic law. In some instances Jesus corrects a wrong interpretation of the OT law. Now that the Christ has come, there is both discontinuity and continuity with regard to the law. Some of the norms of the law continue to be in force with the arrival of the kingdom and the coming of Jesus. Other prescriptions of the law are no longer in force. The entire law must be interpreted in light of the coming of Jesus the Christ.

Luke-Acts

From one perspective, Luke seems to endorse the ongoing validity of the law. Zechariah and Elizabeth are commended for living blamelessly in accordance with the commands of the law (Luke 1:6). Joseph and Mary circumcised Jesus on the eighth day, as the law specifies, and they offered the sacrifices for purification designated in the Mosaic law (2:21–24). Jesus' parents, as the OT enjoins, traveled every year to Jerusalem for Passover, and Jesus traveled with them when he reached the age of twelve (2:41–52). It could be argued that Jesus did not do anything on the Sabbath to violate its prescriptions (6:1–11; 13:10–17; 14:1–6). Jesus teaches that those who love God and neighbor will obtain eternal life (10:25–28). When the rich ruler asked about gaining eternal life, Jesus pointed him to the commands from the Decalogue (18:18–20). Jesus said that the law and prophets were in force until the coming of the Baptist and the kingdom (16:16). Such a statement might imply that the law was no longer in force with the coming of Jesus, but Luke follows up immediately with Jesus' insistence that not even one stroke of the law will pass away (16:17). After Jesus' death, the women did not anoint his body until they had rested on the Sabbath, and Luke adds that they did so in accordance with what the law enjoins (23:56).

An emphasis on keeping the prescriptions of the law can be observed also in Acts. Peter and John continued to worship in the temple, and they came to the temple at a time when the burnt offering was sacrificed (3:1). The accusations that Stephen violated the law are dismissed as false (6:13–14). Stephen turned the tables on his opponents, contending that they had failed to observe the law (7:53). The rules that James expected both Jews and Gentiles to observe stem from OT regulations (15:19–20, 29; 21:25). After reading Galatians, we might expect that Paul would refuse to circumcise Timothy, but he did so (16:3). Apparently, Paul took a Nazirite vow and was traveling to Jerusalem to offer the sacrifices specified by the vow (18:18). When Paul arrived in Jerusalem, he paid for the purification of four men who had taken a vow (21:20–26; cf. Num. 6:14–15). He did so to avoid any suggestion that he taught Jews to abandon the law, or that he himself violated what it enjoins. Such a purificatory rite would also involve the offering of sacrifices, which Paul apparently did not frown upon. When Paul described his conversion to a Jewish audience, he commended Ananias as being "devout . . . according to the law" (Acts 22:12).

The previous texts might suggest that Luke advocates a remarkably conservative stance toward the OT law. When we consider all the evidence in Luke-Acts, however, a distinctly different picture emerges. Luke emphasizes that the prophetic Scriptures find their fulfillment in Jesus of Nazareth, particularly in his death and resurrection (Luke 24:25–27, 44–47; Acts 24:14; 26:22–23; 28:23). The OT, therefore, is interpreted rightly only if it is seen to climax in the ministry, death, and resurrection of Jesus of Nazareth. The law and the prophets point toward the kingdom of God (Luke 16:16). Hence, every letter of the law finds its fulfillment in the ministry of Jesus Christ (16:17). The prohibition of divorce and remarriage that immediately succeeds this saying is instructive (16:18), for the law is now interpreted by Jesus Christ. Jesus did not center on the law; the law centers on Jesus.

The evidence that Luke shares in common with the other Synoptics is significant as well. The cleansing of the leper suggests that Jesus transcends the laws of leprosy (5:12–15). Jesus as the Son of Man is Lord of the Sabbath (6:1–5). Doing good on the Sabbath fits the purpose for which it was instituted (6:6–11; 14:1–6), for Jesus was not required to heal on the Sabbath (13:10–17).

The inauguration of the kingdom through Jesus means that what the law proclaims is fulfilled in him. Such fulfillment does not mean that every aspect of the law is replaced with new content. The command to love God and neighbor remains in force (10:25–28), but even this command cannot be abstracted from Luke's Gospel as a whole. Jesus reminded the rich ruler of the commands of the Decalogue when the latter inquired about gaining eternal life (18:18–22). Nevertheless, the rich man would not enjoy eternal life unless he followed Jesus in discipleship. The injunction to "leave the dead to bury their own dead" (9:60) does not directly abrogate the law. It does confirm, however, that following Jesus is God's supreme demand.

Luke does not think that all the requirements of the law are binding now that Christ is exalted and the Spirit is poured out. For instance, Stephen was charged with speaking against the law and the temple (Acts 6:11–14). Luke informs us that the charges are false. Some scholars have exaggerated Stephen's words in 7:1–53, seeing in them a radical rejection of the temple. Such a view misreads the content of Stephen's speech. Stephen did not actually criticize temple worship, nor did he reject it as if it were contrary to the will of God. What Stephen did was *relativize* temple worship in his speech. He reminded his hearers that God is not beholden to a temple, and that he worked in Israelite history before a temple was erected. God transcends the temple, for as sovereign Lord of the universe, he cannot be contained by a building. Stephen's critique of the law, then, was rather subtle. He suggested a change in the temple's status in light of salvation history's being fulfilled with the coming of Jesus. In sum, Stephen's speech suggests that the law does not play the central role that it did formerly.

Peter's experience with Cornelius and his friends confirms that the commands of the law are not required. Peter's vision on the roof is particularly important (10:9–16). He saw a variety of animals in a sheet lowered from heaven. Some of the animals in the sheet were prohibited, according to the OT food laws (Lev. 11:1–44; Deut. 14:3–21), but God commands Peter to eat them. Luke's point is that food laws are no longer in force at this stage in salvation history. The narrative connects the relaxation of food laws with the gospel's extension to the Gentiles (Acts 10:1–11:18). Peter naturally was puzzled about God's nullifying what previously was a commandment (10:17). But he began to see that the purification of unclean foods was connected to the Gentile mission (10:28). The Gentiles received the Spirit without being circumcised, nor did they conform to Jewish purity requirements (10:44–48; 15:7–11). The Gentiles did not have to conform to the OT law in order to be part of the people of God. By the time of the apostolic council in Acts 15, Peter saw the implications of the Cornelius event clearly (15:7–11). The yoke of the law should not be imposed upon the Gentiles. The only entrance requirement is faith in Jesus Christ, and the gift of the Spirit confirms that they are part of the people of God. Paul's words in 13:38–39 are quite similar. Justification comes not through the law of Moses but rather by believing in Jesus Christ. In the new era of salvation history, forgiveness of sins belongs to those who trust in Jesus Christ instead of those who observe the law.

A controversy arose in the early church over whether circumcision should be required for Gentile believers. Some maintained that circumcision was necessary for salvation because the OT clearly demanded that those who enter into covenant with the Lord be circumcised (Gen. 17:9–14; Acts 15:1, 5). Historical, textual, and theological issues join together to make Acts 15:1–35 complex and controversial. For our purposes here, however, the text as it stands is quite clear. The decision of the council was that circumcision would not be required for salvation. The Gentiles would be considered members of the church through their faith in the Lord Jesus Christ. Luke does not argue that circumcision was a mistake from the beginning, nor does he denigrate the OT requirement. His purpose is to relay that the initiation rite is no longer required at this stage in salvation history. A new era has dawned with the ministry, death, and resurrection of Jesus Christ. Because he is exalted to God's right hand, the Spirit is poured out on all those who believe. The requirements of the Torah are no longer in force since God's promises are being fulfilled and the good news is going out to the Gentiles.

It is clear, then, that Luke does not propose an extremely conservative view of the law. He teaches that justification and forgiveness of sins are obtained not through the law but rather by the grace of the Lord Jesus Christ. Food laws and circumcision, which are normative in the Mosaic law, are no longer necessary for the people of God. The fulfillment of God's promises signals a shift in redemptive history. The so-called conservative texts relating to the law in Luke should be explained within the framework of salvation history. Often believers observed the law for cultural reasons (16:3), not because they felt that the law was required.

Does the so-called apostolic decree contradict what is being argued for here? The council determined that circumcision was unnecessary for salvation but then proceeded to say that Gentiles must "abstain only from things polluted by idols and from fornication and from whatever has been strangled and from blood" (Acts 15:20 NRSV; cf. 15:29; 21:25). The significance and meaning of the decree has long been debated. The Western text omits the things strangled and appears to turn the decree into moral requirements, so that idolatry, sexual sin, and murder are prohibited, and a negative form of the golden rule is added. Such a solution is attractive, but the textual evidence favors including the prohibition of things strangled. Many scholars have maintained that the prohibitions hearken back to Lev. 17–18. Gentiles were to refrain from eating food that was improperly slaughtered, from consuming food with the blood in it, from marrying within the confines prohibited by 18:6–18, and from eating food offered to idols. Barrett (1998: 730–36) suggests that what are prohibited in Acts 15:20 are idolatry, fornication, and murder along with nonkosher foods. It seems to me as well that the decree mixes together moral and ritual requirements, but unlike Barrett, I think that the only moral prohibition relates to sexual sin. In other words, it is difficult to see that the immorality in view hearkens back to the regulations regarding sexual sin in Lev. 18; rather, the reference is to sexual sin in general, for Gentiles had to be taught that sexual sin did not fit with their newfound faith in Christ. The other requirements related to prohibition of nonkosher foods, including foods from which the blood was not properly drained. Such requirements were included to facilitate fellowship between Christian Jews and Gentiles.

The decree was not requisite for salvation, for such a decision would cancel out what was decided with respect to circumcision. James addressed the matter of Jewish sensibilities and requested that Gentiles tolerate Jewish customs for the sake of fellowship. Gentiles would be quite aware of Jewish concerns because the law of Moses was publicly read in synagogues throughout the cities in the Greco-Roman world (Acts 15:21).

The Lukan view of the law is quite complex. The key to untangling it is to interpret it in light of salvation history. The law pointed to Jesus Christ and is fulfilled in him. He is the fulfillment of what was prophesied in the OT. The Lukan view of the law, then, has elements of both continuity and discontinuity. There is continuity in that the law points toward Jesus Christ and is fulfilled in him. Some of the moral norms of the law seem to carry over without any changes. On the other hand, discontinuity exists as well. Circumcision and food laws were no longer required of the people of God. Gentiles were not required to conform to the Jewish Torah in order to belong to the people of God.

The Pauline Literature

Paul clearly teaches that the Mosaic covenant has come to an end, and believers are no longer under it as a covenantal structure. In Gal. 3:15–25 Paul distinguishes the Sinai covenant from the covenant enacted with Abraham. The Abrahamic covenant is foundational, for it was given before any provisions were added from the Sinai covenant. A covenant that was enacted 430 years after the first cannot nullify the provisions of the covenant made with Abraham. In 3:18 Paul contrasts the promissory nature of the Abrahamic covenant with receiving the inheritance on the basis of the law. The covenant with Abraham is established on the basis of God's promise. Hence, the inheritance is guaranteed because it depends not on human performance but rather on the word of God.

The law was intended to be in force only until the seed, Jesus Christ, arrived (3:19). The problem is not the content of the law but rather that human beings were unable to obey what the law demanded and found themselves imprisoned under the power of sin (3:21–22). The law, therefore, was intended to be in force for only a certain period of time. It functioned as "pedagogue" (3:24–25 AT) until salvation history reached its climax with the coming of Jesus Christ. The law was a babysitter or custodian designed for the period of infancy that has ended with the coming of Jesus Christ.

We could easily misconstrue Paul's argument here. He is not suggesting that believers are free from all moral norms, as if life in Christ is free from any moral requirements. His purpose is to argue that the old era of redemptive history under the Mosaic covenant has come to an end. The difference between the covenants is clarified by 4:1–7. Those who lived under the Sinai covenant were like minors who had not yet received the promised inheritance. The inheritance was promised in the Abrahamic covenant, but Israel lived in the period before the promise was realized. In the interval before the promise came to pass, they waited in anticipation for the fulfillment. Israel lived in slavery under "the elements of the world" (4:3 AT). Hence, the law did not restrain sin in Israel but rather contributed to Israel's bondage. Now a new era of redemptive history has dawned with the coming of Jesus Christ. Those who are redeemed by Christ are no longer minors: they have reached full adulthood (4:4–5). They no longer live under the provisional rules of the Mosaic law, for the law functioned as "guardians and trustees until the date set by the father" (4:2 NRSV). They now enjoy the fulfillment of what God has promised, for they have received the Holy Spirit.

Yet grace was not lacking under the Sinai covenant, for God graciously freed Israel from Egyptian bondage, and the salvation won at the exodus became a type of the salvation accomplished by Jesus Christ. Still, Israel as a whole, with the exception of the remnant, did not receive the ability to keep God's law, and thus they lived under the dominion of sin.

Other Pauline texts confirm that the Mosaic covenant was an interim one that passed away with the coming of Jesus Christ. In 2 Cor. 3 the new covenant is contrasted with the old covenant (3:6, 14). The use of the terms "new covenant" and "old covenant" implies that the latter was no longer in force. Paul contrasts the old covenant with the new: the former led to death and condemnation, the latter to life in the Spirit and righteousness. Most significant for our purposes here, the old covenant is said to be "brought to an end," while the new is "permanent" (3:11). The glory that was "brought to an end" on Moses' face (3:13) symbolized the temporary nature of the Mosaic covenant. Christ is both the goal and the end of the law for all who believe (Rom. 10:4). The prescriptions of the law have come to an end through the work of Christ on the cross (Eph. 2:15), so that the long hostility between Jews and Gentiles has been cancelled through the cross.

Nor does Paul think that the observance of days or special festivals is required for believers. Along with foods in Col. 2:16–19, Paul includes festivals, new moons, and Sabbaths (cf. Gal. 4:10). These too are shadows that point to Christ. The inclusion of the Sabbath is particularly noteworthy because it was a regular feature of Jewish life and often commented on by Gentile writers in the Greco-Roman world. Sabbath observance distinguished Jews from their neighbors and was one of the boundary markers of Judaism. For Paul, however, the Sabbath is a shadow that points to Christ (cf. Rom. 14:5). In the same way, observing the Passover is no longer binding for Christians, but such a conclusion does not cancel out the significance of the Passover, for Christ fulfills the Passover sacrifice by his death on the cross (1 Cor. 5:7). Similarly, the command to remove leaven from houses is not mandatory for believers (5:6–8). It does not follow from this that the command about leaven is irrelevant for believers, for it symbolizes the need to expunge evil from their midst and to live with sincerity and truth.

The Pauline perspective on the law is complex. On the one hand, the Sinai covenant and law have passed away; on the other hand, the law is fulfilled in Christ. Because the law has passed away, believers are not obligated to keep the Sabbath, observe food laws, and be circumcised. And yet all these laws are shadows that point to Christ and are fulfilled in him. Hence, circumcision points to the circumcision of the heart accomplished by the cross of Christ (Col. 2:11–12) and the work of the Spirit (Rom. 2:28–29; Phil. 3:3; cf. Deut. 10:16; 30:6; Jer. 4:4). Just as the Passover points to the death of Christ, so too OT sacrifices in general anticipate and reach their fulfillment in Christ's death on the cross (Rom. 3:24–26; Gal. 3:13). Jesus' death fulfills the sin offering found in the OT (Rom. 8:3; cf. Lev. 5:6–7; 9:2 LXX; 2 Cor. 5:21). The blood of Christ hearkens back to the blood spilled in sacrifices in the OT (Rom. 3:25; 5:9; 1 Cor. 11:25; Eph. 1:7; 2:13; Col. 1:20). The temple was considered one of the three pillars of Judaism, but Paul shows no interest in the physical temple. Believers are now the temple of the Holy Spirit (1 Cor. 3:16; 6:19; 2 Cor. 6:16). The language of uncleanness is applied to the ethical sphere. Believers are to separate themselves from evil and live in holiness (2 Cor. 6:17; 7:1). In the OT those who committed certain blatant sins were put to death (Deut. 13:5; 17:7, 12; 21:21; 22:21). Paul does not require, however, that the man committing incest be put to death (1 Cor. 5:13). Still, the OT requirement finds a new fulfillment in Christ. The unrepentant member of the church is to be excommunicated for his sin and failure to repent (5:1–13).

The change of covenants does not mean that all of the moral norms of the OT have passed away for Christians. Paul seems to carry over for NT believers some of the moral norms of the law. The command to honor fathers and mothers still applies to believers (Eph. 6:2). Those who live in love will keep the prohibitions against adultery, murder, stealing, coveting, and so forth (Rom. 13:8–10; cf. 2:21–22; 7:7–8). Those who live according to the Spirit will fulfill the ordinance of the law (8:4), or as Paul says in 2:26, they will keep the precepts of the law. In this latter text as well, such obedience is the result of the Spirit's work (2:28–29). The prohibition against idolatry still obtains, though Paul does not cite any particular OT text (1 Cor. 5:10–11; 6:9; 10:7, 14; 2 Cor. 6:16; Gal. 5:20; Eph. 5:5; Col. 3:5). Paul believes that some of the standards in the OT law are normative, though he does not necessarily specify that they derive from the law: honoring and obeying parents (Rom. 1:30; Eph. 6:1–3; Col. 3:20; 1 Tim. 1:9; 2 Tim. 3:2); murder (Rom. 1:29; 13:9; 1 Tim. 1:9); adultery (Rom. 2:22; 7:3; 13:9; 1 Cor. 6:9; cf. 1 Tim. 1:10); stealing (Rom. 1:29–31; 1 Cor. 6:9–10; Eph. 4:28); lying (Col. 3:9; 1 Tim. 1:10; 4:2; Titus 1:12); coveting (Rom. 1:29; 7:7–8; Eph. 5:3, 5; Col. 3:5).

How do we account for the fact that Paul proclaims the obsolescence of the Mosaic law and yet cites commands from the law as authoritative? Perhaps we can say that the commands are not normative merely because they are Mosaic. Some of the laws in the OT are included in the law of Christ (1 Cor. 9:21;

Gal. 6:2). But the law of Christ should not be restricted to the moral norms of the Mosaic law; nor does the law of Christ call attention primarily to the Mosaic law but rather to the fulfillment of the law in and by Jesus Christ. The self-giving life of Jesus manifested particularly in his death on the cross becomes the paradigm for the lives of believers. In giving exhortations to his churches, Paul does not often cite the OT law. The heart and soul of his ethic is summed up in the command to love one another (e.g., Rom. 12:9; 13:8–10; 1 Cor. 8:1–3; 13:1–13; 14:1; Gal. 5:13–15; Eph. 5:2; Col. 3:14; 1 Tim. 1:5), and many have rightly seen the injunction to love as the center of the law of Christ (cf. John 13:34–35).

Love, however, cannot be separated from moral norms. We learn from 1 Thess. 4:2 that specific concrete directives were given to the churches orally. For Paul, love does not float free of ethical norms but rather is expressed by such norms. Paul does not have a casuistic ethic that prescribes the course of action for every conceivable situation, but neither does he simply appeal to the Spirit and freedom without describing how life in the Spirit expresses itself. The notion that Paul appeals to the Spirit for ethics without any ethical norms is contradicted by his paraenesis. Nor should the Pauline theme of obedience be identified as legalism, for the new obedience is the work of the Spirit in those who are the new creation work of Christ. Nor does it diminish the work of the cross, for the cross is the basis and foundation for the transforming work of the Spirit in believers. Another way of saying this is that the imperative (God's command) is rooted in the indicative (what God has done for believers in Christ). Believers are saved, redeemed, reconciled, and justified even now, and yet we have seen that each of these blessings is fundamentally eschatological. In the interval between the already and the not yet, ethical exhortation is needed. If the priority of the indicative is lost, then the grace of the Pauline gospel is undermined. The imperative must always flow from the indicative. On the other hand, the indicative must not swallow up the imperative so that the latter disappears. The imperatives do not compromise Paul's gospel. They should not be construed as law opposed to gospel. The imperatives are part and parcel of the gospel as long as they are woven into the story line of the Pauline gospel and flow from the indicative of what God has accomplished for us in Christ.

In summary, the law in Paul's thought must be interpreted in light of redemptive history. Now that Jesus Christ has come, the Mosaic covenant and its prescriptions are no longer in force for believers. The new age of salvation history has ushered out the old age, which set boundaries between Jews and Gentiles via laws requiring circumcision, Sabbath observance, and purity. The coming of the new age does not mean that Paul has no moral norms. The law of Christ now functions as the norm for believers, and Christ's self-giving sacrifice functions as the paradigm of this law. At the same time, the law of Christ may be described as the law of love. To say that love is the heart and soul of Paul's ethic does not imply that there are no moral norms that inform the law of Christ. Pauline ethical exhortations are rooted in the tension between the indicative and imperative, with the indicative always functioning as the basis for the imperative. So too, the only means by which believers can fulfill the law of Christ is the power of the Holy Spirit.

Hebrews

When we consider the NT as a whole, we clearly see that the canonical writers believed that the Mosaic covenant was temporary and that believers are no longer obligated to fulfill its stipulations. The author of Hebrews engages in a sustained argument against reverting to the Aaronic priesthood and the Levitical sacrificial cultus. He does not claim that the Mosaic covenant was somehow a mistake from its inception; instead, he hangs his argument on salvation-historical realities. Now that Christ has arrived as the Melchizedekian priest, a return to the Levitical priesthood would constitute a denial of Christ's sacrifice. The Aaronic priests and the OT sacrifices are not rejected wholesale; they are viewed typologically. The OT priesthood and sacrifices pointed to and anticipated the sacrifice of Christ. They are the shadows, but he is the substance. The OT sacrifices cannot forgive, since brute beasts are offered, but Christ's sacrifice is atoning, since he is a willing and sinless victim. The repetition of OT sacrifices reveals that they do not actually forgive sin, whereas the once-for-all sacrifice of Christ definitively and finally atones for sin.

The author of Hebrews maintains that a change of priesthood also constitutes a change of law (7:11–12). Indeed, he claims that the Mosaic law did not bring perfection and was weak and useless (7:18–19). In context it is clear that his point is that the law does not provide a full and final atonement for sin. Indeed, he proceeds to argue that the promise of a new covenant indicates that the Sinai covenant is now obsolete (8:7–13). Once again, the focus is on the failure of the law to provide final forgiveness. A regular feature in Hebrews is the contrasting of the stipulations and/or punishments of the Sinai covenant over against what is required now for those belonging to Christ (2:1–4; 9:6–10, 15–24; 10:26–31; 12:25–29; 13:9–12). Indeed, the very first verses of the letter commend the definitive revelation given in the last days by the Son and contrast it with the partial, preliminary revelation given under the old covenant (1:1–3). The contrast between Moses and Christ articulated in 3:1–6 is similar in this regard.

The author of Hebrews clearly believes that the new covenant has displaced or, perhaps better, "fulfilled" what was promised in the old. Now that the end of the ages has arrived, a return to the old covenant would lead to final destruction. The author is strikingly severe and dogmatic. Those who return to the regulations and sacrifices of the old covenant will be damned, for to do so is to reject the work of Christ on the cross (cf. 6:4–8; 10:26–31; 12:25–29). Hence, he can say that no sacrifice for sins remains for those who turn away from Christ's sacrifice (10:26). This is another way of saying that those who turn back to the Levitical cult have shut themselves off from any possibility of forgiveness. Animal sacrifices have passed away, and yet believers offer to God spiritual sacrifices when they praise God's name and when they share financially with those who are in need (13:15–16).

The author of Hebrews does not charge the Mosaic covenant with legalism, nor does he find fault with the specific prescriptions in the law per se. Rather, the Mosaic covenant and law had a typological and salvation-historical function. The tabernacle points to the true tabernacle in heaven, where God dwells (cf. 8:1–6; 9:1–10). The OT sacrifices and regulations anticipate the sacrifice of Christ and the era that has dawned in the new covenant (9:11–14, 23–28; 10:1–18). The OT sacrifices also point to the need to share with others and to praise God (13:15–16). The promises of land and rest in the OT forecast the heavenly city and the Sabbath rest prepared for the people of God in the age to come (3:7–4:13; 11:9–10, 13–16; 12:22; 13:14).

Is there any continuity between the OT law and the NT fulfillment of the law in Christ in Hebrews? The author cites the new-covenant promise of Jer. 31:31–34, where the law will be written on the hearts of believers (Heb. 8:7–13). The author does not work out what the law written on the heart would mean in terms of giving specific prescriptions from the law. He clearly believes that there is a place for commands and injunctions, as we learn from the exhortations in Heb. 13. What he emphasizes, however, is that through the death of Christ, cleansing of sins has been achieved once for all.

To conclude, Hebrews emphasizes that the new covenant has dawned in Jesus Christ. A new priesthood means that there is a new law, which fulfills what was promised in the old. Now that the new has arrived, believers should not return to the shadows of the old. They live in the age of the fulfillment of what God has promised and have received definitive forgiveness of sins. Going back to the old would be foolish and fatal. Still, believers are called upon to live in a way that pleases God, for God's law is now written on their hearts.

Conclusion

In considering the place of the OT or Mosaic law as it relates to redemptive history, we see the diversity of the NT witness. Many pieces of literature include no direct discussion of the matter or lack a comprehensive treatment of the question. Paul surely includes the most thorough analysis of the role of the OT law. Nevertheless, what is striking is the centrality of salvation history in relationship to the law. The NT writings consistently teach that the Mosaic covenant is no longer in force for believers, or at least they fail to bind their churches with practices that distinguished Jews from Gentiles, such as circumcision, Sabbath, or purity laws. Another regular feature is that the law is seen to be fulfilled in Jesus Christ and points toward his death and resurrection. Such a standpoint is reflected whether we consider Matthew, Luke-Acts, Paul, Hebrews, and so on. The NT writers do not merely argue that the Mosaic covenant is set aside in Jesus Christ; they also teach that the law finds its terminus and goal in him, so that he fulfills what is foreshadowed in the OT law.

Even though the phrase "law of Christ" is found only in Paul, it seems that such a phrase nicely sums up the NT witness regarding the law. The OT law is reinterpreted in light of the Christ event. The central norm of the law is love, and Jesus Christ's giving of himself on the cross is paradigmatic of the love expected of disciples. Such love certainly is filled in by other moral content, so that love does not become a plastic thing, defined in an arbitrary way. Indeed, some of the commands from the OT are included in the definition of love (such as prohibitions against adultery, stealing, murder, and sexual sin). Still, all the norms of the law are related to Jesus Christ, and so we find in the NT letters numerous allusions to the teaching of Jesus in paraenesis. Further, the call to live a new life (the imperative) is always rooted in the indicative of God's saving work in Christ. In addition, the new life is possible only by the work of the Holy Spirit. Hence, when we consider the law, the major themes of this work come together. The OT law must be interpreted in terms of salvation history, and the law is realized only through the saving work of Christ and the empowerment of the Holy Spirit.

Pastoral Reflection

Throughout the history of the church, there has been considerable discussion on the role of the law in the life of Christian believers. Some argue for a moral, ceremonial, and civil division of the law, but we do not find such divisions presented in the NT, even if there is some truth in the categories. Others maintain that the OT law plays no role in the life of Christians, but this seems to exaggerate the theme of freedom from the law. We have seen that the law is both abolished and fulfilled in Christ. It has reached its goal and end in him, and hence the OT law must be interpreted in light of the great events of Christ's death and resurrection.

12

The People of the Promise

Thus far in the book we have considered the saving promises of God that have come to fruition through the work of God and Christ. The previous chapters could give the impression that the NT has an individualistic vision, but God intended to form a people who would bring him honor and glory. God's aim is to display his radiant glory through a corporate people. Previously we have seen that the blessing for the whole world would come through the offspring of Abraham (Gen. 12:3), and clearly the church of Jesus Christ represents the fulfillment of the promise made to Abraham. The NT teaching on the church is restricted in the Gospels since the church is only established with Jesus' death and resurrection. Hence, we find the most substantial discussions in Acts and the epistolary literature.[1]

Matthew

The Gospels do not say much about the church because of their location in salvation history. Matthew forecasts the inclusion of the Gentiles into God's people (cf. 21:43; 28:19). The folding in of the Gentiles manifests itself also in

---

1. Again the discussion is considerably abbreviated. For a fuller treatment, see Schreiner 2008: 675–754.

the story of the magi (2:1–12), and the account of the centurion testifies that belonging to the people of God is not restricted to the Jews (8:5–13). Jesus, as the Servant of the Lord, "will proclaim justice to the Gentiles" (12:18), and "in his name the Gentiles will hope" (12:21). The good seed are sown throughout the whole world (13:37–38) and cannot be restricted to Israel. The feeding of the four thousand most likely occurred in Gentile territory (15:32–39). In the parable of the laborers in the vineyard, the eleventh-hour workers may represent Gentiles (20:1–16).

The gospel is to be proclaimed throughout the whole world (24:14), and this includes both Jews and Gentiles. Jesus commissions his disciples after his resurrection to "make disciples of all nations" (28:19). There are good reasons to think that Jews are included among the nations that are to be evangelized. The people of God, according to Matthew, will be composed of both Jews and Gentiles. The gospel of the kingdom is to be proclaimed to all without exception.

Jesus spoke of the "church" (*ekklēsia*). Indeed, he refers to "my church" (16:18), indicating that the true remnant within Israel belongs to and is governed by him. Intense debate has centered on the words "You are Peter, and on this rock I will build my church" (16:18). Protestant exegesis has traditionally understood the rock to represent Peter's confession of Jesus as Christ, so that Jesus' messianic status functions as the foundation of the church. Roman Catholic exegesis has defended the view that the rock is Peter himself, finding evidence here to support papal supremacy in the church of Jesus Christ. Neither view as traditionally defended is credible. Reading a doctrine of papal supremacy into the text is an anachronism. What we have here is a wordplay on the similarity between Peter's nickname and the Greek word for "rock," so that it is most natural to read the text to say that the church would be built upon Peter as the rock. Peter represents the new community of Jesus. Jesus' new assembly, then, is built upon the apostles with Peter as the first among equals and representative of the Twelve. In saying that the gates of hell will not triumph over the church, Jesus promised that death would not conquer the church.[2]

The other Matthean text that refers to the church is 18:15–20. This paragraph addresses the matter of disciplining believers who need correction, setting forth a process that must be followed in disciplinary cases. The sayings about binding and loosing are rooted in a disciplinary context. Jesus gave instructions to preserve the purity and vitality of the new remnant. Insofar as the church truly gathers in Jesus' name in exercising discipline, they carry

2. For the history of interpretation of "the gates of hell," see Davies and Allison 1991: 630–34. They opt for the view that demonic powers will not conquer the church, but the OT background connects the "gates of Sheol" with death (cf. Job 17:16; 38:17; Pss. 9:13; 107:18; Isa. 38:10; Jon. 2:2; see also Wis. 16:13; 3 Macc. 5:51; Sir. 51:9; Rev. 1:18; 6:8; 20:13–14), so the focus probably is on death, though some connection with the view proposed by Davies and Allison is possible because death and demonic rule are intertwined.

out Jesus' will. Jesus did not grant the church unrestricted authority to carry out every whim. When the church is gathered in Jesus' name, then its binding and loosing fulfill his will.

Luke-Acts

Luke-Acts opens with the promise that the Lord will fulfill the covenantal promises he has made to his people (Luke 1:17). The promises made to Abraham will be realized for Israel (1:54–55, 72–75). At first glance, it appears that the fulfillment of God's promises to Israel will occur in a straightforward way, so that Israel will finally enjoy political and religious supremacy. But Luke emphasizes that many in Israel failed to believe. Furthermore, the message of salvation is to be proclaimed to all nations (24:47; Acts 1:8). The inclusion of the Gentiles is anticipated in Luke 4:25–27. Acts relates the account of the gospel's progress from Jerusalem, Judea, Galilee, and Samaria to the Gentile world, showing the missionary character of the early church.

Acts also emphasizes that important events in the history of salvation were accompanied by prayer, whether the choosing of the twelfth apostle (to replace Judas), the descent of the Spirit, the visit to Cornelius, or the first intentional Gentile mission. Prayer in Acts, in particular, focuses on the mission of the church to bring the good news to the ends of the earth. Further, the regular mention of prayer and the emphasis on being devoted to prayer illustrate the prominent place that prayer held in the life of the early church. Thereby the church indicated its reliance on God for the accomplishment of every good thing.

The church plays a major role in the theology of Luke-Acts. God's covenantal promises were fulfilled in Jesus of Nazareth, so that the saving message was first proclaimed in Israel. Many Jews, however, rejected the good news proclaimed by Jesus Christ, and Jesus himself appointed twelve apostles as the true and restored Israel. Acts relates how the majority of Israel continued to reject the message of salvation, while at the same time the message of salvation expands to include the Gentiles in the story line of the book. Jesus, who in Luke is the bearer of the Spirit, is the one in Acts who pours out the Spirit so that his disciples are empowered to bring the saving message to all peoples everywhere. The church is established on the basis of the teaching of the apostles, the fellowship and generosity of the new community, baptism of new converts, the breaking of bread in the Lord's Supper, and prayer (2:42). By emphasizing these different elements, Luke sketches in the nature of life in the early church.

The Gospel and Epistles of John

Both the Gospel and Epistles of John focus on the individual's relationship to God rather than the church as a corporate community. We should not conclude from this that John had no interest in the corporate life of the church. The limited purposes of his writing should caution us against making confident statements about his lack of interest in the church. In one sense, John shows intense concern about the corporate life of believers. He constantly emphasizes the love that should mark the Christian community. Believers are to love one another just as Jesus loved them in giving his life for their sakes (John 13:34–35; 1 John 3:11–18).

Nor should we conclude that John lacks a theology of mission. Indeed, the focal point of mission in John's Gospel is Jesus himself, for as we have seen earlier, Jesus is sent by the Father for the salvation of the world. Furthermore, just as Jesus was sent by the Father, so also he sends out his disciples for the sake of the world (cf. 15:27; 17:18; 20:21). As Köstenberger and O'Brien (2001: 210) remark, "John describes the mission of the disciples in terms of 'harvesting' (4:38), 'fruitbearing' (15:8, 16), and 'witnessing' (15:27). All of these terms place the disciples in the humble position of extending the mission of another, Jesus." The disciples are sent out to continue Jesus' mission through the work of the Spirit, so that they bear witness to Jesus. Thereby they continue the harvest that Jesus began.

We do not have a full-orbed theology of the church in John. Nothing is said about the structure or leaders of the church, though it is clear that the apostles were authoritative witnesses. Nor does John provide direct teaching on baptism or the Lord's Supper, though his teaching on the salvation that Jesus accomplished points to both of these secondarily. John does emphasize the love that should be the mark of true disciples, pointing to Jesus' self-sacrifice as the paradigm of love.

The Pauline Literature

The term that Paul typically uses to designate the communities that he established is *ekklēsia* (church), which was used in the Greek OT along with *synagōgē* to translate the Hebrew *qĕhal* (e.g., *qĕhal yhwh*, assembly of Yahweh: Num. 16:3; 20:4; Deut. 23:1, 8; 1 Chron. 28:8; and *qĕhal yiśrā'ēl*, assembly of Israel: Exod. 12:6; Lev. 16:17; Num. 14:5). The use of this expression with reference to Paul's converts demonstrates that he conceived of the church as the true Israel, the new people of God, and the fulfillment of what God intended with Israel.

The best-known metaphor for the church in Pauline writings is the body of Christ (1 Cor. 10:16–17; 12:12–27). The body is one and yet has many different members; the variety of members does not nullify the fact that there is one body. In Ephesians and Colossians, Paul speaks of Christ as being the *head* of the body (Eph. 1:22–23; 4:15–16; 5:23; Col. 1:18; 2:19) instead of using the term "head" as he did in 1 Cor. 12:21 to denote a member of the body.

It is "through the church that the manifold wisdom of God" is displayed (Eph. 3:10). The church enshrines God's plan for history, revealing to all creation the wisdom and depth of God's saving plan. The church is the locus of God's glory, the theater in which he displays his grace and love. The church features God's wisdom, declaring to the whole universe that the outworking of history is not arbitrary but rather fulfills God's plan. The corporate people of God, gathered together to hear the word of the Lord and to proclaim the good news, represent God's outpost in the world.

Paul also identifies the church as God's temple (1 Cor. 3:16–17; 2 Cor. 6:16; Eph. 2:21). To have a "religion" without a literal temple, priests, or sacrifices would have seemed quite strange in the Greco-Roman world. The newness of the gospel emerges at this very point. The OT often refers to Israel as God's "people" (*laos*). It is somewhat surprising how little Paul employs this term to refer to the church of Jesus Christ (Rom. 9:25–26; 2 Cor. 6:16; Titus 2:14). The use of the term indicates, however, that the blessings of Israel are now fulfilled in the church of Christ, since in Rom. 9:25–26 Paul picks up the language of Hos. 1:10; 2:23 and applies it to the church.

We certainly recognize that Paul was a missionary-theologian and a missionary pastor to his churches. We see from Acts and his Letters that he traveled constantly to plant churches to further his mission. Paul's theology drove his mission. He desired to proclaim the gospel in virgin areas, so that Christ would be praised where he was previously unknown (Rom. 15:20–24; 2 Cor. 10:13–16). His apostolic sufferings were one of the primary means by which the word of the gospel was proclaimed in new areas (Col. 1:24–29). His sufferings were a corollary of Christ's sufferings, in that his suffering was the means by which the good news was extended to the Gentiles.

Discipline and correction permeate the Pauline Letters, and in some instances severe measures were required. In 1 Cor. 5, Paul mandates expulsion from the church for a man involved in incest; once he is expelled, he enters Satan's sphere (5:3–5). The motive behind such discipline is love, so that the man's "spirit may be saved in the day of the Lord" (5:5). Paul's advice in 2 Thessalonians matches the text in 1 Cor. 5. Those who ignore the instructions in the letter are to be isolated so that they will be shamed into repentance (2 Thess. 3:14–15). Refusing fellowship with the recalcitrant must be motivated by love. There is a kind of admonition that is fraternal and family oriented, which is not rooted in enmity and hatred, and yet discipline is still administered.

1 Peter and Revelation

The General Epistles and Revelation do not contain a detailed discussion on the church. All of these texts are certainly addressed to churches, speaking to the corporate life of the various communities. Since each piece of literature responds to specific circumstances in the churches, the space given to the topic of the church varies. We need to remind ourselves again of the occasional nature of the writings. The failure to say more about the church does not lead to the conclusion that the authors had little interest in the church. For instance, none of the authors mentions the Lord's Supper, but it would be rash to conclude from this that the Lord's Supper was not practiced or that it was rejected. The authors included only what was most pressing in response to situations that arose in the churches.

In 1 Peter the church of Jesus Christ is conceived of as the true Israel, the genuine remnant of God's people. Just as Israel was God's elect people in the OT, now the church constitutes God's elect ones (1:1–2). The theme that the church is the true Israel is emphasized (2:9–10). The church is God's "chosen race." Peter also draws on one of the charter statements of Israel, Exod. 19:6, in designating the church as "a royal priesthood" and "a holy nation." Israel was to serve as God's priest, communicating his glory to the surrounding nations. Now the church of Jesus Christ, as the true Israel, is to mediate God's blessings to the world (cf. 1 Pet. 2:5). The church of Jesus Christ is set apart as God's special and holy people. That the church functions as the true Israel is also communicated in 2:10, where Peter draws from Hos. 2:23. Peter sees this promise fulfilled in the church of Jesus Christ, made up of both Jews and Gentiles. They are the true Israel of God; they are those who were not a people but are now included within the circle of God's blessing.

Not only is the church the true Israel; it also constitutes the true temple. Jesus is both the living stone and the cornerstone of God's temple (1 Pet. 2:4–8). All those who belong to Jesus are also living stones and are being built up as God's spiritual house. The temple in Jerusalem is no longer the center of God's purposes; rather, the church of Jesus Christ, composed of believers from every ethnic background and social class, constitutes the temple of God.

In Revelation, the churches are described as "lampstands" (1:12, 20; 2:1, 5). The two witnesses, which are probably the church, are also designated as two lampstands (11:4). As lampstands, the churches are to manifest the light of God's goodness and supremacy to the world. As witnesses, they proclaim God's lordship over the idolatry of Rome, which demands total allegiance.

One of the fundamental themes in Revelation is that the church is the true Israel. This truth is communicated in a variety of ways. In the OT, Israel was a priestly kingdom (Exod. 19:6), intended to mediate God's blessing to the world. Now, however, God's priestly kingdom is the church of Jesus Christ (Rev. 1:6). Twice in Revelation, Jewish synagogues are called a "synagogue of Satan" (2:9; 3:9). We must locate John's words, however, in their own historical context. John never intended his words to provide a platform for discriminating against Jews or putting them to death. The shocking designation is intended to prevent Christians from committing apostasy and from joining the wrong side. The small community that is loyal to Jesus Christ represents the true people of God. That the church is the new Israel is also communicated in 7:1–8 and 14:1–5. Some interpreters understand the 144,000 as literally referring to Israel, but the twelve tribes of Israel point to a greater fulfillment: the church of Jesus Christ. The 144,000 is symbolic in that it is twelve squared and multiplied by one thousand. It represents, then, the totality of God's people and the fulfillment of God's promises to Abraham. It also represents God's army in that it is comparable to the census of Israel as God's army in the OT. The church of Jesus Christ is, then, the true synagogue of God, the place where his people gather. The church does not cancel out ethnic Israel, for the names of the twelve tribes are on the gates of the heavenly city (21:12). But the true Israel, composed of both Jews and Gentiles, finds its fulfillment in the church of Jesus Christ. Placing the 144,000 (in 7:1–8) next to an innumerable multitude (7:9–17) is no contradiction. John portrays the church with two different pictures to teach that the church is the true Israel, fulfilling Israel's purpose, and also that it is an innumerable host from every tribe, tongue, people, and nation, fulfilling the promise to Abraham that the whole world would be blessed through him (cf. Gen. 12:3). Revelation emphasizes the universality of the people of God. Christ ransomed some from every cultural background (5:9). John emphasizes that in the heavenly city, God resides with human beings so that "they will be his peoples" (21:3 NRSV). The plural "peoples" (*laoi*) celebrates the diversity of God's saving work, which includes human beings from every cultural and linguistic background.

The people of God are also described as the true temple: the dwelling place of God. When John is instructed to measure the temple, a literal temple in Jerusalem is not in view (11:1–2). This is confirmed by the admonition to measure "those who worship there" (11:1). No literal measurement is needed of those who worship in the temple. Those measured represent those who are protected from God's wrath when he begins to mete out judgment from his "temple in heaven" (11:19; 14:15, 17; 16:1, 17).

The people of God in Revelation are also depicted as a woman. The OT antecedents are clear, for often in the OT, Israel is portrayed as the bride of Yahweh (e.g., Jer. 2:2, 20, 24, 32–34; 3:1–2, 6–11, 20; Hos. 1:1–3:5). The Messiah came from God's people (Rev. 12:1–5). God's people presently live in the wilderness of difficulty, where Satan tempts the woman during the 1,260 days of Satan's rule (12:6). The number is half of seven, representing the reign of evil from Christ's death and resurrection until his return. But just as God delivered Israel from Egypt on eagles' wings (Exod. 19:4), so too he will preserve his people in the wilderness from Satan's attacks, so that Satan (under the guise of the Roman Empire) will not triumph over them (Rev. 12:14). Here the time period is described as forty-two months, but that is the same as 1,260 days. The woman is also said to have children, and some have tried to distinguish the identity of the woman and her children (12:17); but the woman here represents the church as a whole, and the children are individual members of the church.

That the church is portrayed as a woman is confirmed by the conclusion of Revelation. The church is the bride of Christ (19:7; 22:17), and she will enjoy the marriage supper of the Lamb (19:7, 9). In Revelation we see that the church represents the true Israel. The church faces a great conflict and temptation, for compromising with Roman imperialism would entail entering the mainstream of society and obtaining economic security. John calls the church to a countercultural stance and to endurance in the midst of a society that persecutes and even kills those who refuse to bow the knee to Rome. Temporary pain will give way to everlasting joy as the church anticipates the marriage supper of the Lamb. The church witnesses to the world in its refusal to capitulate to Rome and in its allegiance to Jesus Christ. Through the church's witness, unbelievers are summoned to flee the economic and political security offered by Rome. They are to find refuge in Jesus Christ, knowing that a promise of a new heaven and a new earth awaits those who are faithful.

Conclusion

The most striking truth about the church in the NT is that the people of God are defined by their relationship to Jesus. The true Israel consists not of ethnic Jews but rather of those who confess Jesus Christ as Savior and Lord. Most often the church is called upon to live in accord with its calling, so that Christ is glorified in the way believers love one another and by the moral beauty of their lives. We see, then, that the church in the NT represents those who belong to Jesus Christ. Sometimes it is called the people of God, other times the body of Christ or the true Israel or the temple of God or God's "assembly" (church) or synagogue. In every instance the church represents those who have experienced God's saving promises, who have repented of their sin and put their faith in Jesus Christ.

We also see that the church is to proclaim the gospel to the ends of the earth. The message of Jesus as the crucified and risen Lord should not be restricted to a certain people or geographical region. All people everywhere are called upon to repent and put their faith in Jesus Christ as Lord and Savior.

Pastoral Reflection

The emphasis on the church is salutary for those of us who have been nurtured in Western individualism. The importance of our corporate life together as Christians is often ignored, and the focus shifts to self-fulfillment and self-actualization. The hard work of serving one another in love and on sacrificing ourselves for others may be trumped by our desires to fulfill our own ambitions.

The Lord does not intend to glorify himself merely through our individual lives but also through the church as the people of God.

Western Christians, who tend to be fiercely individualistic, must heed the biblical witness here on the importance of the church as the body of Christ. The NT does not recognize a Christian faith that exists apart from being vitally involved in the life of the church. A solitary Christian life is an oxymoron, reflecting too often an autonomous and rebellious spirit that refuses to participate in the corporate life to which God has called us as believers.

13

The Consummation of God's Promises

In this work, we have seen that God is a promise-making and a promise-keeping God. The eschatology of the NT has an already-but-not-yet character. In this chapter the focus is on the fulfillment of the not yet—the consummation of God's purposes and promises.[1] The present age is provisional and will give way to the future age, which will never end. The NT writers often cast their eyes to this future, to the day when God's work is completed. In this chapter we consider the second coming of Jesus, the final salvation and reward of his people, and the final judgment of the wicked. These themes are intertwined in the NT since they occur at the same time.

The Second Coming of Jesus

The Gospels and Acts

In the eschatological discourse in the Synoptics (Matt. 24; Mark 13; Luke 21), the second coming of Jesus is closely linked with the destruction of Jerusalem. Unraveling the meaning of Jesus' words when he refers to the coming of the Son of Man is not easy, particularly since they are embedded in a discourse on the destruction of Jerusalem and its temple—a judgment that

---

1. For a fuller treatment of future eschatology in the NT, see Schreiner 2008: 802–64.

was fulfilled in AD 70. Here I will argue that the promise of Jesus' coming
cannot be limited to the events of AD 70.

The text speaks of "the Son of Man coming on the clouds of heaven with
power and great glory" (Matt. 24:30; cf. Mark 13:26; Luke 21:27). The reference to clouds suggests his personal presence when he comes, for all three
parallel passages say that he will be *seen* when he comes. Acts 1:9–11 confirms
that Luke understood the coming to be a physical and personal appearance
of Jesus. The disciples saw Jesus depart from earth on a cloud, and they are
told that just as he was "taken up . . . into heaven," so he "will come in the
same way as you saw him go into heaven" (1:11). Since his departure was seen
as he was lifted on a cloud, it follows that his coming will also be seen as he
arrives on a cloud.

Jesus' coming with glory also suggests a coming that is visible and evident
to all. Indeed, Matthew says that "all the tribes of the earth will mourn"
(Matt. 24:30) when Jesus comes. With this allusion to Zech. 12:10–12, which
elsewhere in the NT refers to the parousia (cf. Rev. 1:7), Matthew says that
the scene encompasses all peoples and should not be limited to the Jewish
people. Further, the gathering of the angels most likely occurs at the end
of history and cannot be explained as the success of the gospel after AD 70
(Matt. 24:3; cf. 13:39, 41, 49). Another argument supporting a reference to
Jesus' personal and visible coming is found in Luke 21:28, where the coming
of the Son of Man is linked to the nearness of redemption for God's people.
Obviously, redemption here cannot refer to conversion or initiation into the
people of God, for the redemption is future and belongs to those who are already members of the people of God. Nor could the destruction of Jerusalem
qualify as the disciples' future redemption, for the razing of that city, although
it vindicated Jesus' words, did not redeem anyone. Therefore Luke must be
referring to eschatological redemption, which occurs when Jesus returns vis-
ibly and physically and ushers in the day of judgment.

The personal and visible character of Jesus' coming is also suggested by
the analogy drawn between his coming and lightning flashing over the entire
sky (Matt. 24:26–27). The illustration is intended to dispel any idea that the
Messiah was hidden in the wilderness or secreted away in some town. The
coming of the Messiah, on the contrary, would be as clear and unmistakable
as lightning that illumines the entire sky. It is doubtful that this image fits with
the destruction of Jerusalem in AD 70, for the issue at stake is the personal
location of the Messiah. The razing of Jerusalem does not answer that particular question, for some will declare that the Messiah is in the wilderness
or some other locality. The rebuttal to such claims is that the return of the
Messiah will be a public event and accessible to all (cf. 26:64).

Even though the Gospel writers often emphasize that Jesus will return
immediately and encourage disciples to be prepared for his coming, there are
some indications of delay before his return (cf. Matt. 24:48; 25:5, 14; Luke

12:45). For instance, Jesus announced that the gospel would be proclaimed to all nations before his return (Matt. 24:14). Clearly, some time must elapse before the gospel can be proclaimed to all. On the other hand, we must beware of imposing a rigid definition of "all nations" upon the Gospels, as if we can engage in eschatological calculation from Jesus' words here. The word "all" is not invariably used in a comprehensive sense (cf. 3:5).

On the one hand, Jesus' coming is relatively soon; on the other hand, it is also stressed that no one can predict or calculate the day of the Son of Man's return. Even the angels and, surprisingly, Jesus himself do not know the time of his return (24:36). Knowledge of the exact time is reserved to the Father alone.

Particularly emphasized relative to Jesus' coming is the warning that his disciples must be prepared for his return (24:45–51; 25:1–30). The readiness demanded does not relate to eschatological calculation, as if faithful disciples could forecast the time when Jesus would return. The disciples demonstrate that they are ready for his return by doing God's will. Hence, when the Son of Man returns in glory, the sheep will receive an eternal reward for their godly and faithful behavior, while the wicked will be punished forever because they have failed to practice goodness (25:31–46).

A fascinating word about the nearness of Jesus' coming is found in Acts 3:19–21. Peter calls upon his Jewish hearers to repent and experience forgiveness of sins through Jesus. If they do so, "times of refreshing" will come, and God will "send the Christ" to them. It seems that a reference to Jesus' return is in view here.

In summary, the Synoptics and Acts clearly teach a future coming of Jesus, though they warn against a kind of eschatological speculation that would try to ascertain the precise time of his arrival. Most important, Jesus' future coming should function as an encouragement and warning for his disciples to be ready.

The Johannine Literature

Scholars have long recognized that the Gospel of John focuses on realized eschatology, and therefore few sayings exist on the return of Jesus. Despite the emphasis on realized eschatology, John does not abandon future eschatology. Jesus promises the disciples that his Father's home consists of "many rooms" (14:2), and that he departs to prepare a place for them. The context clearly indicates that the return of Jesus is intended. (1) Jesus refers to the Father's house that has dwelling places, and this house is not on the present earth. (2) Jesus goes to prepare a dwelling for his disciples in the house of his Father. (3) Jesus does not come, in this context, to reside in the disciples; rather, he comes to take the disciples so that they might be with him. Jesus said, "I . . . will take you to myself, that where I am you may be also" (14:3). The only other reference to Jesus' coming in John's Gospel is incidental (21:18–23), but the fact that it is incidental reveals that it was a part of the worldview of the writer.

In 1 John, the last hour will come to an end when Jesus is revealed (2:28), and John immediately defines this manifestation of Jesus as his "coming." His coming is the day of judgment: those who did not remain in him will experience the shame of judgment. The day of his revelation will also be the day when believers "see him as he is" (1 John 3:2).

In Revelation, John refers often to the coming day of salvation and judgment. The book commences with the claim that it relates to what "must soon take place" (1:1) and indicates that "the time is near" (1:3). It closes with the assurance that the end "must soon take place" (22:6) and that "the time is near" (22:10). John refers to the entirety of his prophecy with these words and not exclusively to the coming of Jesus. Nonetheless, the coming of Jesus is one of the events that will take place soon (cf. 22:7, 12, 20). The promise that Jesus is coming soon occurs elsewhere in the book (3:11) and can justly be said to pervade the message of Revelation as a whole (1:7). The most extended description of Jesus' coming is in 19:11–21. Jesus will ride on a white horse when he comes to judge and make war on those who oppose him.

When we put together the Johannine writings, it is clear that the coming of Jesus was the hope of believers. Revelation in particular emphasizes the nearness of his coming, promising that it will be the day when he rewards his own and punishes the wicked.

The Pauline Literature

The future coming of Christ in Paul's writings, as is typically the case in the rest of the NT, is linked with the day of judgment and reward. The resurrection of Christ is separated by an interval from the physical resurrection of believers, so that the resurrection of believers will take place only when Jesus comes again (1 Cor. 15:23).

Paul uses three different terms to describe the coming of Jesus: his coming (*parousia*), appearance (*epiphaneia*), and revelation (*apokalypsis*). When Paul speaks of the "coming" (*parousia*) of Jesus, he refers to a future event in which Jesus will return personally and bodily (cf. 1 Cor. 15:23; 1 Thess. 2:19; 3:13; 4:15; 5:23; 2 Thess. 2:1, 8). The word "appearance" (*epiphaneia*, 2 Thess. 2:8; 1 Tim. 6:14; 2 Tim. 1:10; 4:1, 8; Titus 2:13) is used especially in the Pastoral Epistles. In Hellenistic thought, the term was used for the manifestation of a hidden deity as the deity intervenes to help the people. In one instance Paul uses it to refer to Christ's first coming (2 Tim. 1:10), but the aforementioned texts indicate that most often the term denotes Christ's second coming. Finally, the word "revelation" (*apokalypsis*) is used twice to refer to Jesus' coming

(1 Cor. 1:7; 2 Thess. 1:7). The word "revelation" implies that Jesus is now hidden from his people but will be unveiled to all on the last day.

If we can speak of the hope of Jesus' coming as the primitive hope of the church, it is evident that this hope permeates Pauline theology. We see this clearly in the use of the Aramaic phrase *marana tha*, which is translated as "Our Lord, come!" (1 Cor. 16:22). In the Pauline writings the coming of Jesus Christ is associated with "the day," whether it is called "the day of the Lord" or just "the day," or "the day of the Lord Jesus Christ," or even "that day" (cf. Rom. 2:5, 16; 1 Cor. 1:8; 3:13; 5:5; 2 Cor. 1:14; 1 Thess. 5:2; 2 Thess. 1:10; 2:2; 2 Tim. 1:18; 4:8). The Pauline language here clearly hearkens back to, and finds its antecedent in, the day of the Lord so often spoken of in the OT (e.g., Isa. 13:6, 9; Joel 1:15; 2:1; Amos 5:18; Obad. 15; Zeph. 1:7, 14).

Jesus' second coming is addressed particularly in the Thessalonian Letters, for clearly the Thessalonians were confused about Jesus' coming and its implications. In 1 Thess. 4:13–18 the Thessalonians are confused about the fate of the believing dead. They apparently were convinced that the believing dead would suffer from some disadvantage when Jesus returned. Paul's main purpose in this text, then, is to provide comfort for those who were grieving over the believing dead, reminding them of the future day of joy when Jesus returns.

In 5:1–11 Paul echoes the Jesus tradition, asserting that the day of the Lord will arrive like a thief. No definite eschatological calculation can determine when he will come. Indeed, he will come at the very time when the world thinks that peace and safety are at hand. For believers, then, the coming of the Lord is a call to spiritual vigilance and alertness. The judgment associated with Jesus' coming is emphasized in 2 Thess. 1:5–10. Jesus will return with a multitude of angels and "in flaming fire" (1:8). He will pour out his vengeance on the disobedient and on those who have no knowledge of God.

When Paul writes 2 Thessalonians, these Christians are still confused about Jesus' coming. Paul is concerned that the Thessalonians might be deluded and instructs them not to lose their heads in eschatological enthusiasm (2:2–7). The Lord will not come before the man of lawlessness appears and a great apostasy occurs.

In summary, Paul reiterates what we have seen elsewhere in the NT. Jesus' future coming will bring comfort and relief to saints and will portend the judgment of the ungodly. Hence, believers are encouraged to endure difficulties and persecution, knowing that the opposition that they face will be short-lived.

Hebrews, James, the Petrine Letters, and Jude

In Hebrews, the second coming of Jesus must not be divorced from the judgment and reward, but the author focuses on the punishment or joy awaiting human beings in order to motivate his readers to persevere and avoid apostasy.

We have two clear references to Jesus' second coming in Hebrews. The day of final judgment and salvation approaches, and it will come, Hebrews declares, when Jesus "appear[s] a second time" (9:28). On this occasion those who are already cleansed by his once-for-all sacrifice will experience the completion of their salvation.

In 10:35–39, the second coming of Jesus is tied to future reward and the coming judgment. The readers are exhorted to persevere in faith and not to abandon their confidence. Those who endure in faith until the end will receive the promised reward, but those who shrink back will face destruction.

The coming of Jesus in 1 Peter must be understood in light of the situation addressed in the letter. The readers were suffering, and Peter reminds them often of their future inheritance, warning them at the same time about the judgment that will be inflicted upon those who do not continue in faith. The suffering faced by believers in the present time produces joy because the authenticity of their faith will lead to a great reward "at the revelation of Jesus Christ" (1:7; cf. 4:13; 5:1, 4). The consummation of God's gracious purposes will be realized when Jesus returns and vindicates his people. Peter uses the noun "revelation" (*apokalypsis*) most often (1:7, 13; 4:13) to denote Jesus' coming. Elsewhere he uses the verb "reveal" (*apokalyptō*; 5:1) and the verb "manifest" (*phaneroō*; 5:4 AT). The noun and verbs relating to revelation suggest that when Jesus returns, the curtain will be pulled back, and God's people will see what has been hidden.

James has only one reference to the Lord's coming (5:7–9). The readers are exhorted to patience until the Lord's coming. The need for patience is compared to farmers who wait for the early and latter rain before harvesting a crop. Given the context, the Lord's nearness almost certainly refers to his promise to come soon. Accordingly, the readers should fortify their hearts and endure to the end. In addition, they should not allow the tension and pressures of their current lives to lead to complaining about others.

The second coming of Jesus is clearly one of the most important themes in 2 Peter. The false teachers denied that Jesus would return, arguing perhaps that OT texts predicting his return were improperly interpreted (1:20). If Jesus does not return, then neither would there be a future judgment, and thus the denial of Jesus' coming opened the door to libertinism and ethical anarchy. The false teachers insisted that it was ludicrous to expect Jesus to return, for the world was marked by uniformity, and life on earth had remained the same since the creation of the world (3:4). They probably also pointed to the long interval between the so-called promise to return and present experience (3:9). The "delay" supposedly demonstrated that the alleged coming of Jesus was a fantasy.

Peter does not consider the denial of the second coming to be a minor error. In 2 Pet. 2:1 he argues that the view of the "teachers" demonstrates that they are "false teachers" and do not belong to the people of God. The transfiguration functions as an anticipation of and prelude to Jesus' second coming because Jesus' majesty was evident, and he received honor and glory from the Father on that occasion (1:16–18). In chapter 3, Peter responds to the objections of the false teachers by which they allegedly refute the second coming; he uses three arguments to rebut the uniformitarian perspective of the false teachers. First, they have failed to perceive the implications of God's creation of the world (3:5). The creation of the world demonstrates that life on earth is not uniform: it had a beginning that constituted a massive break with what preceded. Second, life on earth has not proceeded without intervention since creation: a flood overwhelmed and destroyed the world during the time of Noah (3:6). Third, in the future the world will face judgment by fire, and on that day the unrighteous will face judgment and destruction (3:7). The current world will be consumed with fire, and new heavens and a new earth will dawn (3:12–13).

Second Peter gives two further explanations for the apparent delay in the Lord's coming. First, what seems like a delay from the human perspective is not a delay from God's standpoint, for a thousand years for human beings is, so to speak, only a day for God (3:8). Second, the promised coming is longer from the human perspective than might be expected, but the delay affords human beings the opportunity to repent and be saved (3:9, 15). Hence, the apparent delay serves a merciful purpose and cannot be assigned to a failure of God to keep his promise.

The second coming does not loom as large in Jude as in 2 Peter, though much of the content of the two letters is the same. Jude appeals to a prophecy of 1 Enoch to substantiate the future coming of the Lord (Jude 14–15). The Lord is coming to execute judgment on all the ungodly so that the Lord's triumph over evil will be completed. Thereby Jude assures his readers that victory belongs to the Lord, and the impact of those who pursue wickedness will be short-lived.

Conclusion

The second coming of Jesus is standard fare in NT theology and is indissolubly linked with the future judgment and the reward of God's people. Jesus' coming represents the consummation and fulfillment of God's promises and the dawn of the new creation. In light of the certainty of his coming, believers are exhorted to perseverance, faith, and godly living.

Judgment

The Synoptic Gospels and Acts

We begin by tracing the theme of judgment in the Synoptic Gospels and Acts. The threat of a future judgment for those who disobey and disbelieve is pervasive in the Synoptics and Acts. John the Baptist warned his audiences about the danger of listening to his proclamation while not truly repenting, for God's future wrath would be poured out on the disobedient (Matt. 3:7–10). In the teaching of Jesus, the future judgment is expressed in a variety of ways. Those who do not repent will perish (Luke 13:1–5). Israel, which is represented by the fig tree, will be cut down if it does not produce fruit (13:6–9). Those who censoriously judge others will find themselves on the last day face-to-face with the judgment of God (Matt. 7:1–2). Similarly, those who refuse to forgive others who injure them will not receive forgiveness from God (6:12, 14–15; 18:34–35). Since the Jews are the chosen people, one would expect them to respond positively to the kingdom message of Jesus; yet many will refuse to do so, and so they will be excluded from the end-time banquet (8:11–12). God will consign them to darkness, and they will suffer in agony from "weeping and gnashing of teeth" (8:12).

The phrase "weeping and gnashing of teeth" occurs often in Matthew to express the anguish of future judgment (e.g., 13:40–42, 49–50; 22:11–13). Those slaves who do not live to please the master but rather indulge in evil while he is absent will find that he will return suddenly and punish them (24:45–51; Luke 12:46; cf. Matt. 25:14–30).

Jesus often used the image of fire or hell (*geenna*) for the last judgment, alluding to the valley of Hinnom, south of Jerusalem (Josh. 15:8; 18:16), picking up Jewish tradition in his references to hell (Matt. 5:22, 27–30; 10:28; 18:8–9; 23:15, 33; Mark 9:43–47). In the parable of the sheep and the goats, those who have failed to pursue the good and have lived evil lives will be consigned to "the eternal fire" (Matt. 25:41), a judgment described as "eternal punishment" over against "eternal life" (25:46; cf. Luke 16:19–31).

In Acts, Jesus, as the resurrected one, has been "appointed by God to be judge of the living and the dead" (10:42). In Paul's speech to the Athenians, Jesus' resurrection serves as confirmation of the claim that he would judge the world on the appointed day (17:31). In personal conversation with Paul, Felix becomes spooked when Paul teaches him about the judgment to come (24:25). A day is coming when all God's enemies will be placed under Christ's feet (2:35), and this day is nothing less than the day of the Lord prophesied in the OT (2:20).

In summary, a future judgment is often taught in the Synoptics and regularly appears in Acts. Such a judgment indicates that the decisions made in life are momentous, that human beings are responsible moral agents who must choose goodness over evil. God is a just judge and will recompense those who sin and fail to repent. Such teaching also provides encouragement to the righteous to persevere in trusting the Lord until the final day.

The Johannine Literature

As noted earlier, the Gospel of John fixes its attention on realized eschatology. Nonetheless, the judgment that rests even now on those who refuse to believe in Jesus as the Messiah has a future dimension. God's wrath remains on those who disbelieve in the Son, and so they "shall not see life" (3:36; cf. 9:39–41). This is confirmed by John 5:27–29, where Jesus asserts a future resurrection of the righteous and the wicked: the former will enjoy life, and the latter will suffer condemnation (cf. 8:24).

The Johannine Epistles, like John's Gospel, center on present eschatology. Still, the present world "is passing away" (1 John 2:8, 17), and only those who do God's will remain forever. When Jesus is revealed, the day of judgment will be at hand (2:28). Only those who practice love will enjoy confidence before God when the judgment arrives (4:17).

The theme of judgment pervades Revelation. Not every judgment prophesied relates to the final reckoning, though the judgments in history serve as a prelude and an anticipation of the final judgment. In Revelation, judgment is portrayed in the opening of seven seals (6:1–17; 8:1), the sounding of seven trumpets (8:2–9:21; 11:15–19), and the pouring out of seven bowls (15:5–16:21). The number "seven" designates the completeness and the finality of God's judgment. The seals, trumpets, and bowls increase in severity, so that the judgment of the bowls brings devastation upon the whole earth.

John particularly emphasizes that God's judgments are righteous (15:3–4; 16:5–7; 19:2). Unlike the acts of a crazed deity, drunk with fury, God's judgments are not arbitrary and capricious. His judgments demonstrate that he is holy, true, and just. They do not call into question his goodness but rather verify it. The wicked deserve God's judgments because they have wantonly and maliciously shed the blood of God's people (16:6; 19:2). God's judgments represent his fair and just compensation for the evil that the wicked have inflicted on others.

The last judgment is also portrayed in the impending fall of Babylon (14:8; 16:19; 17:1–19:5). Babylon is described as a whore (17:1, 15–16; 19:2) who has corrupted the world. The use of the term "Babylon" to describe God's enemy draws on the OT, where Babylon is the great city that opposes the things of God (e.g., Isa. 13:1–14:23; 21:9; 47:1–15; Jer. 50:1–51:64).

The final judgment is also described in the "great white throne" judgment (Rev. 20:11–15). Those whose names are inscribed in the book of life will be spared from judgment. All people everywhere will be assessed according to their works (22:12), and those who have practiced evil will be cast into the lake of fire. The final judgment is described as "the lake of fire" (19:20; 20:10, 14–15). The lake of fire is the final habitation of the beast and false prophet (19:20), the devil (20:10), death and Hades (20:14–15), and those whose names are not written in the book of life. The punishment of the lake of fire, as the image of fire suggests, involves eternal torment (20:10; cf. 14:9–11). Further, the lake of fire is identified as the second death (20:14), and the expression "second death" suggests a definitive and final death, from which there is no return. Those who fail to overcome will be destroyed by the second death

(2:11), while those who enjoy the first resurrection will never experience the second death (20:6).

In summary, the Gospel of John and 1 John, with their realized eschatology, focus on the judgment that is actualized by the unbelief and disobedience of human beings. Yet even in these writings there is also the message of a final judgment that brings to completion what has begun in the present age. John in Revelation, on the other hand, focuses on the last judgment, and he expresses its reality in a variety of ways and with fiery intensity. John assures the righteous that wickedness will be punished and that everyone who has embraced evil will be repaid. Further, the message of final judgment also functions to encourage the righteous to persevere. They must remain faithful to the end to avoid the destiny of the disobedient.

The Pauline Literature

The final judgment in Paul's writings is expressed in a variety of ways. Often it is depicted as the outpouring of God's wrath (orgē). Normally for Paul, God's wrath is eschatological, denoting his final judgment. The culmination and final expression of God's wrath are reserved for the day of judgment (Rom. 5:9; 1 Thess. 1:10; 5:9). Those who fail to repent are storing up wrath against themselves in the day to come (Rom. 2:5), and they will experience God's righteous fury (2:8). God's wrath is not arbitrary; it is destined for those who continue in disobedience (Eph. 5:6; Col. 3:6). Christians should refrain from vengeance and wait for God's wrath, which will put all things right in the end (Rom. 12:19). Some scholars have depersonalized Paul's view of God's wrath, maintaining that it should be understood as the natural consequence of sin. Such a view reads Paul through the lenses of Western culture and predispositions; but Paul was nurtured in the OT, where it is clear that God's wrath is personal. Detaching God's wrath from his character reflects a deism that comports with modern sensibilities but deviates from a proper understanding of Paul.

We have seen in our discussion that wrath is closely related to God's judgment. As we noted in terms of God's wrath, his judgment is mainly eschatological. All persons will stand before God at the final judgment (Rom. 3:5; 14:10). He will assess all according to their works (Rom. 2:6; 2 Cor. 5:10; 11:15; cf. 2 Tim. 4:14). Since everything that a person has done will be disclosed accurately and fully (1 Cor. 4:5), God's judgment will accord with the truth (Rom. 2:2): it will fit with the way things really are. Therefore, no one will be able to complain that the judgment is unfair, for God's judgment is "righteous" (2:5). He will impartially judge all in accordance with their behavior (2:6–11). Those who have the law will be appraised by whether they have kept the law, and those who lack the law by whether they have lived according to the law "written on their hearts" (2:12–15). God's judgment of behavior will not fall prey to superficiality, for he evaluates all people in accord with their "secrets" (2:16), so that his final assessment will be indisputable.

In 2 Thessalonians, Paul emphasizes God's justice in judging. God does not judge arbitrarily; rather, he inflicts punishment on those who hate the truth and delight in wickedness (2:10–12). The punishment that the ungodly receive is just, because it is fair compensation for their mistreatment of believers (1:6). Paul reflects here the lex talionis view found in the OT, whereby the punishment is proportional to the crime. The judgment in 2 Thess. 1 occurs at the second coming, when Jesus arrives with his powerful angels (1:7–10). Here we have language that is reminiscent of Jesus' words on hell as given in the Synoptics. Jesus will come with fire and avenge those who do not know God and those who have refused to obey the gospel. Those who are penalized are separated from the Lord's gracious presence forever.

The metaphor of fire is used elsewhere to designate the winnowing process of the judgment (1 Cor. 3:13–15). Often the final consequence of the judgment is designated as "perishing" or "destruction" (*apollymi*, *apōleia*, or *olethros*). We already noted in 2 Thess. 1:9 that those who are unsaved will face "eternal destruction" when Jesus comes. This destruction will come suddenly and without warning (1 Thess. 5:3). Those who make riches their god will end up being destroyed (1 Tim. 6:9). Similarly, those who oppose believers indicate from their opposition that they are headed to destruction (Phil. 1:28). The enemies of the cross, who serve their own appetites and live for earthly things, will be destroyed (3:19). The "man of lawlessness" will flourish for a time, but ultimately he is destined for "destruction" (2 Thess. 2:3). God has even ordained who will experience eschatological destruction (Rom. 9:22). Such a statement, however, can never be abstracted from the remainder of what Paul teaches, for destruction comes because people have sinned (2:12) and because they have rejected the message of the cross (1 Cor. 1:18). Those who perish do not find the message of the cross attractive; they are repelled by it and find it redolent of death (2 Cor. 2:16). So too, Paul can say that those who are perishing do so because they are blinded by Satan (4:4), but the blinding work of Satan does not exempt people from personal responsibility. Paul clearly thinks that those who did not receive the gospel should do so and are rightly held guilty for disobedience.

The consequence of sin is also described as death (Rom. 6:16, 21, 23; 8:6). Death has entered the world and rules over all people because of Adam's sin (5:12–19; 1 Cor. 15:21). The death in view here cannot be limited to either physical death or separation from God, for it entails both.

In summary, in Paul's writings the final judgment is the result of God's wrath and is often described in terms of destruction and death. It represents God's just reprisal on those who fail to believe the gospel and on those who refuse to do his will.

Hebrews

The sermonic character of Hebrews, in which the author exhorts his readers not to apostatize, sets the parameters for the letter as a whole. The exhortations given and the judgments threatened are set within the framework of encouraging and warning his readers not to fall away from the living God. The author tries to motivate his readers by using the image of escaping from judgment. Those who abandon the faith will not escape the one who has accomplished such a great salvation and who has warned them from heaven (2:3; 12:25). The future reward is designated as rest, and those who harden their hearts and continue in disbelief and disobedience will not enjoy God's rest (3:11, 18–19; 4:3, 5). Instead of having rest, they will suffer, so to speak, from eschatological exhaustion and weariness. In 6:7–8 the author provides an illustration from the world of agriculture. Those who commit apostasy are likened to those who have received refreshing rains from God and yet have produced thorns and thistles instead of fruit. Vegetation that produces no fruit will be cursed and burned. The author uses the image of burning to depict the final judgment and suggests that those who turn away will be cursed by God.

Similarly, in the severe warning contained in 10:26–31, the author admonishes the readers of the consequence of deliberately forsaking the sacrifice of Christ. The punishment is worse than the death sentence imposed under the Mosaic covenant. Sinners will experience God's judgment and his consuming fire (10:27; 12:29). Physical death is clearly a result of sin, for Satan holds people in bondage because of the fear of death (2:14–15). Yet the author of Hebrews contemplates the judgment that follows death (9:27), which suggests an even more terrible sentence. God will pour his vengeance and judgment on those who abandon the sacrifice of Christ (10:30). They face the terrifying prospect of falling into the hands of the living God (10:31). Those who fall into God's hands will find that he shows no delight or tenderness toward those who have been too timid to persevere (10:38). Those who shrink back will ultimately experience destruction (*apōleia*; 10:39).

James, 1–2 Peter, and Jude

The future judgment in James is inseparable from the paraenetic character of the letter. For instance, the consequence of sin is death (1:15). If a person in sin does not turn away from evil, death will be the final result (5:20). The rich will experience eschatological humiliation instead of exaltation (1:10). The judgment of the rich is compared to a beautiful flower. When a flower blossoms and stands forth in the richness of its beauty, it seems that it will never fade (1:11). But God's judgment is like the sun, for just as the sun's steady heat day after day causes a flower to wither and fall from the stem so that its beauty is lost, so also the rich will disappear on the day of judgment (cf. 5:1–6). The judgment will occur on the day when the Lord returns (5:7–9).

In his First Letter, Peter refers to the reward that believers will receive far more than he speaks of judgment, perhaps because he seeks to focus on the future blessing promised to suffering believers. Still, some statements about God's judgment do exist. God is an impartial judge, who assesses people according to their deeds (1:17). Jesus did not resort to threats and vengeance when he suffered, for he was persuaded that God would judge justly on the last day those who mistreated him (2:23). God shows his favor to the righteous, but on the day of judgment he turns his face away from those who practice evil (3:12). Those who ridicule and persecute believers may currently enjoy social approbation, but they will have to give a final account to God as judge on the last day (4:5). Even now believers face a purifying judgment through suffering, and thus it follows that the recompense for unbelievers will be far worse (4:17–18).

The theme of judgment pervades the short letters of 2 Peter and Jude. In both letters false teachers have threatened the church, and the authors promise that these teachers will experience adverse consequences for their actions. It seems that in both 2 Peter and Jude the false teachers propounded libertinism (2 Pet. 2:1–3; Jude 4). These teachers were brimming with confidence and authoritatively commanded others (2 Pet. 2:10–12; Jude 8–10), but both authors respond by emphasizing the future judgment of those who practice evil. Both Peter and Jude remind their readers of judgments that God carried out in history: the flood (2 Pet. 2:5; 3:6), the punishment of angels who violated their proper domain (2 Pet. 2:4; Jude 6), the judgment upon Israelites who sinned in the wilderness (Jude 5), the destruction of Sodom and Gomorrah (2 Pet. 2:6; Jude 7). The punishment of angels in history anticipates the final reckoning, which they will receive on the day of judgment (2 Pet. 2:4; Jude 6). The fiery destruction of Sodom and Gomorrah functions as a type of the "eternal fire" (Jude 7; cf. 2 Pet. 2:6).

God's judgments in history, therefore, serve as a prelude to and anticipation of the final judgment. They guarantee that God will condemn the ungodly, for God has prescripted their judgment from the beginning (Jude 4). These examples also demonstrate that even though God's judgments are not immediate, they are certain (2 Pet. 2:9). The delay will not last forever (2:3). God has reserved the present heavens and earth for a fiery judgment, which will spell the "destruction of the ungodly" (3:7). Peter uses the language of the day of the Lord to sketch in the judgment, summoning up a common OT motif (3:10). He also alludes to the words of Jesus, for he says that the day of judgment will surprise the wicked and come like a thief. The current heavens and earth will pass away, and the elements of the world will be dissolved (3:10–12). The false teachers distort both Paul's writings and the OT Scriptures, and hence they will face eschatological destruction (3:16; cf. 2:1). Jude pronounces a woe oracle of judgment on those who imitate Cain, Balaam, and Korah (11). The image of "the gloom of utter darkness" is introduced to describe the impending judgment (13). Interestingly, Jude (14–15) cites a prophecy from 1 En. 1.9 in support of the coming judgment. This prophecy focuses on Christ's coming and emphasizes that all the godless will be judged for their ungodly lives.

Conclusion

The NT writers frequently teach that there will be a future and definitive judgment on the wicked. God will manifest his judgment by punishing those who refuse to believe in the gospel and those who have disobeyed his will. Such a judgment is described in a variety of ways. In any case, it testifies to God's justice, assuring believers that those who practice evil will receive just recompense for their actions. Further, the judgment functions as a motivation for the righteous to persevere, for if they join the wicked, they will face the same destiny that awaits those who have rejected the gospel.

Reward

The Synoptic Gospels and Acts

In the Synoptic Gospels we saw that those who refuse to repent when the message of the kingdom is proclaimed will face judgment, and it follows as a corollary that those who believe and obey will receive a final reward. Many of the Beatitudes promise an eschatological benefit for those who are Jesus' disciples. The sorrowing will receive comfort, the meek will inherit the earth, those hungry for righteousness will be satisfied, the merciful will know God's mercy, the pure in heart will see God, peacemakers will be God's children (Matt. 5:4–9; cf. Luke 6:21).

Jesus did not teach a disinterested Kantian ethic. He promised his disciples remarkable rewards if they followed him (Matt. 6:1–18). As we would expect, the promised reward is conveyed with a number of different images. Those who acknowledge Jesus before other human beings will be acknowledged by Jesus in the Father's presence on the day of judgment (10:32). Giving up one's life for Jesus' sake is a frightening prospect, but ultimately it is worth it because those who surrender their lives will end up finding them (10:39; 16:25). Those who welcome and support prophets, righteous persons, and disciples who belong to Jesus will be recompensed (10:41–42). So too, those who love their enemies will receive a stunning reward in heaven (5:44–48; cf. Luke 12:35–40). The Synoptics do not often speak of the future reward in terms of "eternal life," but the term does occur in the account of the rich ruler (Matt. 19:16), and it is the reward received by the righteous in the parable of the sheep and the goats (25:46). The future reward for disciples can also be described as the reception of the kingdom, with the promise that the Father finds joy in granting the kingdom to his own (Luke 12:32). Jesus speaks of those who are justified or vindicated before God by their words (Matt. 12:37).

The missionary preaching of Acts naturally concentrates upon the resurrection of Jesus from the dead, demonstrating that his resurrection was rooted in OT prophecy and eyewitness testimony (1:22; 2:24–32; 3:15, 26; 4:2, 10, 33; 5:30; 10:40–41; 13:30–37; 17:3, 18, 31–32). The future resurrection will consummate the expectation of the righteous and introduce the day of judgment for those who have given themselves to evil.

In summary, reward for the righteous is communicated in a variety of colorful ways in the Synoptic Gospels and is confirmed in Acts as well. The reward is nothing other than eternal life, but it is described in terms of receiving mercy, inheriting the earth, being satisfied, enjoying the messianic banquet, being raised from the dead, and seeing God. By the wondrous future that is promised to them, believers are motivated to continue to believe and obey.

The Johannine Literature

In John "eternal life" refers to the reward that believers will enjoy forever, for the word "eternal" intimates that the life given never comes to an end. The future character of eternal life is confirmed by its collocation with the future resurrection. Jesus is "the resurrection and the life" (11:25). Nor can this resurrection be defined only in terms of realized eschatology: on several occasions in John's Gospel, eternal life is linked with the future resurrection. Those who have eternal life will be raised by the Son from the dead on the final day (6:40, 44, 54; cf. 5:28–29).

Those who remain in the Son and the Father will receive eternal life as promised (1 John 2:25). Eternal life is prominent in John's Gospel, and so the promise of eternal life in 1 John links the two documents (1:2; 3:15; 5:11, 13, 20; cf. 5:12). What believers will be when Jesus returns has not been fully disclosed; yet moral transformation is promised to them so that they will be like Jesus when he is revealed, and they see his face (3:2–3).

Just as Revelation dwells upon future judgment, so too the future reward of believers occupies much of John's attention. Suffering believers are reminded of the consequence of failing to endure and of the great blessing that will be theirs if they remain faithful. Those who "die in the Lord" will receive blessing and eschatological rest because their deeds demonstrate that they truly belong to God (Rev. 14:13). So too, those who are vigilant and are clothed with goodness will be rewarded with blessing when Jesus returns (16:15). The end-time blessing is reserved for those invited to the Lamb's marriage supper (19:9; cf. 3:20). Those who enjoy the first resurrection are blessed (20:6), for they have been faithful to Jesus and have refused to worship the beast (20:4).

Those who belong to God and the Lamb will never suffer from hunger, thirst, and intense heat (7:16). Every tear will be wiped from their eyes (7:17;

21:4). Mourning, crying, and pain will be only a memory (21:4). The Lamb will satisfy his thirsty people with the springs of the water of life (7:17; 21:6; 22:1, 17). The glory and beauty of the future prepared for God's people are symbolized in the white robes and fine linen that will be worn (3:4–5, 18; 6:11; 7:9, 13–14; 19:8, 14).

All the blessings promised to believers can be summed up in the promise that God himself will dwell with his people (21:3). God's abiding presence with his people represents the fulfillment of all his covenantal and saving promises and is the climax of all of redemptive history. God fulfills his promises in a new creation, where he creates a new heaven and new earth (21:1). The promise of a new heaven and new earth is rooted in the OT (Isa. 65:17–25).

John devotes his energy to describing the new Jerusalem, and the language employed indicates that he writes symbolically, for he is stretching to describe the indescribable, to capture a coming world beyond human imagination. Probably the most important thing about the city is that it redounds with God's glory (Rev. 21:11). Those who inhabit it and gaze upon it behold God's beauty, loveliness, power, and might. The beauty of the city is compared to a precious jewel that dazzles (21:11). The indescribable beauty of the city is conveyed by its wall being made of jasper, the city bedecked with translucent gold, the foundations of the wall with stunning jewels, and the gates with dazzling pearls (21:18–21). The stones represent paradise restored (Gen. 2:11–12; Ezek. 28:13) and fulfill the prophecy regarding the new Jerusalem (Isa. 54:11–12).

In summary, John's Gospel and 1 John describe the reward of believers in terms of eternal life, and the life that believers now enjoy will culminate in the resurrection. In the book of Revelation the future reward of believers is described with a kaleidoscope of images. John calls his readers' attention to the astonishing reward that awaits believers who persevere until the end, encouraging them thereby to continue to endure persecution. The sum and substance of the reward, however, is the presence of God with his people—seeing God's face. And yet it is not only God who takes center stage, but also the Lamb. Hence, one of the major themes of this book is evident in the final reward of believers, for the joy that awaits saints is the luminous presence of God and the Lamb forever.

The Pauline Literature

The final reward of believers is described by Paul in various ways. Believers will enjoy relief and freedom from the sufferings and afflictions that characterize this present evil age (2 Thess. 1:7; cf. Gal. 1:4). They will rest in the comfort that God reserves for his own (2 Cor. 1:3–7). When Christ comes, believers will be full of joy and gladness; they will rejoice in the Lord and in other believers (Phil. 4:1; 1 Thess. 2:19–20; 3:9).

Eternal life is granted only to those who do what is good, and it will not be the portion of those who practice evil (Rom. 2:7; 6:22–23; 8:6; Gal. 6:8; 1 Tim. 6:19). On the other hand, eternal life is God's gift and is not earned by anyone. The final reward is described in terms of inheritance, and Paul links the inheritance of believers with entrance into the kingdom of God (cf. 1 Cor. 6:9–11; Gal. 5:21).

Believers will be glorified (Rom. 8:17, 30; Col. 3:4) on the day Christ returns. Therefore, believers will be astonished and seized with joy when they finally receive the glory that God has promised and reserved for them from the beginning (Rom. 9:23; 1 Cor. 2:7; 1 Thess. 2:12; 2 Thess. 2:14). Paul promises those in Christ that they will obtain immortality or incorruption (Rom. 2:7; 1 Cor. 15:42, 50, 53–54; 2 Tim. 1:10). The promise of immortality, however, is rooted in the Pauline conception of the resurrection. In Jewish thought the resurrection spelled the coming of the eschaton, the inauguration of the age to come, and therefore the passing away of this present evil age. In Paul's theology the age to come has arrived with the resurrection of Christ (Rom. 1:4; 2 Tim. 2:8). One of the most fascinating texts on the resurrection is 1 Thess. 4:13–18. Paul assures the Thessalonians that the believing dead are at no disadvantage and will be raised before living believers are snatched up. He comforts believers with the truth that they will be with one another and the Lord forever.

In summary, Paul emphasizes the future reward of believers. Those who put their faith in Jesus Christ and manifest their faith by good works will receive eternal life. They will be saved from God's wrath on the final day. They will find peace and joy forevermore. When Christ appears, they will marvel, be astonished with joy, and shine with glory. Believers will be raised from the dead and will inhabit the new creation that God has promised. In a variety of ways Paul traces out the joy set before believers, inspiring them to continue to believe and obey until the day of redemption.

Hebrews

One way that the author of Hebrews dissuades his readers from committing apostasy is by reminding them of the reward that will be theirs if they persevere in faithfulness. Indeed, the theology of reward figures largely in Hebrews. The author asserts that one cannot even please God unless one is convinced that God "rewards those who seek him" (11:6). If they do not forsake their allegiance to Christ, they will receive "a great reward" (10:35). Since God is faithful, those who persist in believing will receive what he has promised (10:36). The promise, as 10:39 makes plain, is nothing less than salvation, for it is contrasted with eschatological destruction. The blessing that God has for his people is the hope of inheriting all that he has promised (6:7, 18). The future reward is also described as an unshakable kingdom (12:28), signifying the inviolability of God's promise. God will bring his children to glory, so that the corruption and imperfection of the present world will vanish (2:10). The future blessing is also designated as "rest" (3:11, 18; 4:1, 3, 5, 8–11). The rest culminates when life ends, when human beings cease from their works on earth (4:10), when the Sabbath rest of the OT finds its fulfillment in the heavenly rest.

The reward of believers is also described in terms of the heavenly city to come (11:10, 13–16; 12:22–23; 13:14). The present created order will be shaken (12:25–29), and a new, unshakable order will be introduced. This thought seems quite similar to Revelation's promise of a new heaven and a new earth. The old creation will give way to the new creation, the city of man to the city of God. Hebrews, then, encourages believers to persevere, knowing that a great reward lies before them, so that they, like Jesus, should endure because of the joy set before them (12:2).

James, 1–2 Peter, and Jude

James only glances at and does not dwell on the future reward of believers. Those who respond to trials in a godly way will be perfected morally (1:4). This is quite similar to John's promise that God's children will be like Jesus (1 John 3:2). Those who endure trials will be given "the crown of life" (James 1:12), and here the crown refers to the promise of eternal life, which will belong to those who are truly the Lord's. In the same way, believers are inheritors of God's kingdom (2:5). God also promises that those who are humble will receive eschatological vindication (1:9). A day of reversal is coming in which the humble will be rewarded for their faith and obedience.

The future reward of believers looms large in 1 Peter, for Peter desired to comfort persecuted believers with the certain hope of final reward. From the outset of the letter, Peter thus reminds believers of the "living hope" that is theirs "through the resurrection of Jesus Christ" (1:3). The resurrection of Jesus Christ is the inauguration of the age to come and functions as the promise, by implication, of the final resurrection of believers. The end-time reward of believers is designated an inheritance (1:4; 3:9), and it is emphasized that the inheritance cannot be defiled or stained, so that nothing can diminish the joy that awaits believers. The life of the future is one of remarkable joy and gladness (4:13), when believers will be exalted instead of humiliated (5:6). They will then enjoy eschatological salvation (1:5, 9), and praise, glory, and honor will redound to them (1:7; 2:7). The good days that all humans long for will be theirs forever (3:10).

According to 2 Peter, the participation in the divine nature, which belongs to believers even now, will consummate in the fulfillment of all of God's promises to his people (1:4). Just as the Lord saved Lot and Noah in the midst of wicked generations, so too will he preserve his people so that they will receive what is promised on the last day (2:5, 7, 9). Those who practice godly qualities and truly live out their faith will not fall short of receiving what is promised; they will receive the reward of entering into the kingdom of Jesus Christ (1:10–11).

They will be found in him as blameless on the last day and inherit salvation (3:14–15). In other words, they will enjoy the new heavens and new earth that God has promised (3:13). The brevity of Peter's Second Letter is such that he does not elaborate on the nature of the new heavens and new earth. Righteousness will reign supreme in the new world or new creation.

Jude looks forward to the coming of Jesus Christ, who will show mercy to his own and grant believers the gift of eternal life (21). In the last day they will stand, unblemished, with inexpressible joy before God (24). The perfection that believers long for will then be a reality.

Conclusion

The promised new creation will become a reality at the coming of Jesus Christ. God's covenantal promises will then be fulfilled, and the groaning of the old creation will end when the new world dawns with all its stunning beauty. What will make the new creation so delightful is a vision of God and his dwelling with his people. Believers will enter the new creation with the resurrected bodies that they have been eagerly awaiting in the interval between the already and the not yet. They will receive the reward of eternal life and the kingdom promises that they grasped by faith while on this earth. The final inheritance and salvation for which they longed then become a reality. Conversely, those who refused to believe in Christ and to obey his word will face a final judgment. Their destruction will be concomitant with the destruction of Satan. The arrival of God's kingdom in its fullness will involve not only reward for believers but also punishment for the wicked, who resisted the gospel and mistreated believers. The new world and new universe will have arrived, and God will be all in all. Believers will worship and enjoy the Father, the Son, and the Spirit forever.

Pastoral Reflection

What C. S. Lewis (1982: 3) said about demons is true about the future as well: We may fall into "two equal and opposite errors" relative to the future. On the one hand, we may live only for the future so that we do not avail ourselves of present opportunities. On the other hand, we may so invest ourselves in the present that we ignore the future day of judgment and reward. Such a truncated view of reality betrays a failure to understand the eschatological character of the NT message, for it is blinded to ultimate reality. Those who have a proper understanding of the future live most effectively in the present, for they understand that in all things the goal of believers is always to honor God in Christ.

Epilogue

I have argued that the NT focuses on the fulfillment of the saving promises of God given in the OT. The NT represents the climax of the story begun in the OT, but it is a bit like a mystery novel because the story is fulfilled in an astonishing way. God's promises are fulfilled in Christ through the Spirit, and yet we still await the fullness of what was promised. There is an already–not yet character to the fulfillment. The promises are inaugurated but not yet consummated.

We must also see the main characters in the story. The promises that are coming to pass are the promises of God, who, as the Lord of history, is working out his plan. In particular, he has sent his Son, Jesus Christ, as the one who fulfills the promises made to Abraham, Moses, David, and the prophets. Jesus is the son of Abraham, the prophet greater than Moses, the true David (the Messiah), the Son of Man, the Lord, and the Son of God. Indeed, he is divine. It is through him that God's promises have become a reality. He is the one sent by the Father, the one who has come to do his Father's will. But also, the promises were brought to fruition through Jesus in a way that subverted human expectations. Jesus conquered sin and death by taking on the role of the Servant of the Lord. He conquered evil by submitting to suffering and at the cross absorbing the punishment due his people. The NT writers, using words such as "salvation," "reconciliation," "justification," "redemption," and "adoption," burst at the seams in trying to express what Jesus the Christ did at the cross. Further, the NT fulfills the OT because the salvation that God promised has been effected by the Spirit, who was promised in the OT. Jesus was both the bearer of the Spirit and the one who poured out his Spirit on God's people. He carried out his ministry in the power of the Spirit, and after his resurrection and exaltation, Jesus gave that same Spirit to those who belong to him.

The rest of the NT explains how the story of God's promise works itself out in the lives of human beings. Human beings need God's liberating work because of the power of sin and death. Sin and death are the two towers of evil that devastate human beings, and human beings are not merely pawns of sin but rather have actively given themselves over to it. Hence, to enjoy the victory that Jesus won over evil, they must repent of their evil and put their trust in Jesus Christ as Savior, Redeemer, and Lord. This repenting faith is a persevering faith, a radical faith, a faith that honors God and Christ in surrendering one's life to God and Jesus Christ. Hence, those who live under the reign of God and Christ live a new kind of life. Indeed, the church of Jesus Christ is a new community in which the love of Christ is displayed. They are now the true Israel, and they are to display God's beauty in how they relate to one another and to the world as they proclaim the good news of Christ's salvation to the world.

Finally, the story is not over yet. Believers still await the consummation. They await the new creation, the completion of the new exodus, and the final fulfillment of the new covenant. Jesus will come again and transform the universe. There is a new world coming, a new creation, a new heavens and a new earth. In that coming world, God will be all in all, and Jesus Christ will be honored forever and ever. The paradise that was lost will be regained—and more than regained, it will be surpassed. And we will see God's face (Rev. 22:4), and his glory will be magnified through Christ forever and ever.

Bibliography

Avemarie, Friedrich. 1996. *Tora und Leben: Untersuchungen zur Heilsbedeutung der Tora in der frühen rabbinischen Literatur.* Texte und Studien zum antiken Judentum 55. Tübingen: Mohr Siebeck.

———. 1999. "Erwählung und Vergeltung: Zur optionalen Struktur rabbinischer Soteriologie." *New Testament Studies* 45:108–26.

Barr, James. 1988. "*'Abbā'* Isn't 'Daddy.'" *Journal of Theological Studies* 39:28–47.

———. 1999. *The Concept of Biblical Theology.* Minneapolis: Fortress.

Barrett, C. K. 1973. *A Commentary on the Second Epistle to the Corinthians.* Harper's New Testament Commentaries. New York: Harper & Row.

———. 1978. *The Gospel according to St. John: An Introduction with Commentary and Notes on the Greek Text.* 2nd ed. London: SPCK.

———. 1998. *Acts 15–28.* International Critical Commentary. Edinburgh: T&T Clark.

Bauckham, Richard. 1999. *James: Wisdom of James, Disciple of Jesus the Sage.* New York: Routledge.

Bietenhard, H. 1976. "Ὄνομα." Pages 648–56 in vol. 2 of *New International Dictionary of New Testament Theology.* Edited by Colin Brown. 4 vols. Grand Rapids: Zondervan, 1975–85.

Borsch, F. H. 1992. "Further Reflections on 'The Son of Man': The Origins and Development of the Title." Pages 130–44 in *The Messiah: Developments in Earliest Judaism and Christianity.* Edited by J. H. Charlesworth. Minneapolis: Fortress.

Buckwalter, H. Douglas. 1998. "The Divine Saviour." Pages 107–23 in *Witness to the Gospel: The Theology of Acts.* Edited by I. H. Marshall and D. Peterson. Grand Rapids: Eerdmans.

Burge, Gary M. 1987. *The Anointed Community: The Holy Spirit in the Johannine Tradition*. Grand Rapids: Eerdmans.

Capes, David B. 1992. *Old Testament Yahweh Texts in Paul's Christology*. Wissenschaftliche Untersuchungen zum Neuen Testament 2/47. Tübingen: Mohr Siebeck.

Carson, D. A., Peter T. O'Brien, and Mark A. Seifrid, eds. 2001. *The Complexities of Second Temple Judaism*. Vol. 1 of *Justification and Variegated Nomism: A Fresh Appraisal of Paul and Second Temple Judaism*. Wissenschaftliche Untersuchungen zum Neuen Testament 2/140. Tübingen: Mohr Siebeck; Grand Rapids: Baker Academic.

Das, A. Andrew. 2001. *Paul, the Law, and the Covenant*. Peabody, MA: Hendrickson.

Davies, W. D., and Dale C. Allison. 1991. *Commentary on Matthew VIII–XVIII*. Vol. 2 of *A Critical and Exegetical Commentary on the Gospel according to Saint Matthew*. International Critical Commentary. Edinburgh: T&T Clark.

Dunn, James D. G. 1992. "The Justice of God: A Renewed Perspective on Justification by Faith." *Journal of Theological Studies* 43:1–22.

Elliott, Mark A. 2000. *The Survivors of Israel: A Reconsideration of the Theology of Pre-Christian Judaism*. Grand Rapids: Eerdmans.

Ellis, E. Earle. 1992. "Pseudonymity and Canonicity of New Testament Documents." Pages 212–24 in *Worship, Theology and Ministry in the Early Church: Essays in Honor of Ralph P. Martin*. Edited by M. J. Wilkins and T. Paige. Journal for the Study of the New Testament: Supplement Series 87. Sheffield: JSOT Press.

Fitzmyer, J. A. 1998. *The Acts of the Apostles*. Anchor Bible 31. New York: Doubleday.

Gasque, W. Ward. 1989. *A History of the Interpretation of the Acts of the Apostles*. Peabody, MA: Hendrickson.

Gathercole, Simon J. 2003. *Where Is Boasting? Early Jewish Soteriology and Paul's Response in Romans 1–5*. Grand Rapids: Eerdmans.

Goldsworthy, Graeme. 2000. "Kingdom of God." Pages 615–20 in *New Dictionary of Biblical Theology*. Edited by T. Desmond Alexander and Brian S. Rosner. Leicester, UK: Inter-Varsity; Downers Grove, IL: InterVarsity, 2000.

Hamilton, James Merrill, Jr. 2006. *God's Indwelling Presence: The Holy Spirit in the Old and New Testaments*. NAC Studies in Bible and Theology. Nashville: Broadman & Holman.

Harris, Murray J. 1992. *Jesus as God: The New Testament Use of* Theos *in Reference to Jesus*. Grand Rapids: Baker Academic.

Hartman, Lars. 1991. "Ὄνομα." Pages 519–22 in vol. 2 of *Exegetical Dictionary of the New Testament*. Edited by H. Balz and G. Schneider. 3 vols. Grand Rapids: Eerdmans, 1990–93.

Hemer, Colin J. 1989. *The Book of Acts in the Setting of Hellenistic History*. Edited by C. H. Gempf. Wissenschaftliche Untersuchungen zum Neuen Testament 49. Tübingen: Mohr Siebeck.

Hurtado, Larry. 2003. *Lord Jesus Christ: Devotion to Jesus in Earliest Christianity*. Grand Rapids: Eerdmans.

Jeremias, Joachim. 1967. *The Prayers of Jesus*. Studies in Biblical Theology 2/6. London: SCM Press.

Jervell, Jacob. 1996. *The Theology of the Acts of the Apostles*. Cambridge: Cambridge University Press.

Knight, George W., III. 1992. *The Pastoral Epistles*. New International Greek Testament Commentary. Grand Rapids: Eerdmans.

Köstenberger, Andreas. 2004. *John*. Baker Exegetical Commentary on the New Testament. Grand Rapids: Baker Academic.

Köstenberger, Andreas J., and Peter O'Brien. 2001. *Salvation to the Ends of the Earth: A Biblical Theology of Mission*. Downers Grove, IL: InterVarsity.

Lau, Andrew Y. 1996. *Manifest in the Flesh: The Epiphany Christology of the Pastoral Epistles*. Wissenschaftliche Untersuchungen zum Neuen Testament 2/86. Tübingen: Mohr Siebeck.

Lewis, C. S. 1982. *The Screwtape Letters with Screwtape Proposes a Toast*. Rev. ed. New York: Macmillan.

Marshall, I. H. 1970. *Luke: Historian and Theologian*. Grand Rapids: Zondervan.

McKnight, Scot. 1992. "The Warning Passages in Hebrews: A Formal Analysis and Theological Conclusions." *Trinity Journal*, NS, 13:21–59.

Meier, John P. 1994. *Mentor, Message, and Miracles*. Vol. 2 of *A Marginal Jew: Rethinking the Historical Jesus*. New York: Doubleday.

Michel, Otto. 1966. *Der Brief an die Hebräer*. 12th ed. Kritisch-exegetischer Kommentar über das Neue Testament. Göttingen: Vandenhoeck & Ruprecht.

Mounce, William D. 2000. *Pastoral Epistles*. Word Biblical Commentary 46. Nashville: Nelson.

Peterson, David. 1982. *Hebrews and Perfection: An Examination of the Concept of Perfection in the "Epistle to the Hebrews."* Society for New Testament Studies Monograph Series 47. Cambridge: Cambridge University Press.

Sanders, E. P. 1977. *Paul and Palestinian Judaism: A Comparison of Patterns of Religion*. Philadelphia: Fortress.

Schreiner, Thomas R. 2003. *1, 2 Peter, Jude*. New American Commentary. Nashville: Broadman & Holman.

———. 2008. *New Testament Theology: Magnifying God in Christ*. Grand Rapids: Baker Academic.

Schweitzer, Albert. 1931. *The Mysticism of Paul the Apostle*. New York: Henry Holt.

Seifrid, Mark A. 2000. *Christ, Our Righteousness: Paul's Theology of Justification*. Downers Grove, IL: InterVarsity.

Stettler, Hanna. 1998. *Die Christologie der Pastoralbriefe*. Wissenschaftliche Untersuchungen zum Neuen Testament 2/105. Tübingen: Mohr Siebeck.

Thompson, Marianne Meye. 2001. *The God of the Gospel of John*. Grand Rapids: Eerdmans.

Wallace, Daniel B. 1996. *Greek Grammar beyond the Basics: An Exegetical Syntax of the New Testament*. Grand Rapids: Zondervan.

Wrede, William. 1962. *Paul*. Repr., Lexington: American Theological Library Association.

Scripture Index

Old Testament

Genesis
1 73
1–3 112
1:1 73
1:1–2:3 155
1:2 140
1:3 73
1:26–27 20, 89
2:11–12 242
2:15–17 20
2:19 128
3:15 20
11:1–9 137
12:1–3 20
12:3 18, 30, 41, 148, 217, 223
15:6 193
17:9–14 208
18:18 20
18:19 96
21:1–7 132
22:17–18 20
26:3–4 20
28:12 68
28:14–15 20
35:12–13 20
49:9 128

Exodus
3:6 71
3:14 55, 71
3:19 53
4:22 69, 89
12:6 220
15 56
15:3 107
16:7 117
16:10 117
19:4 223
19:6 222
20:3 40
20:7 62
21:22–27 205
23:4 206
23:5 206
24:6–8 119
24:17 117
25:40 31
28:41 63n1
29:2 63
29:7 63n1
29:36 63
30:30 63n1
33:3 162
33:5 162
33:19 96
34:5–7 62
34:9 162
34:29 60
40:13 63n1
40:15 63n1

Leviticus
2:4 63
4:2 189
4:3 63n1
4:5 63n1
4:16 63n1
4:22 189
4:27 189
5:6–7 LXX 212
6:20 63n1
7:12 63
7:36 63n1
8:12 63n1
9:2 LXX 212
9:6 117
11:1–44 208
16 114
16:17 220
16:32 63n1
17–18 209
17:7 120
18 209
18:6–18 209
19:17–18 206
24:17–22 205
26:41 162

Numbers
3:3 63n1
6:14–15 207
12:6–8 112
14:5 220
15:30 189
16:3 220
19:4 119
19:18–19 119
19:21 119
20:4 220
23:19 65
23:24 128
24:9 128
35:25 63n1

Deuteronomy
4:34 53
5:15 53
6 44
6:4 40
6:4–5 40
6:13 44
6:16 44
6:21 53
9:6 162
9:13 162
10:16 162, 212
10:17 128
13:5 212
14:1 69
14:3–21 208
17:7 212
17:12 189, 212
18:15–22 60
19:15–21 205
21:21 212
21:23 83
22:21 212
23:1 220
23:8 220
24 205
24:1–4 205
25:1 99
28:10 118
30:6 212
32:5 162
32:6 69
32:13 69
32:43 LXX 116
33:2 123

Joshua
15:8 234
18:16 234

Judges
9:8 63n2
9:15 63n2

1 Samuel
1:1–28 132
2:10 63n2

253

6:12 177, 234
6:14–15 43, 176, 234
6:18 46
6:19–21 44
6:24 44
6:26 42
6:28–29 42
6:28–30 41
6:32 46
6:33 41, 44
7:1–2 43, 234
7:7–8 173
7:11 42
7:13–14 176
7:15–20 176
7:17–19 160
7:19 43
7:21 46
7:21–23 61, 176
7:22 62, 118
7:24–27 176
8:5–13 218
8:10 174
8:11–12 22, 174, 234
8:12 43, 234
8:17 75
8:18–22 175
8:20 66
8:23–27 61
8:29 70
9:2–5 60
9:2–8 61, 174
9:6 66
9:12–13 160, 173
9:13 61
9:14–17 204
9:22 174
9:27 64
9:28–30 174
9:35 21, 25
10:7–8 25
10:15 43
10:22 177
10:23 67
10:28 43, 234
10:29–31 42
10:32 240
10:32–33 46, 160, 177
10:37 61
10:37–39 176
10:38–39 61
10:39 61, 240
10:40 61
10:41–42 240
11:2–6 23
11:6 23, 160
11:19 66
11:20–24 43
11:25 46
11:25–26 42
11:27 70

12:1–14 204
12:8 66
12:18 218
12:21 62, 218
12:28 22
12:32 28, 66
12:33 160
12:33–37 176
12:37 241
12:46–50 61, 175
12:50 44, 46
13 24
13–15 160
13–44 24
13:1–9 24
13:11 24
13:18–23 24, 175
13:22 28
13:24–30 24
13:31–33 24
13:36–43 24
13:37 66
13:37–38 218
13:39 228
13:39–40 28
13:40–42 234
13:41 228
13:41–43 67
13:44–46 41
13:49 28, 228
13:49–50 234
13:52 25, 204
13:53–58 60, 174
14:13–21 60
14:25 61
14:33 69
15:1–11 44
15:1–20 204
15:6 42
15:22–29 174
15:29–31 45
15:32–39 218
16:13–20 63
16:16 69
16:18 218
16:21 60, 67n1
16:21–23 64
16:24–26 175
16:25 61, 240
16:27 46, 67
16:28 22, 67
17:5 60, 75
17:9 67
17:12 67
17:17 174
17:22–23 60, 67n1
17:27 123
18:3–4 175
18:8–9 176, 234
18:15–20 218
18:20 61, 62

18:21–35 43, 176
18:34–35 234
19:3–12 205
19:14 175
19:16 28, 240
19:17 44
19:21 175
19:24 28
19:26 41, 177
19:28 67
20:1–16 218
20:17–19 60
20:18–19 67n1
20:28 67, 75, 204
20:30–31 64
21:9 64
21:11 60
21:12–13 60
21:19–21 60
21:40–41 43
21:43 217
21:46 60
22:11–13 234
22:11–14 43
22:18 60
22:23 80
22:29 41
22:37–40 44
22:41–46 65
23:2–3 204
23:9 46
23:15 234
23:16–22 205
23:22 46
23:23–24 204
23:33 234
24 60, 204, 227
24:3 28, 228
24:13 177
24:14 21, 218, 229
24:20 204
24:26–27 228
24:27 67
24:30 67, 228
24:35 60
24:36 46, 229
24:37–39 67
24:44 67
24:45–51 176, 229, 234
24:48 228
25:1–13 176
25:1–30 229
25:5 228
25:14 228
25:14–30 176, 234
25:31 67
25:31–46 22, 229
25:34 22
25:41 234
25:45 176

25:46 176, 234, 240
26:2 67n1
26:28 75, 177
26:29 22
26:34 60
26:45 67n1
26:53 46
26:54 74
26:56 74
26:62–63 75
26:63 41
26:63–64 64
26:64 68, 228
27:12–14 75
27:43 42
28:16–20 60
28:19 46, 62, 70, 132, 139, 217, 218
28:20 28, 62, 70

Mark

1:1 70
1:11 70
1:14–15 21
1:15 175
2:7 42
2:10 66
2:17 61, 173
2:28 66
3:11 70
3:31–35 61
4:19 28
4:26–29 24
4:41 61
5:7 70
5:34 174
5:36 174
6:7 118
6:48 61
6:52 160
7:1–23 204
7:19 204
8:17 160
8:21 160
8:31 67n1
8:35 61
8:38 67
9:7 60, 70
9:9 67
9:12–13 67
9:31 67n1
9:33–37 160
9:43–47 234
9:43–48 43
10:18 42, 44
10:30 28
10:33–34 67n1
10:35–45 160
10:45 67, 75
10:52 174

Subject Index